This photo, taken in Tilton (Sussex, UK) in 1927, sums up the contents of this book. John Maynard Keynes, the most influential economist of the last century, opponent of laissez-faire and proponent of expansive monetary and fiscal policies in support of full employment, is flanked by two younger Cambridge economists. Like guardian angels, to the right of Keynes stands Dennis Robertson, who later became warden of economic orthodoxy, and to the left, Piero Sraffa (devil rather than angel) representing heterodoxy. Keynes, significantly, is in the middle.

Heterodox Challenges in Economics

Sergio Cesaratto

Heterodox Challenges in Economics

Theoretical Issues and the Crisis of the Eurozone

 Springer

Sergio Cesaratto
Department of Political Economy and Statistics
University of Siena
Siena, Italy

ISBN 978-3-030-54447-8   ISBN 978-3-030-54448-5   (eBook)
https://doi.org/10.1007/978-3-030-54448-5

This Springer imprint is published by the registered company Springer Nature Switzerland AG.
The registered company address is: Gewerbestrasse 11, 6330 Cham, Switzerland

Acknowledgements

I thank Tony Aspromourgos, Giancarlo Bergamini, Dirk Bezemer, Roberto Ciccone, Matteo Deleidi, Stefano Di Bucchianico, Eladio Febrero, Saverio Fratini, Vladimiro Giacché, Sergio Levrero, Gary Mongiovi, Antonella Palumbo, Riccardo Pariboni, Susan Pashkof, Marco Passarella, Fabio Petri, V. Ramanan, Annalisa Rosselli, Ernesto Screpanti, Paolo Trabucchi, Attilio Trezzini, Giuseppe Vandai and Gennaro Zezza for reading, commenting on and helping me to clarify various points and to improve the style of the two Italian editions and the present one. The publication of this book in Argentina (*Seis classes sobre economia*, Universidad Nacional de Moreno Editora, 2018) was the initiative of Alejandro Fiorito.

I thank Helen Ampt for her skill and patience in translating the book. Special thanks go to

(Italian Association for the study of economic asymmetries, www.asimmetrie. org) for supporting the project. I also thank the University of Siena and the director of the Department of Political Economy and Statistics, Prof. Salvatore Bimonte, for additional financial support (Piano sostegno alla ricerca).

Contents

About the Author

Sergio Cesaratto is a full professor at the University of Siena where he teaches European monetary and fiscal policy and economics of growth. He has published many articles in leading international heterodox journals on various topics, including the theory of income distribution and growth, pension systems, monetary analysis and the eurozone crisis.

He is a well-known participant in the Italian and European debate on the fate of the eurozone. The Italian edition of this book has been well received and has had two editions and several reprints. Another book on this subject is currently being translated into German for Springer.

Abbreviations

AES	Alternative economic strategy
APP	Asset Purchase Programme, ECB's securities purchasing programme, also known as QE; it includes Public sector purchase programme (*PSPP*), Asset-backed securities purchase programme (*ASSPP*) and Covered bond purchase programme 3 (*CBPP3*)
BTP	Buono del Tesoro Poliennale (Italian 10-year Treasury Bond)
Buba	Nickname given to *Bundesbank*, the Central Bank of Germany.
CAC	Class action clause
CBPP	Covered bond purchase programme (ECB's bank bond purchase programme)
CGIL	Confederazione generale italiana lavoratori (the Italian left wing union)
DB	Deutsche Bank
DM	Deutsche Mark
ECB	European Central Bank
EDIS	European deposit insurance scheme
EMS	European Monetary System (European system of fixed but adjustable exchange rates 1979–1998)
EMU	European Economic and Monetary Union
EONIA	Euro OverNight Index Average (interbank interest rate)
ESM	European Stability Mechanism (financial fund by the euro area Member States to rescue euro area countries in severe financial distress)
EU	European Union
Fed	Abbreviation of Federal Reserve, central bank of the USA
FMI	International Monetary Fund
GDP	Gross domestic product
IOU	Abbreviation of *I owe you*; document acknowledging debt
LTRO	Longer-term refinancing operations (long-term operations by the ECB to provide reserves to the banking system); they include Very longer-term

	refinancing operations (*VLTRO*) and Targeted longer-term refinancing operations (*TLTRO*)
MMT	Modern Money Theory (ultra-Keynesian theory)
MRO	Main refinancing operations (short-term operations by the ECB to provide reserves to the banking system)
OMT	Outright market transactions (a programme of the ECB consisting of the direct purchase by the *ECB* of short-term sovereign bonds issued by EMU countries with macroeconomic difficulties, under certain conditions)
QE	Quantitative easing (popular definition of the APP)
SMP	Securities Markets Programme (ECB sovereign bond purchase programme 2010–2012)
Target2	Trans-European Automated Real-Time Gross Settlement Express Transfer System, electronic platform for the euro area interbank payment system
ZLB	Zero lower bound

1

Economics: A Political and Mathematical Discipline

If not completely right, almost nothing wrong.

Fabrizio De André

Abstract This introductory chapter discusses the nature of the economic discipline. Economics has to do with the production and reproduction of the material living conditions of society, and is therefore at the crossroads between natural, quantitative and political sciences. The central theme of economics is income distribution, how output is distributed among the components of society. This theme has obvious political implications, and it is not surprising that in the history of economic thought several theories have arisen in this regard. These theories influence our social–political beliefs. The issue of income distribution has implications for other central themes, such as economic development. We introduce two approaches: the surplus approach characteristic of the classical economists of the eighteenth and nineteenth centuries and of Marx; and the neoclassical or marginalist approach that arose as a reaction to the former at the end of the nineteenth century, which is mainstream today. There is also a third theory, that of John Maynard Keynes, which brought a considerable upheaval in the dominant theory and is, in many ways, closer to the surplus approach.

Finally, the chapter presents our work plan, from the analysis of distribution theories, through monetary analysis, to the debate on the eurozone crisis.

© Springer Nature Switzerland AG 2020
S. Cesaratto, *Heterodox Challenges in Economics*,
https://doi.org/10.1007/978-3-030-54448-5_1

1.1 Economics and Politics

The aim of these chapters, or lessons as they were called in the Italian edition, was to answer the simple question: "What should an informed and committed citizen know about economics?" The lessons were also directed at students of economics and other disciplines who are bored with conventional teaching or are simply curious. They were also aimed at many opinion leaders and politicians who express views on everything, but who privately confide that they have never understood economics. Above all, they were for the thousands of people who in these difficult years, particularly in Italy, have done their best to grasp and then clear away the mountain of lies that has buried us, primarily the idea that fiscal austerity was necessary in the name of Europe. My aim was to reinforce this effort by providing a sound analytical background for rejecting mainstream economic recipes. In this context, I wanted to convince my friends that support Modern Money Theory (MMT) that heterodox economics is much broader than they believe (I will return to the MMT in the fifth chapter).

The purpose of this English edition is to share these considerations with a larger international public interested in a fresh combination of theoretical and political arguments in view of the euro area crisis.

Economics actually does not have enormous entry requirements. The mathematical latinorum with which it is often adorned is designed to intimidate people, making them feel inept and keeping them away from the truth (and lies) that are basically simple to understand. Knowledge and counter-information are annoying to those in power. They prefer people to think that their pronouncements issue from mysteries reserved for the initiated, administered by modern wizards or high priests called economists. We shall see, for example, that all mainstream economic analysis is based on a handful of accessible concepts, the foundations of which were laid in the late nineteenth century and have been handed down unchanged. Two distinguished heterodox economists, Aldo Barba and Giancarlo De Vivo, likened mainstream economics to the goldfish that lives happily in its glass bowl since its memory is so short that it discovers a new world each time it goes round.[1] I do not know whether this is true, but it certainly applies to the serious economist who prescribes us solutions that are one and a half centuries old, while presenting them as cutting-edge science. But don't be surprised if the alternative I offer has even older intellectual roots in the ideas of "classical economists" at the turn of the eighteenth and nineteenth centuries. In the day of these

---

[1] Barba and De Vivo (2010).

economists, economic conversation consisted of reasoning and disputes between learned people interested in politics and culture. Marx admired them greatly, and for obvious reasons considered it also fundamental that truths and lies in economic theory be disclosed to the working class (to ordinary people, if you prefer less militant language). It is of course true that economic analysis of any orientation has complex aspects that may require sophisticated mathematics. But it is also true that any reasonably informed person, used to reading good books, can master the core of economic analysis irrespective of his or her level of education, and indeed should be invited to do so as an informed citizen. After all, what is politics about? In the words of an amusing morning programme on Italian Radio 24, it is about "heart and money", that is to say, civil rights and economic policy. Now Europe only lets us discuss the former, which is a good reason to delve into the latter.

Economics *and* politics then!

But Prof, if economics is a key to politics (and vice versa), can it be considered a science?

Good question! Alfred Marshall (1842–1924), one of the founders of mainstream theory, introduced that strange creature, the *representative firm*.[2] I fear that you, as a *representative reader*, will ask many questions during my exposition. Let us distinguish two aspects of your question.

Firstly, many economic phenomena have a quantitative manifestation. Thus we speak of prices, quantities produced, incomes, investment, saving and so forth. This numerical manifestation not only invites statistical quantification, but also representation of its interactions by variably complex logical/mathematical models. This gives economics a certain analytical rigour, a pattern of consequential reasoning. In conversation I often hear the comment: "I can tell you are an economist". I like both aspects of economics: rigour in reasoning combined with strong political implications—a founder of the discipline, William Petty, called it Political Arithmetic—but certainly, mathematics is not everything. The true pleasure of economics is above all in its strict verbal reasoning. A famous suggestion from Marshall is to use maths as abbreviated notation and for checking ideas, not as an end in itself. The results must be translated into words and checked against the facts.[3] In fact, Marshall skilfully pursued the social penetration of mainstream theory by presenting it comprehensibly and linked to the real world. Leaving aside his promotional motives, we can agree with the method Marshall suggests.

---

[2] In 1930 Marshall's representative firm was the subject of a famous symposium in the "Economic Journal", then directed by Keynes (Robertson et al. 1930).

[3] Alfred Marshall had a degree in mathematics. His indications on the use, or rather against abuse, of mathematics in economics are in Pigou (1966).

Secondly, the quantitative relations studied in economics are not just interactions between numbers, but are the ultimate manifestations of the relations between individuals, social groups, institutions, and the evolution of these relations. Prices represent relations between producers and consumers; wages express a relation between entrepreneurs and workers; the balance of payments expresses a relation between countries and so forth. The organization of economic life cannot be separated from the political institutions that give it legitimacy. Think of economies founded on slavery or serfdom that derived their legitimacy from a given political order; but also a market economy draws its legitimacy from the legal institutions that protect material and intellectual property rights.

Whether our analysis starts from the individual, or from society as an arena of interactions between social groups depends on the theories in use. The ABC of the philosophy of science warns that we interpret the world through the lens of a theory, even when we are unaware of doing so. The theories of classical economists and of Marx led them to talk about social classes, that is of groups of individuals defined on the basis of property relations with the instruments of production: the class of landowners; capitalists, owners of means of production; workers, owners of nothing but their own labour. In general, "modern" economics prefers to move from the individual. Famously Margaret Thatcher, inspired by Friedrich Hayek, maintained that "there is no such thing as society", that is to say, society is the result of individual choices, from which analysis should therefore begin. Nonetheless, even for mainstream economists, it is impossible to avoid referring to social classes, grouping people on the basis of the different nature of their income, e.g. wage earners and capitalists receiving profits. (Of course, mainstream economists prefer to refer to less politically sensitive social groupings such as consumers or savers.)

Once income distribution between the social classes is introduced, economics becomes politics, and in politics (to return to our previous simplification) two things are discussed: how to divide the pie produced (and perhaps how to increase it), and civil rights. The current mainstream theory actually tries to expunge politics from economics by speaking of a *natural* distribution of income, meaning that there are economic laws that indicate exactly what slice of the pie must go to workers and what slice to capitalists (and related classes). There is a "natural" division of the pie: that is, to each his own; end of story. In this way, politics is relegated to the debate on civil rights.

Summing up, social relations and political choices (often) manifest in economics through quantitative relations of a logical/mathematical nature. While this makes the economic discourse more precise, we should not let it cause us to forget the deep bond between economics, history and politics, of which these relations are manifestations.

Does the involvement of politics in economics make the latter less scientific? Not according to David Ricardo (1772–1823), the most refined of the classical economists, nor according to his "pupil" Marx (1818–1883). On the contrary, for Ricardo the laws governing income distribution are what economic investigation is about. Ricardo is a good example of what we want to say: he shows that there is an inverse relation between wages and profit (if one grows, the other declines) that can be expressed mathematically. Behind the mathematics, this inverse function represents a social relation between labour and capital. At what point on the curve a society will historically lie—that is, what the actual distribution of income will be—will depend on the balance of power between the two social groups, workers and capitalists. That's politics, baby! In fact, in mainstream theory it is the opposite, politics must adapt to laissez-faire, it is economics that dictates to politics. That's the market, baby!

Certainly, Prof, it is complicated to talk about scientific research in economics with all the interests at play! Yes, Marx had no doubts on the subject and it is worth citing a famous passage in the Preface the first German edition to *Das Kapital*:

> In the domain of Political Economy, free scientific inquiry meets not merely the same enemies as in all other domains. The peculiar nature of the materials it deals with, summons as foes into the field of battle the most violent, mean and malignant passions of the human breast, the Furies of private interest.[4]

In other words, specific material interests condition "free inquiry". And how could it be otherwise if the object of study is no less than the conflict between material interests?

Marx has very clear ideas about when political economy ceased to be science. This happened after the death of Ricardo in 1823. Ricardo had given logical/mathematical expression to the conflict between the capitalist bourgeoisie and the rural landlords in England. The latter lobbied for duties on cheaper imported corn, so as to make their own crops, from which they extracted land rent, more competitive (corn is the expression used at the time to refer to cereal grain, such as wheat and barley). However, duties on cheap imported corn would have increased corn prices in England, especially for workers whose subsistence depended above all on corn (used, for example, to

---

[4] Marx (1974 [1887], p. 21).

produce bread and beer). This would force manufacturing capitalists to pay higher wages, reducing their profits.

Ricardo, who was also a member of parliament, sided with the capitalists and not the rural landholders, because he held that the accumulation of capital, namely the investments that would advance the economy, depended on profits. He was therefore in favour of corn imports. The rentiers would suffer but profits and accumulation would benefit.

However, Marx recounts that once it had achieved political power, the bourgeoisie rejected Ricardo's economic theory, and for good reason. Indeed some early socialists had begun to realise that if there was no natural distribution of income between rents (landed aristocracy) and profits (capitalists), this principle also applied to distribution between wages (workers) and profits (capitalists). In the first case, it was a question of power balance between industrialists and landed aristocracy in Parliament, and between industrialists and workers in the labour market in the second case. The term "exploitation" began to appear well before Marx, such that a few years after Ricardo's death an American economist, Henry Carey (1793–1879), defined Ricardo's theory as the theory of class "discord".[5] For the same reasons, George Poulett Scrope (1797–1876), an English economist, defined the spread of Ricardian theory as a "crime".[6] Thus Marx concludes in the Afterword to the Second German edition to *Das Kapital*:

> In France and in England the bourgeoisie had conquered political power. Thenceforth, the class struggle, practically as well as theoretically, took on more and more outspoken and threatening forms. It sounded the knell of scientific bourgeois economy. It was thenceforth no longer a question, whether this theorem or that was true, but whether it was useful to capital or harmful, expedient or inexpedient, politically dangerous or not. In place of disinterested inquirers, there were hired prize fighters; in place of genuine scientific research, the bad conscience and the evil intent of apologetic.[7]

But is this enough to criticise mainstream economics? Evidently not. Indeed the same accusation of bending scientific inquiry to ideological prejudices or to class interests can easily be turned back on the critics of mainstream economics. We must, therefore, work hard to demonstrate that mainstream

---

[5] Henry Carey writes that: "Mr. Ricardo's system is one of discords ... its whole tends to the production of hostility among classes and nations" in Carey (1963 [1848], pp. 74–75).

[6] See Blaug (1958, pp. 149–150).

[7] Marx (1974 [1887], pp. 24–25).

theory has serious analytical inconsistencies, namely it is analytically wrong and not just ideologically biased.

The "mainstream theory" facing Marx was actually a hotchpotch of post-Ricardian theories that he defined as "vulgar". In fact, it was not until towards the end of the nineteenth century that bourgeois economists sorted out a new and more coherent theory. To give it some noble blood, it was later defined neo-classical, though it had little to do with the classics, and for reasons we shall see, it would be better to give it its early label of *marginalist theory*. But Marx did not become aware of this theory, the full-blown form of vulgar economics.

Marginalism encountered two great challenges in the course of the twentieth century. The first was the "Keynesian revolution" initiated by the *General theory of employment, interest and money* that John Maynard Keynes (1883–1946) published in 1936. The second was brought by the great Italian economist Piero Sraffa (1898–1983), who in the 1960s shook the analytical foundations of the marginalist edifice. We rely mainly on the work of these two economists to see what is analytically wrong with mainstream theory.

1.2 Through the Lens of the Theories

For the next three chapters I have decided to follow a historical line. I will show how mainstream theory emerges at the end of the nineteenth century as a reaction to the theory of Ricardo and Marx. Note that Marx could be seen as a close follower of Ricardo, as well as a critic. Since the nucleus of his economic theory was the same as that of Ricardo, who was considered the most rigorous bourgeois economist until then, Marx could honestly say that he did not invent anything on the basis of anti-bourgeois prejudice: it was already all in Ricardo! This made Marx's theory very dangerous. Naturally, Marx gives a historical context to the theory of Ricardo, as he did not consider the laws under which bourgeois society worked to be eternal and immutable. However, the economic theory of Marx is basically that of Ricardo. After explaining the approach of classical economists and Marx in Chap. 2, in the third we look at mainstream theory, showing its implications for contemporary debate, for example, on the flexibility of the labour market and on the economic constitution of Europe. In Chap. 4, we see how the combination of classical theory and the critique of Keynes are a formidable instrument for analysing economic crises. In Chap. 5, we discuss the role of money, seeking to show that there is nothing mysterious or mystical about it. In this chapter, we also illustrate what for non-conformist economists is the central node of economic policy, the balance of payments constraint (here my MMT friends will disagree with me). Fortified by these notions, in the last two chapters we return to the question of Europe and the crisis in the eurozone.

If at the end of these chapters I hear you say: "I already felt I knew all this, but now it is clearer", I will have fulfilled my goal. In these years, under the impulse of the European crisis, there has been a massive amount written about economics, favoured also by the social media. The aim of these chapters is to strengthen the analytical background of the work done in these years with a group of tenacious heterodox economists, starting with the topic of Europe. We shall never lose contact with reality, hopefully confirming that knowledge is first and foremost a pleasure that confirms our convictions, preparing us for the political struggle for change.

Let me end this introduction by commenting on two possible sources of misunderstanding about economics.

When like many young people I began my economic studies in the 1970s, we were very interested in the theoretical debates that raged at the time. We were well aware that the world is interpreted through the lens of theory. We implicitly agreed with Keynes in this regard (although we studied Marx more). According to Keynes, politicians (and for that matter everyone) argue, without realising it, on the basis of theories formulated by some economist who died decades earlier. In the post-ideological epoch we believe we belong to, young people regard theoretical debates with less tolerance and consider certain social categories, such as capital and labour, to be things of the past. My impression is that this leads them to consider economics a purely empirical science, and indeed they are often good at econometrics (the discipline that seeks to estimate theoretical models empirically), viewing theory as a toolkit, a menu with a little of everything that can be ordered *à la carte*. This idea of economic theory as a toolkit is also found in Keynes, confirming his mental versatility, which was sometimes, however, muddled. The empirical testing of theories is obviously important, and historical analysis and mere observation of data are often much more important than the mechanical methods of econometrics, but preliminary theoretical analysis is just as important. In fact, those economic debates conducted solely in the empirical-econometric dimension are often the most inconclusive (the results depend on what data and variables are considered, and on the estimation methods applied to enormous masses of data, ignoring historical and political contexts, etc.). In any case, no empirical test can be taken as valid if conducted on the basis of a wrong theory. "He who speaks ill, thinks ill", the Italian film director Nanni Moretti once said. Being able to point out the inconsistencies of theories makes it easier to settle practical questions. If I succeed in convincing a few young people to be more sensitive to theoretical analysis, this book will have achieved its aim.

One example is the growing inequality, an issue that certainly fascinates the most politically sensitive young people. Superficially it does not seem to require any complex theoretical analysis, but only statistical measurements. But in actual fact the theme cannot be tackled without understanding the transformations of capitalism, without having a theory. After all, the French scholar Thomas Piketty, who has made the subject even more popular, adopts rather neoclassical patterns of thought, which can only make the interpretation of its important empirical findings spurious.

Another misapprehension regarding economics, perhaps the most popular above all among the grandchildren of the anti-globalisation movements, comes from confusing Fairtrade, microcredit, zero-miles products, local currencies, *empresas recuperadas* and so forth with "alternative economics". Attempts to create a non-capitalist economy are meritorious, albeit often rather ingenuous. Economics, as we shall endeavour to understand it together, belongs to a more macro level concerned with the dynamics of output and income distribution, rather than the micro level of single experiences. If you think this is too abstract, this book is not for you. But remember that you run the risk of adopting the ideas of someone you have delegated to think for you. Small exemplary experiences are destined to remain just that, for the very reason that they lack a broader and more informed (and therefore realistic) political and economic perspective. A finger pointing at the moon is not the moon.

Polanyi moment. Ricardo gives a very clear definition of economic science: "In different stages of society, the proportions of the whole produce of the earth which will be allotted to each of these classes, under the names of rent, profit and wages, will be essentially different... To determine the laws which regulate this distribution, is the principal problem in Political Economy".[8]
Also for the marginalists the question of the distribution of income is central, but it is better to mask it a little, so Lionel Robbins (1898–1984) in the Thirties took charge of giving the "official" definition of economics according to the dominant theory: "Economics is the science which studies human behaviour as a relationship between ends and scarce means which have alternative uses".[9] In other words: humanity suffers from a scarcity of resources—more specifically of the "production factors" labour, capital and natural resources—which have a limited endowment in each period of time, so their use must be chosen rationally, for example, between the satisfaction of current needs (consumption) or greater future well-being (investment). These choices include the distribution of the product obtained from those resources to their owners, i.e. to labour (wages),

---

[8] Ricardo (1951 [1817], p. 5).
[9] Robbins (1932, p. 15).

capital (interest/profits) and natural resources (rent). All these rational choices will depend on objective factors such as the initial endowments of the "production factors", the prevailing tastes of consumers, and technology. There is no room for social conflict. As we shall see, objective laws will dictate "to each his own". Economics is reduced to an "engineering" exercise on how to allocate scarce resources between alternative purposes.

Karl Polanyi (1886–1964), a well-known economic anthropologist, is famous for criticizing the anthropological foundation of liberalism according to which the inborn drive of economic activity is, following Smith, the "propensity to barter, trade and exchange one thing for another".[10] On the contrary, says Polanyi: "In spite of the chorus of academic incantations so persistent in the nineteenth century, gain and profit made on exchange never before played an important part in human economy. Although the institution of the market was fairly common since the later Stone Age, its role was no more than incidental to economic life".[11] Polanyi looked at welfare state institutions as a defensive reaction of the working classes to the unleashed laissez-faire. In this sense he spoke of society's "double movement": to an extension of laissez-faire, society reacts by trying to rebuild institutions of solidarity. The success in the last decade of "populist" movements, have been interpreted as a reaction in the direction foreseen by Polanyi, a social ¡Ya basta! Polanyi had also foreseen that the reaction to unleashing of the free market could also take equivocal right-wing expressions.

The considerations on the eurozone crisis in the last 10 years were still current events at the time the book was written, but are history in light of the COVID-19 pandemic. However, what Europe does or does not do in the face of this unprecedented crisis can be better understood in the light of that first dramatic experience that revealed all the political fragility of the old continent. We do not yet know whether a new and better chapter will open for Europe, or a worse one in continuity with the past.

Further Reading

I have borrowed from the textbooks of Augusto Graziani (1933–2014), a great Italian heterodox economists, the idea of concluding the chapters with small guides to the literature. The reading recommendations complement the main text and roughly follow the order in which the subjects are presented. Old Italian textbooks, like Graziani's, compared the different theories progressively formulated in the history of thought. This comparison

---

[10] Smith (1904 [1776], p. 15).
[11] Polanyi (2001 [1944], p. 45).

was useful to have clearer ideas and to acquire a better appreciation of the world. My university department prescribes the Core Team (2017) as an introductory economics text with the idea of stimulating the interest of young students of economics. Edited by S. Bowles, W. Carlin and M. Stevens, the first edition was funded by the Institute for New Economic Thinking (INET). The strategy of the Core Team is to "be realistic", to refer to "hard facts", especially inequality. Arguably, what is missing from the most popular mainstream textbooks is not empirical evidence. What is missing is a serious discussion of the different theories, such as to allow us to interpret the economic "facts" and thus place our understanding of capitalism and inequality on solid foundations. Fortunately, INET also supports more courageous lines of research.

The difference between the *vulgar* economists of the late classical period and marginalists is that the former had no theory underlying their argument that everything is determined by supply and demand. That is why Marx called them vulgar. Since marginalism constructed a theory to justify these statements, it is not strictly vulgar in the Marxian sense. Marshall even tried to establish continuity between the new marginalist approach and classical economics. For a critique of this attempt, see Bharadwaj (1986). Highly esteemed by Piero Sraffa, Krishna Bharadwaj (1935–1992) was an extraordinary Indian economist who applied her passion for classical political economy to the study of the concrete problems of her country. This small volume is of enormous value because it is based on conversations with Sraffa.

A critical analysis of Piketty's influential book (Piketty 2014) can be found in Stirati (2016), where other unorthodox reviews including those of Gary Mongiovi and Tony Aspromourgos are cited.

As the foundation of economic relations, Polanyi replaced Smith's innate "propensity to barter, trade and exchange" with other innate values such as altruism, reciprocity and gifts. However, in the volume cited above, Krishna Bharadwaj argues that like the marginalists, Polanyi slips from the primacy of production proper of the classical economists to that of "circulation", the term Marx uses to indicate the sphere of exchange of goods. One must look to the sphere of production, where control of the means of production is defined, in order to understand the social relations of a society (see Cesaratto and Di Bucchianico 2020).

Finally, good histories of economic thought are Screpanti and Zamagni (1993) and Roncaglia (2005), while a summary of the theories presented in this book is in Cesaratto (2019).

References

Barba, A., & De Vivo, G. (2010, July 26). *I pesci rossi e le lune di Giove, Il Sole 24 Ore*. Retrieved April 28, 2020, from https://st.ilsole24ore.com/art/commenti-e-idee/2010-07-26/pesci-rossi-lune-giove-161232.shtml

Bharadwaj, K. (1986). *Classical political economy and the rise to dominance of supply and demand theories* (2nd ed.). Calcutta: University Press India (1st. ed. Orient Longman, 1978).

Blaug, M. (1958). *Ricardian economics: A historical study*. New Haven, CT: Yale University Press.

Carey, H. (1963 [1848]). *Principles of social science* in three volumes. New York: Augustus M. Kelley.

Cesaratto, S. (2019). The modern revival of the Classical surplus approach: Implications for the analysis of growth and crises. In T. Gabellini, S. Gasperin, & A. Moneta (eds.), *Economic crisis and economic thought—Alternative perspectives on the economic crisis* (pp. 111–134). Abingdon: Routledge (Working Paper Version, Quaderni DEPS, No. 735/2016).

Cesaratto, S., & Di Bucchianico, S. (2020). The surplus approach, Polanyi and institutions in economic anthropology and archaeology. Quaderni DEPS, N. 828 (forthcoming in *Annals of the Fondazione Luigi Einaudi*, special issue "Marshall Sahlins's Stone Age Economics, a Semicentenary Estimate").

Core Team. (2017). *The economy: Economics for a changing world*. Oxford University Press. Retrieved April 28, 2020, from https://www.core-econ.org/

Marx, K. (1974 [1887]). *Capital—A critical analysis of capitalist production* (Vol. I). London: Lawrence & Wishart [English edition 1887].

Pigou, A. C. (Ed.). (1966). *Memorials of Alfred Marshall*. New York: A. M. Kelley.

Piketty, T. (2014). *Capital in the twenty-first century*. Cambridge, MA: Belknap Press.

Polanyi, K. (2001 [1944]). *The great transformation: The political and economic origins of our time*. Boston: Beacon Press.

Ricardo, D. (1951 [1817]). *On the principles of political economy and taxation*. In P. Sraffa (ed.), *The works and correspondence of David Ricardo* (Vol. I). Cambridge: Cambridge University Press.

Robbins, L. (1932). *Essay on the nature and significance of economic science*. London: Macmillan.

Robertson, D. H., Sraffa, P., & Shove, G. F. (1930). Increasing returns and the representative firm. A symposium. *Economic Journal, 40*(157), 79–116.

Roncaglia, A. (2005). *The wealth of ideas: A history of economic thought*. Cambridge: Cambridge University Press.

Screpanti, E., & Zamagni, S. (1993). *An outline of the history of economic thought*. Oxford: Clarendon Press.

Smith, A. (1776). *An inquiry into the nature and causes of the wealth of nations*. Edited by R. H. Campbell & A. S. Skinner. Indianapolis: Liberty Classics.

Stirati, A. (2016). *Piketty and the increasing concentration of wealth: Some implications of alternative theories of distribution and growth*. Centro Sraffa Working Papers No. 18.

2

The Surplus Approach

Abstract This chapter introduces the surplus approach. The surplus is that part of the social product that is available to the community, or its élite, once it has set aside what is needed to reproduce the same output, that is, for replacement of the means of production and for the subsistence of the working class. The chapter examines some applications of the concept in relation to the birth of ancient civilizations and German mercantilism. Next, it explains the evolution of the ideas of the classical economists and Marx. These economists shared the idea that income distribution depends on power relations between the social classes. A solution to some of the difficulties they encountered was suggested by Piero Sraffa, an economist who was close to Gramsci, Keynes and Wittgenstein. In addition to rediscovering the classical approach, Sraffa also challenged mainstream theory on the basis of analytical problems in its fundamentals. In the 1960s, this criticism led to the so called "two Cambridges controversy", which involved the brightest economists of the time. The most prominent, Paul Samuelson, admitted that the criticism was correct. Today the controversy is rarely mentioned in university courses, evidently because it has uncomfortable implications for mainstream theory.

2.1 The Classical Surplus Approach

Theories of surplus-value is the title Marx gave to what was to be the fourth volume of *Capital*, his history of economic thought. He defined the prevalent theories up to Ricardo as surplus theories. The concept of surplus will be

© Springer Nature Switzerland AG 2020
S. Cesaratto, *Heterodox Challenges in Economics*,
https://doi.org/10.1007/978-3-030-54448-5_2

central in all chapters, so it is a good idea to master it now. The simplest definition is:

Social surplus is that part of the product that society can freely use once the amount needed to reproduce the same output in the next period has been set aside.

To master the concept, let us ask the following question.

Many of our ancestors were farmers. What did our peasant ancestor, or if you are one of the lucky few, your princely landlord ancestor, do with the corn he produced?[1] Let us consider the latter case, so we have two classes, peasants and landlords (and don't call me a communist, although I won't be offended if you do). Once the corn produced has been harvested, the landlord set aside an amount to sow next season and a part to feed the peasant families until the next crop. He could then do what he liked with what was left, the surplus: make bread and pastries for the family and maintain the servants; exchange it for other goods, such as elegant clothes and books; or he could cultivate more land or make technical innovations to his fiefdom, in other words invest it, that is use the surplus as new capital. The surplus is, therefore, the difference between the final product and the replacement of what was consumed to produce it, namely what is necessary to repeat production at least on the same scale (corn to sow and to feed the peasants):

$$Social\ product - Replacements = Social\ surplus \qquad (2.1)$$

Does this seem banal? Let us see some fascinating applications of this simple idea.

2.2   In the Beginning Was the Surplus

It is not always easy to be a "heterodox" economist. One is often assailed by doubts about how one can be right when most of the profession has another opinion, at least on basic topics. Reading a book that many of you already know has nevertheless strengthened my convictions. It is the famous work by Jared Diamond *Arms, steel and germs*.[2] Dear me, I shouldn't have mentioned it, if you start reading it you will certainly lay my book down. Diamond, a

---

[1] The word "corn" in nineteenth Britain indicated all cereals grains like wheat or barley; corn has also become a favourite "representative product" for economists since it is both a wage-good and an investment-good, when used to sow.

[2] Diamond (1997).

multidisciplinary biologist, ambitiously sets out to explain why different areas of the world developed differently, to the extent that some civilisations prevailed over others. Diamond does not cite any economists. So, his multidisciplinarity stops on the threshold of the Department of Economics of UC Berkeley, the university where he teaches. We will explain this. So that you are not distracted by reading Diamond directly, here is a brief summary.

Until about 11,000 years ago, the human population consisted of hunter-gatherers. Agriculture and domestication of animals, and with them more stable and complex sedentary social structures had not yet developed. Indeed, only with agriculture did humans begin to produce a storable food surplus that enabled them to reduce mortality, increase in numbers and support a larger population, part of which consisting of a class of "unproductive" workers dedicated to political–military organisation and to the discovery and preservation of knowledge: food surplus makes it possible to support unproductive groups of bureaucrats, scholars and soldiers, but also artisans. The emergence of the surplus is therefore also associated with the appearance of social stratification.

The production of a food surplus did not however occur in all the regions inhabited by *Homo sapiens*. Leaving aside the fact that homo sapiens arrived at different parts of the earth at different times, giving a head-start advantage to some, according to Diamond only some regions had a sufficient variety of plants and animal species suitable for domestication to make it worthwhile for hunter-gatherers to become farmers. With regard to agriculture, consider that only a tiny minority of the thousands of plant species are edible, nourishing and suitable for cultivation, or otherwise allowing a range of crops that could be readily cultivated with a high yield. These species did not occur in all regions of the world. Only in a few areas was there an array or *package* of varieties with nutritional properties (for example, the right combination of carbohydrates and proteins), cultivability and yield such as to make farming more advantageous than hunting and gathering. The discovery that plants could be grown from seeds was not enough to convert humans to farming; it was the geographical availability of suitable varieties that determined which populations developed agriculture and which did not. Similar considerations hold for animals, of which only very few species can be raised in captivity, and among these even fewer large ones can be domesticated for transport, work and war, as well as for producing milk, hides, etc. A substantial package of such animal species only occurred in certain parts of the world due to appropriate climatic conditions, giving those fortunate populations another enormous advantage. Food surplus generated population growth and a surplus of manpower that could be diverted from material reproduction and allocated to higher activities such as politics (yes!), war and the accumulation of knowledge, among the latter the invention of writing and numbers (probably emerging from the need to keep records of the amount of agricultural surplus in storage). Sedentary life rendered advantageous the development of constructions and complex artefacts that could not be transported and were therefore of no use to nomadic peoples.

The generation of a food surplus occurred in the Fertile Crescent (Mesopotamia), China, Central America, the Andes and what is now the eastern United States. Mesopotamia developed the "wheat-barley-peas-lentils" package, China "rice-millet-soy", and central America the less nutritious "maize-beans". The number and quality of animal species suitable for domestication made the difference: in the Americas, there were only turkeys and lamas (the latter in the Andes). In those lands, there were no beasts of burden and so the wheel was not invented or at least not used, and their absence also held back agriculture and the development of ploughing, transport and so forth. There was also a lack of close contact with domestic animals. In other places, this proximity transmitted major epidemic diseases such as smallpox, measles, influenza and the plague to man, leading to resistance and immunity in survivors. The spread of these viruses in lands conquered by Europeans amounted to a biological weapon that almost exterminated native populations.

The geographical disposition of Eurasia also enabled a faster spread of natural species and human knowledge between regions with a relatively similar climate at similar latitudes. In contrast, the longitudinal disposition of the Americas, interspersed with deserts, impeded this spread. And of course, other lands were isolated by oceans.

The thesis of Diamond is therefore that agriculture was the fundamental step by which certain populations achieved demographic growth and the possibility of supporting an unproductive élite (in the sense that they were not involved in subsistence production). Besides politicians and soldiers, this unproductive part of population included what Adam Smith would have called the class of "philosophers", producers of knowledge. The larger populations in turn increased the scale on which activities were conducted and the probability of innovative ideas. The limited number of useful domesticable plant and animal species only made this possible in certain parts of the world.

In conclusion, notice the language used by Diamond—surplus, subsistence, productive and unproductive labour —the same we find used by classical economists. As I said, Diamond does not cite any economist, classical or marginalist. This demonstrates how little use "modern" economics was to him. At the same time, however, we can presume that Diamond was hardly exposed to the ideas of classical economists like Anne-Robert-Jacques Turgot (1727–1781) and Adam Smith (1723–1790) who advanced theories that anticipated that of *Arms, steel and germs* on the basis of the first reports from the new lands just then discovered. For example, Turgot wrote[3]:

Without provisions, and in the depths of forests, men could devote themselves to nothing but obtaining their subsistence,

while among farmers

the land can sustain many more men than are necessary to cultivate it. Hence people who are unoccupied; hence towns, trade, and all the useful arts and accomplishments; hence more rapid progress in every sphere, for everything follows the general advancement of the mind; hence greater skill in war than in the case of barbarians; hence the division of occupations and the inequality of men; hence slavery in domestic form, and the subjection of the weaker sex (always bound up with barbarism), the hardship of which increases in proportion to the increase in wealth. But at the same time a more searching enquiry into government begins.

The search for the lost ark. Since Turgot, even since Montesquieu (1689–1755), there is a long tradition in archaeology and economic anthropology anticipating Diamond. Its most fascinating exponent was the Australian Vere Gordon Childe (1892–1957), the greatest archaeologist of the last century. Childe was the typical English-style intellectual: pipe, eccentric, snob... and Marxist—not exactly Indiana Jones! It was he who coined the term "Neolithic revolution", the transition from the state of hunter-gatherers to agriculture. This laid the foundations for the emergence of surplus, social stratification and the "urban revolution", which manifested with the great civilisations in the near east. Many modern archaeologists and anthropologists, not only Diamond (who quotes Childe), continue to use the notion of surplus.

Prof, I have a concern. If the origin of the élites presupposes the appearance of a surplus, it occurs to me that the extraction of a surplus presupposes the existence of an élite. Yes, this is a very complicated issue. The anthropologist Karl Polanyi and his school were in fact very critical of the vision that sees social stratification as a semi-automatic result of the emergence of a surplus. The answer suggested by many studies in modern archaeology is that in fact the first communities of both hunter-gatherers and farmers were quite egalitarian. If the community produced in excess of subsistence, this surplus was dissipated at

---

[3]Turgot (2011, pp. 351 and 355).

feastings or even destroyed. Anthropologists even suggest social practices in primitive communities aimed at ridiculing any attempt to place themselves too much above others. The adoption of agriculture also presupposed the storage of crops so as to make subsistence available throughout the year, or even over several years, compensating for good and bad years. It is likely that the élites rose up from the social group (such as priests) assigned by the community to control and manage the warehouses. From being administrators of the surplus to community service, these individuals and their entourage became élites served by the community.

2.3   From the Neolithic to Schäuble[4]

Let us look at another application of the concept of surplus that allows us to link it to current political debate. It is now quite common to accuse Germany of being "mercantilist" and wanting to sell abroad without buying. Mercantilism was a vast international school of thought that developed from the sixteenth century until the publication of *The Wealth of Nations* by Adam Smith, who in 1776 deceived himself into thinking he had sung its *de profundis*. It inspired many writers, often men of commerce and sometimes scholars we met in high school, like John Locke (1632–1704) and David Hume (1711–1776). William Petty (1623–1687), highly esteemed by Marx, had a clear conception of surplus as in relation (2.1): Social product − Replacements = Social surplus (for the sake of the argument, let us call it "domestic surplus"). However, the other mercantilists had another surplus in mind, the trade surplus, namely a positive trade balance. This is defined as difference between exports and imports:

$$Exports - Imports = Trade\ balance$$

It is generally thought that mercantilists see the wealth of a nation as measured by its trade surplus (let us call it "external surplus"). According to the greatest scholar of this early school of economic thought, Eli Heckscher (1879–1952), the mercantilists were tormented by "fear of goods", the fear that unsold goods might accumulate in national warehouses (many mercantilists were actual merchants for whom this is understandable): hence the need to sell abroad.

---

[4] Wolfgang Schäuble was the German minister for finance at the peak of the crisis 2007–2017.

In some ways, however, identifying national prosperity with the trade surplus is absurd. An increase in wages would suffice to sell domestically any excess of goods in warehouses, increasing the well-being of most citizens! Yes, but unfortunately, if we increase wages, profits will decrease and capitalists or merchants do not want this.

Prof, help us gather the threads. Capitalists produce in aggregate a certain amount of commodities in a year. A part goes to replacing means of production consumed in the last production cycle; a part goes to workers as wage-goods; the rest remains as surplus in their warehouses. Yes. Of course, capitalists consume some themselves (yachts, villas, Ferrari cars, etc.), but not enough to dispose of the entire surplus and transform all of it into profits, namely into effective monetary gain.

And of course, if we understand correctly, it would never occur to capitalists to give a bit more to workers through an increase in wages—lest it made them lazy. Exactly, and indeed most mercantilists preached low wages.

A solution for the capitalists is therefore to try to export the surplus? That's right. And here the mercantilist precept is far from absurd: exports are a way for capitalists to place the part of the surplus they themselves do not consume on the foreign market. The idea of trade as "vent for surplus" was present also in Adam Smith, although he was a fierce critic of mercantilism.

Prof, but what do capitalists gain from this? There are two possibilities: (1) they obtain gold and other precious materials (as in the heyday of mercantilism) or strong currencies or financial assets (as happens now), in other words, they accumulate financial wealth; or (2) they, in turn, buy foreign luxury goods, i.e. capitalists of different countries exchange surplus domestic goods: Brunello for Champagne, Rolexes for caviar, and so forth. Clearly, only the first behaviour, the truly mercantilist one, is globally harmful, because in accumulating financial wealth, capitalists depress world demand (by selling but not buying) and unload debt on foreign countries. Yes, as Germany does. We return to this in Chap. 6. With the second behaviour, capitalists export in order to import: they exchange a surplus of Brunello against a surplus of Champagne, and since they sell in order to buy, they do not depress global demand.

Actually, very few mercantilists have come to reason in this way. Only one late mercantilist, William Hay, presumably influenced by Petty, identified a clear connection between domestic surplus and foreign trade surplus:

> The source of wealth is from the number of its inhabitants; … the more populous a country is, the richer it is or may be … For the earth is grateful and repays their labour not only with enough but with an abundance … Now whatever

they have more of than they consume, the surplus is the *riches* of the nation. This surplus is sent to other nations and is there exchanged or sold, and this is the trade of the nation. If the nation to which it is sent cannot give goods in exchange to the same value they must pay for the remainder in money; which is the balance of trade; and the nation that hath that balance in her favour must increase in wealth.[5]

In other words, Prof, the scheme suggested by mercantilists is that a policy of low wages generates a surplus for capitalists, who since they cannot sell it on the domestic market, try to place it abroad in exchange for luxury goods and financial wealth. Exactly.

Arguing that wealth is obtained through low wages smells somewhat of Marxism, doesn't it? In effect an important historian of mercantilism, Edgar Furniss, sees the seeds of socialist doctrine in it, whereas Heckscher defines the low-wage economy as the tragedy of mercantilism. Since everyone today wants to imitate the German mercantilist model, Europe is experiencing this tragedy.

Thus we see that classical economics based on the concept of surplus provides elements for criticism of capitalism. It is after Ricardo, that the bourgeoisie realised the subversive implications of the surplus approach, and quickly discarded it.

2.4   The Global Minotaur and the European Minotaur

While there are mercantilist countries that live below their means, there are also countries that live beyond their means. Former Greek Finance Minister Yanis Varoufakis gave the name *global Minotaur* to the model in which the imperial power, the United States, generates global demand through its domestic market, absorbing the trade surpluses of China, Japan, Germany, South Korea, Taiwan and so forth.[6] In turn, countries in surplus agree to recycle the net proceeds, investing them in public and private US stock and shares. In this way, the stability of the dollar is ensured since its collapse would not be to anyone's benefit ("The dollar is our currency but your problem", is a famous comment attributed to Nixon's Treasury Secretary, John Connally). The metaphor of sacrifices to appease the voracious Minotaur refers to the

---

[5] The quote is taken from Furniss (1920, pp. 19–20, italics in Furniss).
[6] Varoufakis (2011).

tribute that the rest of the world pays to the insatiable US consumer in exchange for the *Pax Americana*, for the political and monetary order guaranteed by the hegemonic power and consumer of last resort. With the global financial crisis of 2007–2008, the financial mechanisms by which the United States ensured expansion of its demand, mainly through consumer credit (including home loans), seized up. These mechanisms had compensated the increasing inequality in the distribution of wealth that severely hobbled middle-class purchasing power in the decades that followed the conservative presidency of Ronald Reagan. These issues are associated with secular stagnation, a topic to which we shall return in Sect. 4.10.

In exchange for the role of global Minotaur, the United States exercised what the great international economist Charles Kindleberger (1910–2003) called imperial leadership, guaranteeing monetary stability and markets for the global economy. It is amusing (if not tragic) to observe how the Minotaur worked in reverse in Europe in the first 10 years of the euro: the local imperial sub-power, Germany, generously fuelled purchase of its goods by European peripheral countries through credit (vendor finance). In Europe, the function of Minotaur, namely absorber of surplus, was not conducted by the leading power but by the vassals. When the German Minotaur realised that the vassals could not pay, it starved the vassals. The German élite regards itself as heir of the Holy Roman Empire, but it never understood the meaning of Pax Imperialis. An ugly tale.

Through these three examples (Diamond's picture of how civilisation emerged, the meaning of mercantilism and the global Minotaur), I set out to show you the power and versatility of the concept of surplus from the Neolithic to Schäuble. However, roses have thorns. The surplus theory encounters many problems that I have yet to explain. First, however, let us take a deviation along Adam Smith avenue. We do so because Smith laid the foundations for the modern economic discourse.

2.5   Adam Smith, Judicious Laissez-Faireism

Adam Smith was not fond of mercantilists, regarding them as sly merchants who under the guise of defending national trade and interests, demanded privileges and protection of their own business through import duties, while ignoring the interests of consumers. The figure of the consumer in economics begins with Smith and achieves its full stature in subsequent marginalist analysis. In actual fact, Smith was not a naive advocate of laissez-faire and the class conflict has a full role in *The Wealth of Nations* (1776).

The Scottish philosopher and economist is indissolubly associated with the concepts of division of labour and invisible hand. The two concepts are closely related. Smith takes the concept of the division of labour from previous authors and makes it the key to the wealth of nations. The division of labour is, first of all, an organisational innovation, a more rational distribution of functions so that each worker has a single task in which she specialises. Thus time is not wasted changing tools or moving about (if anything, the object being produced moves on the production line) and tasks are done more rapidly. Above all, dividing a process into many simple functions favours the invention of industrial machinery that replace human work. Indeed, if today an industrial robot can do many functions, at the time of Smith fragmentation of a process into a few simple operations was a premise for the introduction of machines. Smith also sees the progress of the division of labour as depending on the expansion of markets (an ante litteram "Keynesian" approach to innovation!). This is logical. When I was a child, small villages used to have an emporium (I remember them in my beloved Friuli), a small shop that sold a little of everything. Only in cities was the market sufficiently large to support many specialised shops.

Smith asked who coordinates an economy where there is division of labour, namely an economy in which production is carried on by many firms in a variety of industries? Here Smith is truly innovative: it is the invisible hand of the market that coordinates the division of labour, guiding producers in the choice of how much of each commodity to put on the market. The invisible hand is also not particularly ethereal, since it manifests itself through prices. Let us see how it works.

When is an entrepreneur happy? Put yourselves in her (or his) shoes: she is satisfied when she sells all the goods she takes to market at a price that enables her to cover what she spent, including remuneration of the capital employed. These expenditures are production costs. It is important to understand why production costs include not only wages, materials and so forth but also remuneration of capital. Many of you may once in a lifetime have thought, perhaps after the boss's nth injustice: "Ah, if I had capital I would set up on my own". Well then, if an old forgotten aunt who emigrated to Australia left you some capital, you could invest it in something safe (once it was US treasury bonds) or set up a business, such as a little vegan restaurant (to be in fashion). Clearly, you would want the money to return at least as much as a safe investment, if not more because the restaurant may not be successful and you took the risk of opening it. You would, therefore, set the prices of the vegan dishes to include remuneration of your capital among the production costs, as you would if a bank had lent you the money against interest. If the capital is yours, you pay yourself interest.

An entrepreneur is therefore satisfied when she sells her goods at the expected price, the price that covers production costs including normal or expected remuneration of capital. If, however, you have to lower prices below those expected in order to fill the restaurant, it means that you set up in an area where there is already much supply or little demand. This tells you (or some of your competitors) that you should pack up and go elsewhere. On the other hand, if you easily fill the tables, you will be tempted to raise your prices, or more likely to expand the premises to prevent potential competitors from opening another restaurant in the same street. In brief, by comparing the *normal* price—the one that allows you to recover your costs and remunerate the capital inherited from your aunt—with the *effective* or *market price* you are able to realise, you can tell whether the restaurant is going well, and may perhaps be expanded, or whether you should move.

The invisible hand acts through prices. But what is hiding behind the invisible hand? The answer is *competition*. The competition between producers to meet demand acts in such a way that in the long period, each one takes to market exactly the amount required at the normal price.

Prof, but what do you mean by "long period"? How long is the long period for economists, someone once ironically asked? Long period means that the processes of economic adjustment take time. When we talk about convergence towards long-period equilibria (or positions), we mean that some forces prevailing in those circumstances are making the economy tend towards that outcome. Perhaps this is not achieved, because other circumstances change in the meantime. Through economic analysis we must be content to express trend laws: if in situation A we introduce a shock x, the economy will *tend* towards state B. The adjustment will be complete if nothing else changes in the meantime (the famous ceteris paribus clause). However imperfect, this method is a guide for us to predict, for example, the effects of certain economic policy measures. Of course, step by step, we can make the model more complex. The method was once called comparative statics.

The "rate of profit" is different from "profits". Think of your saving (if any). Certainly, you will try to invest it where it earns the highest interest rate. The interest rate is the ratio of interest earned to capital invested (and it is usually expressed as a percentage: 5% is better than 2%). In the same way, the rate of profit is the ratio of profits to capital advanced. Interest rate and rate of profit both indicate the rate of remuneration of capital. The former is used with reference to financial capital, the latter in relation to real capital of firms. But beware! Real capital and financial capital are flipsides of the same coin, at least to a first approximation. The financial flipside of real capital of firms is share capital. To a first approximation, the terms *interest* and *profit* are also interchangeable, at least with reference to private capital.

2.6   Smith the Equaliser

According to Smith, the invisible hand of competition makes the economy gravitate towards an equalisation of rates of profit in the various activities. The levelling effect is due to the tendency of capital to move towards the sectors where the rate of return is highest. Let us see in more detail.

Economists are notorious for their ad hoc hypotheses. A famous joke begins: "An economist, an engineer and a physicist were shipwrecked on a desert island. They find a tin of tuna…" If you don't know it, you can easily find it online, as I am no good at telling jokes (but do not blame me if economics is known as the "dismal science"). The sense of the story is that while the other two are thinking up practical ways to open the can, the economist reflects and says, "Let us assume we have a can-opener". This would of course be a silly suggestion, but it happens in many economic models in which what is demonstrated (how to open a can) is implied in the initial assumptions (let us assume we have a can-opener). Further on we encounter the so-called *Ricardian vice*, namely seeking to reduce a problem to its essential elements. This vice can indeed be a can-opener for a problem, and it is a feature of economics that I like. So let us assume (Ricardian vice) two sectors, corn and textiles (cloth for simplicity). If the rate of profit in producing cloth is higher than that of producing corn, capital would slowly shift away from the corn sector towards the cloth industry. The output of cloth will thus increase and its prices fall. How long will the process last? Until the rate of profit levels out in the two sectors. Exactly like water in a bucket that, after being shaken, finds its level, in the same way capital mobility leads to uniformity of the profit rate (if you are familiar with the principle of communicating vessels, it is an even better metaphor).

This level of the rate of profit is defined as "normal" by economists (the word normal, from norm or mean, means here "the level to which an economic magnitude gravitates under the action of competition"). Initially, the rate of profit was above normal in the cloth sector and below normal in the corn sector, and this indicated that the economy produced too little cloth and too much corn. The invisible hand of competition between capitals, all seeking the highest remuneration, therefore acts to move capital so as to increase textile production and decrease corn production. At the equilibrium point or normal position of the economy, corn and cloth are sold at a price defined as normal, since at that price there is the same normal rate of profit in both sectors.

At this point, I ask you not to make any moral judgments about the efficiency of laissez-faire on the basis of what we have just seen. What Smith proposes is an effective description of how the invisible hand of the market works. Nobody expressed it well before him, and his description is still perfectly valid as a basis for many other considerations. Let us examine two.

In the first place, our bucket of water seems to be travelling on a bus in Rome, vibrating with every hole in the road (thanks to bad city administrations but also to the European austerity policies). Then there are the ups and downs of the seven hills of Rome, but the water will still find its level. Outside the metaphor, this means that the levelling trend continues even in the middle of economic cycles, waves of optimism and pessimism, innovations, obstacles to free competition and all the rest. The existence of waves, tides or the greenhouse effect does not prevent us from talking about "sea level". This is an important point because many pseudo-heterodox economists confine their criticism of capitalism to the fact that it is chaotic, unplanned, unbalanced and so forth. These are superficial critiques that Marx would perhaps have called vulgar. These economists reject the idea that economic science is concerned with equilibrium positions, without realising that only by proceeding in an orderly manner can one understand where imbalances come from. Be wary of disequilibrium economics!

In the second place, although Smith believed that letting the market operate was a good way to improve consumer well-being, nowhere does his theory of the invisible hand imply that this necessarily happens. In Greece, the invisible hand has continued to act in recent years in the midst of tragedy; just as it acts in Denmark in the midst of widespread well-being. Holding that the invisible hand is a good first approximation to how the market functions under free competition does not mean condoning laissez-faire.

Adam Smith the Marxist. Marx is certainly the father of the concept of the alienation of labour. What did he mean? Marx's idea was that in modern subordinated labour there is a rift between product design and its realization. Craftsmen design and produce, whereas factory workers execute a design made by others. Moreover, this execution is organised in such a way that the worker has no control over execution times. This point was developed by a great American Marxist, Harry Braverman (1920–1976)[7] who had himself been a worker. If technological knowledge is left in the hands of the worker, she will also continue to control working time. Think of when you take the car to the mechanic or when the dishwasher repairman comes to the house: he knows what the problem is, you do not. You are in his hands. He can tell you whatever he likes: that it will take 10 min to fix the problem or half a day (economists call it information asymme-

---

[7] Braverman (1974).

try). Do you think that capitalists could leave production in the hands of workers who were still in control of execution times? According to Braverman, the scientific organisation of labour espoused by Frederick Taylor (1856–1915) is designed to divide workers' tasks into operations that are so simple that their execution time can be measured exactly (does anyone remember the film by Elio Petri "The working class goes to heaven" (US "Lulu the Tool")?) The worker had to be controlled exactly like a machine. Alienation is complete. Smith anticipates all this clearly, contending in the first pages of *The Wealth of Nations* that differences in talent between men are the fruit and not the cause of the division of labour, and later that monotonous simplified tasks can only dull the minds of workers. Not bad for the supposed prophet of laissez-faire!

Very well, Prof, in capitalism there is alienation, but Smith argues that the system of prices is a good way to coordinate economic activity… True. However, Smith is aware of certain limits of laissez-faire. Neither his theory nor that of the other classical economists suggests that the free market leads to full employment. However, you touched the raw nerve of the progressives. Like it or not, with the fall of the Soviet central planning model, the left has jettisoned the idea of an economic model alternative to the market.

A great economist, Dennis Holme Robertson, who collaborated with Keynes at Cambridge in the 1920s but later became critical of the Keynesian revolution, said that the market leads to the economisation of altruism.[8] As Smith remarked, in the market "It is not from the benevolence of the butcher, the brewer or the baker, that we expect our dinner, but from their regard to their own interest. We address ourselves, not to their humanity but to their self-love, and never talk to them of our own necessities but of their advantages".[9]

It must be acknowledged that at the moment the progressive left does not have any radical alternative to capitalism. Many of us would actually be happy with a form of capitalism well-regulated by the State, as we largely saw in the 1950s and 1960s, and in an exemplary manner in the Scandinavian countries. Unfortunately, since the demise of the Soviet Union, capitalism has run wild and power relations between capital and the labour movement have changed radically in favour of capitalists. However, we do not see the gift-economy and altruism, utopian ideas cultivated by certain social forum economists, as a viable alternative at least at the macroeconomic level.

---

[8] Robertson (1956).
[9] Smith (1776, pp. 26–27).

2.7   The Price of the Class Struggle

Smith makes an enormous step forward in the analysis of the nature of the normal (or natural) price of commodities.

Prof, you must admit that you economists are truly without ideals to be concerned with the "nature of the price of commodities". Excuse our ignorance, but what do we citizens or students concerned with social and political issues care about "the nature of prices"? Paraphrasing Oscar Wilde, it is in fact said that economists know the price of everything and the value of nothing. Actually, we shall soon see that price is a microcosm of the class conflict. When I was a politically committed student in the 1970s, we chose economics to know more about the "theory of prices and of income distribution" that since high school we've been hearing fiercely debated among the various schools of thought.

We said above that in the long period, the price of a commodity coincides with its production costs, which include the normal remuneration of capital, hence the normal rate of profit. It also includes remuneration of the labour used to produce the good, for example, your normal wage as manager of the restaurant and that of your employees, as well as the rent you pay the owner of the premises. The price also includes the cost of the materials you use and depreciation of your equipment (ovens, refrigerators, etc.). The price of a commodity is therefore truly a complex issue: to know it we have to know the rate of profit, wages, rent, the price of the other goods we buy to produce the commodity in question. Truly a brainteaser. Let us say that Smith leaves us with the idea that ultimately the price of commodities depends on the remuneration of what we utilized to produce them: capital, labour and resources like buildings or land—the remuneration of these resources is known as rent. What you should now realise is that the nature of prices is closely linked to the topic of the distribution of income between wages, profits and rent (for the sake of simplicity let us ignore rents).

For Smith, the natural price of a commodity depends on the natural wage rate, the natural rate of profit and the natural rate of rent. According to him, in the end everything that goes to produce a good, including intermediate goods and equipment can be reduced to the wages, profits and rents paid to produce them. We must, therefore, ask what the natural wage and rate of profit depend on.

By *natural* wage, rate of profit and rents Smith meant that they are determined by natural laws, including social laws regarding class conflict that can be detected scientifically. In this sense for Smith and the classical economists, natural does not mean invariant, as if nature prescribed a certain income distribution which the subjectivity of social forces would do well not to change, almost as if it were the work of a divinity in the book of creation. On the contrary, "modern" economic theory uses the term natural precisely in this second more mystic sense.

Regarding the rate of profit, the origin of profits as evoked by relation (2.1) is less evident in Smith than in the previous theories of Petty and the Physiocrats. Further progress on the question had to wait until Ricardo.

However, Smith was clear on one thing: the wage level depends on power relations between workers and capitalists, whom he calls the masters. Smith had no doubts about who was stronger: the masters were few in number and could easily reach agreement to resist worker demands; the workers had no accumulated wealth and could not sustain lengthy disputes. Smith did not seem to be without sympathy for the workers. Unlike Margaret Thatcher and the *Adam Smith Institute*, famous for their statement "There is no such a thing as society", Smith strongly believed in human society and considered it to be based on natural empathy between individuals. Indeed, Thatcherism is based more on marginalism than on Adam Smith.

2.8   Ricardo and His Vices

David Ricardo (1772–1823), businessman and politician, was an author of intransigent logic, nicknamed the Prince of Economists. In a certain sense, he is the inventor of abstract reasoning in economics, where problems are reduced to their essential elements, a practice dubbed "Ricardian vice" by Austrian economist and historian of economic thought Joseph Schumpeter (1883–1950). There is actually nothing wrong with simplifying problems to make them clear. Be wary of those who criticise abstract reasoning, especially if used to reveal the deep conflicts of our society! This was precisely the case of Ricardo, who was interested in conflict between the landed aristocracy and industrialists in Britain. As we mentioned in Chap. 1, the landowners favoured a duty on corn imported from European countries, where it was produced more cheaply, so that they could sell domestically produced corn at a higher price. However, Ricardo held that if the price of corn increased, industrialists would have to pay higher wages, and this would mean a lower rate of profit and would discourage investment. To make his point, Ricardo needed to demonstrate that there is an inverse relation between wages and profit. Without meaning to, in this way Ricardo ended up talking about the class struggle (between capital and labour). Bourgeois economists will never forgive him.

Now there is something more difficult to understand, but if you don't panic, you will not have difficulty. Let us return to relation (2.1): Social product − Replacements = Social surplus.

Replacements are the portion of the social product that the ruling classes allocate for worker subsistence—necessities or necessary consumption—and to replace means of production destroyed in the previous production cycle. Like Smith, Ricardo holds that since the means of production (machines, materials, etc.) are also produced by labour, it is possible to say that in the end what needs to be set aside to start a new production cycle consists only in necessities for workers (here Ricardo commits an error, as we shall see). So we can rewrite relation (2.1) as follows:

$$Social\ product - Necessary\ consumption = Social\ surplus \qquad (2.2)$$

or in symbols:

$$P - N = S$$

where P is the social product, N is necessities and S is the social surplus.

Clearly, if necessary consumption coincides with workers' wages, the surplus coincides with the profits of the masters (remember that we are ignoring rents). In other words, relation (2.2) can also be written as:

$$Social\ product - Wages = Profits$$

We saw earlier that the rate of profit is the ratio of profits to capital invested. If, as we postulate here, profits coincide with surplus and the capital invested consists only of necessary consumption (wages) for workers, we can write the rate of profit as follows:

$$r = \frac{Social\ product - Necessary\ consumption}{Necessary\ consumption} \qquad (2.3)$$

or in symbols:

$$r = \frac{P - N}{N} = \frac{S}{N}$$

You don't need a degree in mathematics to see that if wages and therefore necessary consumption N increase for a given social product P, then surplus S and rate of profit r decrease, and there is thus an inverse relation between wages and profits. For example, if $P = 1000$ and $N = 500$, r comes to be 100% (ignore the plausibility of the numbers). If N increases to 750, r falls to 33%.

However, there is a problem. The social product consists of many different commodities, as does necessary consumption. Would you ask your son to do this division?

$$\frac{10 \; pears + 8 \; apples}{6 \; pears + 2 \; apples}$$

No, of course not. Surely you must remember when in the first year of primary school we were taught to solve the following problem: "Your mother goes shopping and buys 10 pears and 8 apples. If the pears cost €1 each and the apples 50 cents, how much does mother spend?"

I know how to do that, Prof! The answer is €14. Right. And if mother buys 6 pears and 2 apples? *I know sir, seven euros!* Good.

If we know the prices, also the preceding ratio can be calculated and comes to €14/€7=2, or:

$$\frac{10 \; pears \; x \; pears \; price + 8 \; apples \; x \; apples \; price}{6 \; pears \; x \; pears \; price + 2 \; apples \; x \; apples \; price} = \frac{14 \; €}{7€} = 2$$

What we did before summing pears and apples was to express them in the same units. If we were biologists we might have summed the vitamins; as economists we used their prices. So, to correctly calculate the rate of profit by relation (2.3) we have to know the price of the commodities that make up *P* and *N*.

What a mess, Prof! In the light of what you explained earlier, to know the price of goods we must, among other things, know the rate of profit. Indeed, it is a vicious circle: to calculate the rate of profit we first have to know prices, but these are unknown if the rate of profit is not known. So it isn't true that economists know the price of everything and the value of nothing. Here they seem to know nothing. So the problem is to measure *P* and *N* without first knowing prices. Ricardo tries two routes.

2.9   Ricardo the Land Surveyor

Along the first route Ricardo examines the agricultural sector and in particular its most important product, corn, which presumably constituted the main wage-good (recall that "corn" in nineteenth-century Britain indicated all cereal grains like wheat or barley, presumably produced using similar technologies).

If P and N consist of corn, then the rate of profit in agriculture r_a can easily be calculated. For example, if P is one million tons of cereals and N half a million tons, r_a will be:

$$r_a = (P - N)/N = \left(10^6 - 5 \times 10^5\right)/5 \times 10^5 = 100\%$$

And the rate of profit of the manufacturing industry? According to Ricardo it can only line up with that of agriculture. It is easy to see why. Once the rate of profit of agriculture r_a is given, the general rate of profit of the whole economy cannot but level out with it, given the tendency of rate of profit to become uniform. So, for instance, if the rate of profit of industry were lower than that of agriculture, capital would move from industry to agriculture, and vice versa in the case of a higher rate of profit of industry. These inter-sectoral movements in capital lead to the levelling of profit rates.

However, also in response to criticism from Robert Malthus (1766–1834), Ricardo admits another problem: if, as one must expect, wages include not only cereals, but also industrial products, such as clothes, the homogeneity of P and N would again be lost and we go back to the problem with pears and apples. To calculate N when it is composed of corn and cloth, we have to know their respective prices, and we are back to square one. Like the land surveyor in *The Castle*, we are again in a situation worthy of Kafka.

2.10 Ricardo the Labour Supporter

Ricardo then resorts to a second quite different measurement of P and N: he measures their "labour content". The product P this time includes the whole set of agricultural and industrial products, many of which are also included in the "necessities" N. Measuring P and N in labour units means measuring them in terms of all the labour respectively used to produce them.

For each product, the labour used to produce it, or "embodied" in it as it is commonly referred to, includes both the live labour used directly in its production, and that spent indirectly to build the means of production utilized in the production process. The engineer can tell us the sum of direct and indirect labour (in principle, of course... a little mental elasticity, please), and this does not require an a priori knowledge of prices. Ricardo can now measure P and N through the following formula, without first knowing prices:

$$r = \frac{P - N}{N} = \frac{\textit{Labour embodied in P} - \textit{Labour embodied in N}}{\textit{Labour embodied in N}} \tag{2.4}$$

Let us take an example. If P is produced with one million hours of labour and N is produced with half a million, the equation gives us $r = 100\%$. If wages increase and N becomes 0.75 million hours of labour (i.e. workers with the higher wages buy and consume more necessities and therefore N contains more hours of work), we obtain $r = 33\%$; the rate of profit has decreased, as expected.

Summing up, Ricardo's distribution theory works like this. Wages settle at a historically determined subsistence level (more about this soon). Given the worker's wage and the number of workers employed, then we also know the wage-bill (total wages) paid in the economy. In real terms, the wage-bill is composed of many different commodities (bread, eggs, blue jeans, etc.), but all can be measured in terms of the direct and indirect labour needed to produce them. So N is easily calculated. We can then also measure the social product P in terms of the labour employed to produce the commodities that compose it. Finally, we can calculate r using relation (2.4). It is evident that if wages increase, N increases and r falls.

2.11   Ricardo the Criminal

The "subversive" content of this theory did not pass unnoticed in the emerging workers' movement (particularly among so-called Ricardian socialists) or among the "hired prize fighters" (Marx's term) defending bourgeois interests. According to Henry Carey (one of the latter), Ricardian theory created havoc among the classes, while George Scrope declared the spread of Ricardo's ideas a crime (we encountered both economists in Chap. 1).

Indeed, in Ricardo there is no Iron Law of wages, like the one Marx later fought on the basis of Ricardo's teachings, that fixes a certain "equilibrium" or "natural" distribution of income between wages and profits (natural in the second of the two senses illustrated in the previous box). And furthermore, the origin of profits is in a quota of the social product not paid to workers, who basically created that product. There is no specific contribution of "capital" to production. Obviously, production equipment (machinery, factory buildings, etc.) is essential for production. However, it contributes to production at any level of the rate of profit and this rate, therefore, does not measure a "relative contribution" of capital: the same equipment would be equally useful also with a rate of profit of zero, for example, if "capital" was owned collectively by the workers, who at that point would also take possession of the surplus. Capitalists only earn profits because they own the capital. And the amount they earn depends on power relations, that is on the relative bargaining power of labour and capital. In the end, even capitalists are rentiers. Certainly, many capitalists are also captains of industry, entrepreneurs and managers. In this capacity they, too, are workers who earn a wage, which according to the customs of the country, is relatively low (as in Sweden) or relatively high (as in Italy), compared to that of an ordinary worker.

But was the labour theory of value without defects? Unfortunately not: the rigorous Ricardo saw that there were problems and so did Marx, who adopted Ricardo's theory of value. These problems cannot be corrected, and to save the surplus approach we will have to abandon the labour theory of value, which is nonetheless a milestone in classical economic theory. Before discussing the problems with the labour theory of value, let us first point out two or three other contributions by Ricardo to the classical theory of surplus.

Typical of the classical approach is that the real wage is taken as given when determining the rate of profit, while determination of the real wage is left to a different "theoretical stage" where more historical and institutional circumstances are taken into account. The same approach is taken with respect to social output, as we shall see shortly. The classical economists advanced different theories of wages.

In Smith, we saw a conflicting theory of wages based on the power relations between capitalists and workers. Ricardo completes this approach, arguing that an increase in wages and hence in workers' standard of living, if persistent in time, becomes second nature for workers (as expressed by Robert Torrens [1780–1864]). Although Ricardo spoke of "subsistence wage", this does not mean that he considered workers to be anchored to a miserable and immutable standard of living. He regards the subsistence wage as historically determined. This is the wage level considered decorous in a particular historical period. Until a few years ago, for example, in Italy a decent wage for an ordinary family would have included decent housing, a car, and a month of holidays per year at the seaside or in the home village. Now that is no longer true: holidays may be reduced to a week and the car… well it has 150,000 km but is still going. The power relations between capital and labour have changed.

2.12 Ricardo the Anti-Keynesian

As already mentioned, in classical economics the level of social output P is also taken as given when determining the profit rate (P must be known in order to calculate r with relations 2.3 or 2.4). As in the case of wage theory, the classical economists also advanced different theories of the determination of the social output. We saw, for instance, that Adam Smith regarded the division of labour as the key determinant of the stage of economic growth. Ricardo's opinion on how the social product P is determined is slightly more problematical. Ricardo believed in Say's Law, which takes its name from Jean-Baptiste Say (1767–1832), the French economist who formulated it. We shall see that Marx and Keynes both criticised Say's Law.

Was Ricardo therefore an anti-Keynesian before Keynes? Yes and no. But let us first clarify what is meant by Say's Law or the Law of markets. It arises from a very simple and useful approach—as a first approximation—to the circular working of the economy as a whole. When firms produce, they distribute income to workers (wages) and to capitalists (profits). These incomes are then spent and the flow of money returns as it were to firms. Say's Law states that from a macroeconomic viewpoint, the economy works as a repeating "income-expenditure" circular flow. The key idea is that in an economy based on the division of labour, since everyone produces to obtain an income to buy other commodities, everything produced is therefore sold. If such an economy produces for a value of a thousand billion euro, a thousand billion in income will be distributed, a thousand billion will be spent and all of the production sold.

$$Production\,(1000) \rightarrow Income\,(1000) \rightarrow Expenditure\,(1000)$$

or

$$Aggregate\ supply\,(1000) = Aggregate\ demand\,(1000)$$

In the first year of university, Say's Law was taught to us and summarized by the expression "supply creates its own demand". Now it is no longer explicitly taught, though its message is conveyed surreptitiously so that it is assimilated subliminally. Economics is no longer taught to stimulate critical inquiry.

The most straightforward objection to the optimistic view that under capitalism aggregate demand always matches aggregate supply, is that part of incomes will be saved, especially in the wealthier classes who enjoy incomes much larger than their nonetheless opulent consumption. Actually, we have already seen this: it is improbable that capitalists and satellite classes consume all the surplus that they allocate to themselves and this causes a problem of demand. In the previous example, if only 800 billion euros is spent on consumer goods and 200 billion is saved, 200 billion euros' worth of production remains unsold.

$$Production\,(1000) \rightarrow Income\,(1000) \rightarrow Expenditure\,(800) + Saving\,(200)$$

or

$$Aggregate\ supply\,(1000) > Aggregate\ demand\,(800)$$

The unsold commodities will remain for a time in the warehouse, but if nothing is done, the firms will reduce production and, as a consequence, unemployment will increase.

However, Ricardo has in mind an economy in which it is true that people save, but they do so in order to invest. In other words, capitalists who save 200 billion of their profits do so to buy 200 billion's worth of capital goods (equipment, plant, etc.), so that in the end the whole income is spent, 800 consumed and 200 invested.

$$Production\,(1000) \rightarrow Income\,(1000) \rightarrow Consumption\,(800) \\ + Investment\ 200)$$

or

$$Aggregate\ supply\,(1000) = Aggregate\ demand\,(1000)$$

Thus we return to equilibrium between aggregate supply and demand. (In the meantime, please note that in this vision banks intermediate saving by transferring it from depositors to investors.)

Keynes's criticism of Ricardo was that in a modern economy, decisions regarding saving are separate from those regarding investment. When the wealthy local professional decides what to do with her ample saving, she does so on the basis of her own motivations (to enjoy her old age, miserliness or whatever), whereas the immigrant laundromat owner at the end of the road decides whether or not to buy new equipment on the basis of other considerations (obsolescence of the current machinery, market trends, etc.). The professional may not necessarily decide to save exactly as much as "beautiful laundrette" decides to invest, and vice versa. There is no relation between the two decisions. And if the professional decides to save more than the proprietor of the laundromat decides to invest, the economy may be in crisis due to a lack of aggregate demand.

However Marx, who understood Ricardo much better than Keynes did, does not judge Ricardo's agreement with Say's Law a sufficient reason to discard all Ricardian theory, especially the theory of surplus. In fact Marx demonstrates that it is not only possible to agree with the theory of surplus while rejecting Say's Law, but also that the surplus approach can underpin the most innovative conclusions of Keynes much better than the vulnerable theoretical basis adduced by Keynes himself.

The proof is that while agreeing with Say's Law, we do not find in Ricardo market mechanisms that could automatically lead to full employment. In a chapter on machines, for instance, he endorses the opinion that motivated the Luddite movement, that is, the belief that mechanisation can reduce employment over the long run, and advances an idea that was annoying for the establishment: there is no automatic market mechanism by which workers made redundant due to technological innovations will find work elsewhere. For Ricardo, technological unemployment is a fact.

Unfortunately, Keynes put Say, Ricardo and the marginalists in the same pot, defining them all as "classical". In so doing, he created more confusion than clarity. Incidentally, Marx was somewhat acknowledged as an antecedent of his theory, but relegated by Keynes in the "underworld" of crank economists. To Marx we now turn.

2.13   Marx the Ricardian

Marx followed Ricardo's surplus approach. Marx's historical–philosophical perspective, called historical materialism, is broader than that of Ricardo. Marx regarded economic formations as historically determined, and just as feudalism was subverted by the bourgeoisie, the fate of capitalism was to be subverted by the proletariat. He also firmly believed that mainstream theories serve the interests of the ruling classes. If his first prophecy has not materialised (though we have been close), mainstream economic science is certainly there to confirm the second proposition.

Marx's theory of distribution is the same as Ricardo's, with an important innovation: the consideration of *physical capital* advanced by capitalists in relations (2.3) and (2.4). This is not complicated. We have already seen that like Smith, Ricardo makes capital advanced by capitalists coincide with the aggregate wage bill advanced to workers. This is not quite correct since capitalists also advance what is needed to buy machinery (fixed capital) and raw materials (circulating capital). Rigorous Ricardo knew this, but it was Marx who took it fully into account. Get used to following me as if we were doing a puzzle. The full figure only emerges at the end.

Fixed capital consists of capital goods that last several production cycles, while circulating capital goods are consumed in a single cycle; the treatment of fixed capital is very complicated and we will, therefore, assume only circulating capital.

Marx calls the labour embodied in the goods that compose the wages advanced to workers *variable capital* (*v*) (in relation 2.4, we called it *N*) and the labour content of physical capital advanced by the capitalist *constant capital* (*c*). He calls the labour contained in *v living labour*, and that contained in *c, dead labour*. Let us see why.

Marx states that capitalists only extract profits, which he also calls surplus value (or surplus labour), from variable capital *v*, i.e. from living labour. What does he mean? Marx says that in capitalism, labour is a commodity that, like the others, is bought and sold. It cannot be otherwise because capitalists own the means of production, whereas workers only have their work to sell in order to eke out a subsistence. Wages are the price of the *labour commodity*. For Marx, in continuity with the classical economists, the price of this particular commodity is equal to its cost of production. How much does it cost to produce a unit of the labour commodity, for example, a day of work? Well, it costs the wage necessary to keep the worker alive and efficient for a day.

Marx points out that the wage must also cover the "reproduction cost" of the worker, i.e. he must be able to reproduce his own species, and must, therefore, be able to support family and offspring. This is true for labour just as it is for equipment. As everyone knows, firms depreciate their machinery, building an amortization fund, so that when the machinery no longer functions they can scrap and replace it. Hence the cost of labour is not just the food to keep the worker going (bread and cheese in the lunch break), but also depreciation (dinner for the spouse and offspring) in order to have fresh labour available after so many years. In the same vein, Keynes held later that pensions were the counterpart of the cost of scrapping used equipment.

Let's suppose, therefore, that capitalists paying a daily wage buy a 10-hour working day. Let us also assume that the wage contains 5 hours of labour, namely that 5 hours of work are needed to produce the wage-goods necessary to sustain the worker and his family for a day. It is as if the worker worked the first 5 hours to produce his subsistence goods and the other 5 hours for the master. In other words, the working day bought by capitalists can be divided in two: in the first part the worker works for himself, in the second he works for the master:

$$10 \text{ hour working day} = labour \text{ embodied in wage - goods 5 hours} + surplus \text{ 5 hours}$$

Prof, this reminds me of the saying that we work a good share of the year for the state and the rest for ourselves. This is a different story in support of tax evasion and the flat tax. In many countries, until late Spring we work to pay the wages of public healthcare personnel and our children's teachers. Certainly some are loafers, but this is another story.

So the capitalist pays 5 hours, the variable capital advanced as wage to the worker, and obtains 10 hours of performance, the whole working day. Is she stealing then? No, Marx says, the capitalist has bought the labour commodity or the 10 hours of work, at its production and reproduction cost, i.e. the wage required to sustain the worker and his family. She is not stealing anything. There is no difference between buying a day of work or a pear. Do not take your boss to court for exploitation, therefore, you will only waste your money (even if you can expect extravagant verdicts from Italian judges). So v is wages (the 5 hours of work of the example) from which the capitalist extracts surplus labour s (the 5 hours of work of the example, also called surplus value). The capitalist pays v and obtains $v + s$, all in perfect observance of market logic. This is the origin of profits, according to Marx. The theory is exactly that of Ricardo although expressed in a slightly different language.

But Prof, isn't the same game possible with constant capital (c), the physical capital that the capitalist advances? To answer the question, let us take a small step ahead.

For Marx and Ricardo alike, the price of a commodity is equal to the labour that goes directly and indirectly to produce it. Repeating the above example, let us suppose that a commodity contains 10 hours of direct labour (of which the worker works 5 hours for himself and 5 hours for the master) and another 10 hours of indirect labour, that contained in physical capital (equipment), so that the value of this commodity is 20 hours. We have:

$$Direct\ labour = 10\ hours = v + s$$

$$Indirect\ labour = 10\ hours = c$$

$$Value\ of\ the\ commodity = Direct\ labour + Indirect\ labour = 10\,h + 10\,h$$
$$= 20\ hours = c + v + s$$

As we can see, the capitalist's profits (surplus value) only come from direct labour, whereas indirect labour passes unchanged into the price of the commodities and this is why indirect labour is defined as constant capital. The capitalist does not extract any surplus value from indirect labour, i.e. from constant capital c. This is why Marx calls it dead labour. He calls v living labour because the capitalist can extract surplus labour from it.

We see that for Marx the value of a commodity is equal to its production costs: cost of physical capital c and wages v plus profits s, all the quantities measured in labour content.

On this basis Marx calculates the rate of profit r completing the surplus relation (2.3) or Ricardo's relation (2.4) (in which the term c did not effectively appear). In other words, r is given by profits (surplus value s) on capital invested (constant and variable, c and v, respectively), with quantities s, c and v measured in terms of labour content:

$$r = \frac{Surplus\ labour}{Labour\ embodied\ in\ constant\ capital + Labour\ embodied\ in\ variable\ capital} \quad (2.5)$$

or in symbols:

$$r = \frac{s}{c+v}$$

This is Marx's version of relations (2.3) and (2.4).

2.14   Marx the Cost Accountant

The labour theory of value has some problems and the astute Ricardo was aware of this as well as Marx. You do not have to be an economist to understand why. For many of our arguments, it suffices to reason as you would for your daily affairs, small or large. The point is this: in a certain sense, Marx was wrong to say that the capitalist only extracts profits from living labour, i.e. this year's labour used to produce goods. In some ways the opposite is true: he extracts more from dead labour, i.e. last year's labour used to produce equipment. Let's take an example from everyday life. If you put your capital in the bank for a year, you will earn interest for 1 year at the agreed rate of interest. If you leave it for 2 years you will earn interest for 2 years plus the interest on the interest (compound interest), and so forth for many years. The longer you keep an investment, the higher its final value. Let us now return to our capitalist. She produces today using both direct labour (variable capital) provided today, and equipment and materials produced yesterday with indirect labour (constant capital), i.e. labour delivered yesterday. Simplifying, to know today's value of constant capital produced yesterday we need to know the rate of profit: *just as* the capital of €100 you invested last year at an interest rate of 5% (or 0.05) is now worth €100 × (1 + 0.05) = €105, and in general €100 × (1 + i) if capitalised at interest rate i; *in the same way*, a capital of €100 invested yesterday for 1 year by the capitalist in labour that produced the equipment, today is worth €100 × (1 + 0.05) = €105 (for a rate of profit r = 0.05). In other words, the capitalist who advances capital for a year has to earn a normal rate of profit on it, otherwise, he would have invested in safe bonds without taking the risks of a commercial investment.

So the hours of labour contained in c and v are not part of the value of a commodity in the same way: the hours contained in c must be capitalised and to do so we have to know the rate of profit (or the rate of interest, synonyms of the "rate of return on capital" to a first approximation).

Correctly calculated, if direct labour $v + s$ and indirect labour c are both 10 hours, the value (or price) of the commodity is not 20 hours but $(v + s) + c$ $(1 + r)$ = 10 hours + 10 hours $(1 + r)$ = ? We cannot solve this simple equation without knowing the rate of profit r at which to capitalise the capital advanced the previous year. But on the other hand, if we do not solve the equation, we cannot determine r.

Ricardo the cheesemaker. Another example from everyday life can help. We all know that matured parmesan cheese (or aged whisky) costs more. You already know why. The maturation process costs money: capital is held immobile and interest must be calculated on it. Two forms of parmesan produced with the same amount of work but with different maturations therefore have different prices. Ricardo is clear on this:

> Strictly speaking, then, the relative quantities of labour bestowed on commodities regulates their relative value, when nothing but labour is bestowed on them. When the times are unequal, the relative quantity of labour bestowed on them is still the main ingredient which regulates their relative value, but it is not the only ingredient; for besides compensating for the labour, the price of the commodity must also compensate for the length of time that must elapse before it can be brought to market. All exceptions to the general rule come under this one of time ....[10]

But Prof, these vicious circles in economics are a genuine vice! True, but Marx suggests a way to solve the question. Later Piero Sraffa achieved the same goal independently. We deal with this in the Appendix to this chapter.

---

[10] Ricardo's letter to McCulloch, 13 June 1820, quoted by Bharadwaj (1986, p. 23).

Marx dead or alive. What we said above is actually how Ricardo (not Marx) realised there was a problem. Moreover, Ricardo thought that the error of considering current (direct) labour to be the same as past (indirect) labour provided in previous years to produce the means of production was a minor mistake. But a theory is right or wrong; it cannot be approximately true! Would an engineer send a shuttle into space on the basis of a theory of trajectories that was more or less true? Only a dictator could recruit the astronauts for the mission!

Marx became aware of the problem in a different way. In line with the labour theory of value, according to which profit is only extracted from living labour, Marx realised that living and dead labour are not in the same proportion in all industries and those that use proportionally more living labour have an advantage and enjoy a higher rate of profit. Let us provide an example. In "light" industries such as clothing, relatively more direct, living labour (variable capital) is used than indirect, dead labour (constant capital), whereas in "heavy" industries such as steel, where plant are enormous, relatively more dead labour is used than living labour. Intuitively, since surplus value is only extracted from living labour, the light industries have an advantage, that is a higher profit rate. Being a good economist, Marx knew that structural differences in rates of profit between sectors would violate the principle of the tendency to a uniform rate of profit: as in physics (I guess), the first task of economic science is to model the centre of gravity, i.e. normal prices having a uniform rate of profit—later it can be concerned with perturbations to the gravitation process. So Marx realized that the centre of gravity cannot be determined from labour values.

2.15 Sraffa the Simultaneous

At the beginning of his studies on the theory of value and distribution, Piero Sraffa was very suspicious of the labour theory of value because he saw in it, especially in Marx, a weight of political–philosophical considerations, which however suggestive, could deflect correct economic analysis. Labour as "the substance of value" assigned an immediate ethical-philosophical content to the theory of prices (profits were unpaid labour). It is no coincidence that the title of Sraffa's famous book was *Production of commodities by means of commodities*.[11] Indeed, Sraffa took a very materialistic view of the theory of surplus, closer to the material calculations of surplus found in Petty, the Physiocrats and Ricardo the Surveyor (in a certain sense also in Jared Diamond) rather than the measurements of embodied labour of Ricardo and Marx. To

---

[11] Sraffa (1960).

give you an idea, Sraffa regarded labour as an input of the production process like any other commodity (coal, machinery, etc.), and the quantity of this input is, therefore, to be measured through the quantity of commodities that enter in the form of wage-goods (the famous necessities) in the wages of the workers employed. Rather than measuring wage-goods in terms of labour, Sraffa measured labour in terms of wage-goods. If we wished to philosophise on the subject, an exercise dear to the radical left, this view is perfectly coherent with the idea that in capitalism labour has been reduced to a commodity. In this regard, Sraffa was struck by a passage written by James Mill (1773–1836), a classical economist contemporary with Ricardo and father of the famous economist and philosopher John Stuart Mill:

> The agents of production are the commodities themselves … They are the food of the labourer, the tools and the machines with which he works, and the raw materials which he works upon.[12]

The orphans of the labour theory of value may note Sraffa's ultra-materialism. But perhaps this is what a certain left does not like: materialism leaves little space for mental ruminations and issue shifting.

With Sraffa the economic system seems like a process in which commodities enter as "agents of production" (input) and exit as production (output). The difference between the net quantity of commodities produced (after subtracting the commodities necessary to replace worn out means of production), and the commodities that go to workers as wages, is the surplus.

But Prof, we are back at square one, at relation (2.1)! In some ways, yes. What Sraffa does, however, and what Marx was close to doing, is to express this economic process by a system of simultaneous equations in which, given the wage-rate (as the basket of commodities composing it) and the production techniques, the prices of all commodities and the rate of profit are determined (see Appendix). The pivot is the idea that the wage-rate is determined by the power balance between workers and capitalists as suggested by Smith, Ricardo and Marx.

A few years after the publication of Sraffa's book in 1960, this idea was adopted by the more militant wing of the Italian unions with a famous slogan: "the wage-rate is an independent variable". Although this is strictly speaking a misrepresentation—even a left-wing government could not set a wage level without any consideration for the surrounding economic situation—the

---

[12] Quoted by Kurz (2012, p. 1542).

shop-floor militants borrowed Sraffa's idea that there is no fixed distribution of income, which depends, rather, on power relations.

Sraffa also suggested that the central bank could intervene in the distribution conflict by fixing the rate of interest (we see how in Chap. 5). This rate of interest would be a benchmark for the rate of profit desired by capitalists (you did the same calculation when you opened the vegan restaurant with the inheritance from your Australian aunt). For example, a higher rate of interest and of profit would increase prices, as it increases the cost of capital used to produce the commodities, leading to a consequent decrease in real wages.

As you can see, Sraffa's theoretical framework is fully coherent with the classical approach; what is perhaps lost with his simultaneous equations is the conceptual clarity of relation (2.3) and of Ricardo's and Marx's similar relations (2.4) and (2.5), respectively.

Sraffa who? Sraffa's famous booklet *Production of commodities by means of commodities* came out in 1960. He had been working on it since the mid-1920s. Born in Turin and studying under Luigi Einaudi, he befriended Antonio Gramsci (1891–1937) in the years of *Ordine Nuovo*, to which he contributed. While still a young university professor, his open anti-fascism and some of his articles denouncing the misconduct of the Italian banking system irritated Mussolini, eventually forcing him to flee Italy in 1926. He was welcomed to Cambridge University by Keynes, to whom he had been introduced by the socialist exponent and scholar Gaetano Salvemini. In Cambridge, he became part of the select circle of young academics close to Keynes, and among other things, exercised great influence on Ludwig Wittgenstein. He visited and gave intellectual and material assistance to Gramsci during his difficult prison years. His rediscovery of the classical surplus approach was expounded in 1951 in the Introduction to the complete works of David Ricardo, at which he had worked meticulously for 20 years. In 1961 Sraffa was awarded the Soderstrom gold medal of the Swedish Academy of Science for this edition of the works of Ricardo, an honour the Italian economist shared with Keynes and few others. Sraffa's sponsor was Gunnar Myrdal (1898–1987), a great Swedish economist and one of the intellectual fathers of Scandinavian social democracy. As we shall underline further on, it was clear to Myrdal, as it was to Sraffa, that there was no idea of a natural distribution of income in Ricardo and that this could be changed to the benefit of workers in the framework of a social compromise. In addition to rediscovering the classical approach, Sraffa also challenged mainstream theory on the basis of analytical problems in its fundamentals. In the 1960s, this criticism led to the so called "two Cambridges controversy", which involved the brightest economists of the time (see Sect. 3.10). The most eminent, Paul Samuelson, admitted that the criticism was correct. Today the controversy is rarely mentioned in university courses, evidently because it has uncomfortable implications for mainstream theory.

Sraffa published very little during his lifetime, but left many manuscripts concerning the long road that led him to reformulate the theory of surplus. These are important, since as he wrote, in economic theory the conclusions are sometimes less interesting than the path by which they are reached.[13] As in life, for that matter. Heinz Kurz of the University of Graz, who has been coordinating the publication of the Sraffa manuscripts since the death of Sraffa's literary executor, Pierangelo Garegnani (1930–2011), defined him as "one of the greatest economists and deepest thinkers of the twentieth century". Garegnani was Sraffa's favourite pupil (and my teacher).

2.16   The Orphans of Labour Value

In the 1940s, once Sraffa had perfected his equations, he returned to the labour theory of value and reappraised it if not for ethical–philosophical content, at least for its role in the search for a provisional solution to the problems of measuring the quantities of relation (2.3). Indeed Sraffa appreciated Marx's "superhuman effort" in understanding the classical theory, at a time when classical ideas were being clouded by "vulgar theories" that emerged after Ricardo, culminating in today's mainstream economics.

Nonetheless, the more orthodox wing of Marxism felt that Sraffa had defrauded the theory of its ethical-moral content. Actually, the idea that surplus is derived from exploitation emerges with solid clarity in Sraffa's work, while nothing of the other aspects of Marx, especially historical materialism, are damaged. Today defence of the labour theory of value seems an anachronistic exercise, often based on bad economics.

2.17   Marx in Crisis

We have already mentioned that the surplus approach provided an explanation of the crises linking unequal distribution of income with problems of aggregate demand (those with teeth have no bread; those with bread have no teeth—Italian proverb). Marx actually proposes various crisis theories.

We will deal immediately with one, namely the idea that crises are due to the anarchic nature of capitalist production which leads to errors, waste and bankruptcy. This is certainly a fact. However, the invisible hand of Smith suggests that albeit among errors and uncertainties, firms tend to produce what

---

[13] See Kurz (2012, p. 1535).

the market demands at the natural or normal price. Say's Law, which evokes a crisis-free laissez-faire economy, would not be easy to criticise solely on the basis of the uncertainty under which entrepreneurs make their decisions. Uncertainty is also an argument that has nothing to do with inequality as the ultimate cause of crises. Nonetheless, many modern heterodox economists still think that the anarchic nature of capitalism, in particular the uncertainty surrounding investment decisions, is at the root of crises. Unfortunately Keynes fed these beliefs. More about this later.

A second theory of crises still enjoys credit among more orthodox Marxists. This is the so-called *Law of the tendency of the rate of profit to fall*. It is not difficult to intuit. As we know, living labour is the source of surplus labour (the part of the working day worked for the capitalist) and of surplus value, i.e. of profits. Besides, Marx thinks that progressive substitution of workers with machines is likely under capitalism, hence substitution of living labour with dead labour. The latter, however, is not a source of surplus value. By pursuing their immediate interest of getting rid of workers—always indolent or inclined to strike—capitalists would dig their own grave: with the progressive substitution of living with dead labour, the source of profits would dry up, and with it the zeal of capitalists to accumulate capital. Capitalism would fall like a ripe pear.

Marx himself was cautious in judging that law, which he guardedly labelled "tendential". The basic objection to the law is that Marx's theory of the rate of profit based on the labour theory of value is defective. The validity of the Law of the tendency of the rate of profit to fall must therefore be reconsidered on the basis of a more correct theory of determination of the rate of profit. In this regard, Sraffa's reformulation of the classical theory disproves the "law": if it is worthwhile adopting a new productive method, then this will always raise the rate of profit for a given real wage.

The question is not without political implications. For orthodox Marxists the law implies that struggles to improve the condition of workers under capitalism, struggles supported by socialist reformers, are useless since they seek improvement in a system which is terminally ill by nature; it is only necessary to wait. In contrast, once the law has been demonstrated false, the idea of worker battles to improve their lot and increase their bargaining power through full employment seems quite justified.

Retro-Marxism or the "Legend of the tendency of the rate of profit to fall". In a talk to the International Monetary Fund in 2013, Larry Summers, previous president of the University of Harvard and Secretary of the US Treasury, took up the old thesis of the secular stagnation of capitalism, motivating it with the structural weakness of aggregate demand (more about this in Sect. 4.10).

Recently some Marxists endorsed this thesis by appealing to the "law" under discussion. They also presumed to find empirical confirmation of it. The problem, like the devil, is in the details and especially in the fact that Marxist empirical analyses focus upon the *actual* rate of profit (the one effectively realized), which is not the relevant one for appraising the law. Indeed, what counts is the *normal* rate of profit, which is the rate Marx refers to in his law. Technically the normal profit rate is the rate expected for newly installed capital goods, calculated on normal input and output prices, obtained with the dominant technique and using productive capacity at a rate considered normal (the dominant technique is the most up-to-date and profitable in the given circumstances). Now, there's no doubt that during a depression the *current* rate of profit drops. But that does not imply that the *normal* profit rate follows the same trend.

In practice, if no attempt is made to correct the effective profit rate for cyclic variations in the degree of utilization of the stock of capital installed, there can actually be a tendency of this rate to fall, due solely to the onset of stagnation, when lower demand reduces sales figures, profits and, for a given capital invested, the effective rate of profit. Let us take a US case as example: at the end of the 1970s the Federal Reserve raised interest rates to extremely high levels, causing a sharp contraction in economic activity. This made the effective rate of profit fall, without necessarily affecting the normal rate of profit, indeed quite the opposite. It is therefore easy to base one's arguments on spurious relations (the effective rate of profit), which are different from the truly relevant analytical category (the normal rate of profit). This is what I meant earlier by "bad economics".

It also shows why "looking at the figures" is not enough: the figures must be filtered and interpreted through a good theory.

Analysis of capitalist trends can actually benefit in two ways from discarding the "law". First of all, much more weight is given to the role of aggregate demand in the processes of growth and accumulation, instead of seeing Keynesian policies as useless palliatives that only delay the end of capitalism. In second place, it opens the way to authentic Marxist analysis based on historical and political factors. The power relations between opposing interest groups (social classes) are the main determinant of the distribution of income and the rate of profit, which does not in fact follow any mechanical long-period trend—like in the controversial "law"—unrelated to the social conflicts historically prevalent. In brief, more space for politics!

In effect, Summers also explains the structural shortage of aggregate demand on the basis of increasing inequality in the years of globalisation. This seems to confirm Marx's law on the relative impoverishment of the proletariat. The improving living standard of the masses in the golden age (1950–1979) seemed to belie this law and to bury Marx. Actually, however, that growth was due to historical circumstances that favoured worker bargaining power, for example, the Soviet model's challenge of capitalism. Once those circumstances ceased, history seems to have continued along the paths foreseen by Marx.

Fortunately, Marx has a third theory of crises based on the rejection of Say's Law. A large part of aggregate demand comes from workers, who spend all their wages, whereas capitalists may not spend all their income (as Say and Ricardo assume). Part of the production can then remain unsold. Marx refers to this as the "realization problem". He argues that all capitalists hope that other capitalists will pay high wages in order to maintain the demand for goods, but at the same time keep the wages of their own workers low, so as to pocket higher profits. In other words, a case of wanting their cake and eating it too. In the end, capitalists seek to pay the lowest possible wages, at the expense of the demand for goods. Indeed, their primary objective is a high rate of profit, even if depressed demand leads some firms to close down.

2.18   The Proletariat Has ~~No~~ Nation...

Marx actually has a fourth theory of crises, which was based on the concept of the *industrial reserve army*. The aim of capitalists is to valorise capital (make it increase in value) according to a sequence also dear to Keynes:

$$M - C - M'$$

where M is initial (monetary) capital, which when used to buy and then sell commodities (C), increases in value, i.e. is "valorised" so *that $M' > M$*. How does this happen? According to Marx, the mercantilists believed that those more skilled at trading would trick their counterparts, achieving a higher price and therefore selling their goods at a price higher than the normal cost of production. Actually, he continues, the valorisation of capital occurs in a market, the labour market, where capitalists purchase the labour–commodity that yields surplus value, as we have seen. This is the secret of the valorisation of capital.

However, when the rate of accumulation of capital increases, the demand for labour goes up, the bargaining power of workers increases and wages tend to be higher, making the rate of profit fall. According to Marx, for capitalism to function well, a constant pool of unemployed workers, an industrial reserve army as it were, is needed to moderate the labour market. It is typically composed not only of unemployed males, but also of females, immigrants, elderly workers, and, in Marx's time, vagabonds, children and invalids. These workers are often kept out of the labour market, but are called back into service when the thrust of the labour force composed of mature males fails to meet the needs of accumulation, with the risk that their bargaining power grows and their wages increase. In the long period, also fertility falls into line with the needs of accumulation, but this takes a long time (and we now know that the link between fertility and economic growth is extremely complex). Importation of migrant labour is typically a much faster way to moderate wages. The introduction of machines is another method used by capitalists to create unemployment and preserve the industrial reserve army. Finally, a crisis is a further way in which by increasing unemployment, capitalists replenish a dwindling industrial reserve army. Non-orthodox economists, for example, hold that the high unemployment in western countries since the end of the 1970s was a deliberate choice of capitalism after the prevalence of full employment in the previous two decades and the consequent union indiscipline at the end of the 1960s.

In Chap. 3, we look at conventional theory and momentarily set aside heterodox economics. To defeat the mainstream, we need to know it.

Appendix

Marx the Transformer

Marx was a great economic scientist and this is evident from how he approached what is known as his "transformation of values into prices". This problem is also a good exercise in how to "do" economics.

We saw that Marx and Ricardo were aware of the problems of the labour theory of value. In Marx's terms, if goods were exchanged according to the labour embodied in them, those from "light" sectors that use more living (direct) than dead (indirect) labour (the one incorporated in means of production) would enjoy a higher rate of profit (r) than "heavy" sectors that use more dead than living labour. This is because living and not dead labour is the source of surplus value (i.e. profit). Marx and Ricardo were also both aware that in actual fact, capitalists calculate the profit rate in relation to the total capital they advance, alive or dead, whether in the form of direct or indirect labour. However, Marx does not want to give up the idea that only direct (living) labour gives rise to surplus value. He then strives to prove that although goods are *not* exchanged according to the principle of embodied labour, surplus value is still only determined by direct labour. Let us see how he reconciles the fact that the rate of profit is actually calculated on variable capital (living labour) as well as constant capital (dead labour) with the idea that its ultimate source is only variable capital.

Marx starts by writing prices as if they were determined by embodied labour. Let us assume (Ricardian vice):

- an economy with only two commodities, corn and steel;
- that the price of a unit of corn is p_c and that of a unit of steel is p_s;
- that for each commodity the unit is chosen so that it incorporates one unit of labour (e.g. if the unit of labour is a labour year, the unit of corn is the quantity of corn such that its production requires 1 year of direct and indirect labour);
- finally, let us assume that in both industries constant capital consists of steel only and variable capital (wages) of corn only.

Using the notation of Sect. 2.12, we write the two labour value/price relations:

$$\begin{cases} p_c = c_c + v_c + s_c = 1 \\ p_s = c_s + v_s + s_s = 1 \end{cases} \quad (2.6)$$

In relations (2.6), the price of each commodity is the sum of the labour values, i.e. of the indirect or dead labour contained in the constant capital and of the direct or live labour embodied in the variable and surplus labour (or surplus value) respectively employed in the two sectors. The indirect or "dead labour" used in the two sectors is c_c and c_s, respectively, and the direct or "living labour" is $l_c = v_c + s_c$ and $l_s = v_s + s_s$, respectively. For instance, c_c is the quantity of labour embodied in the steel used to produce one unit of corn, and $v_c + s_c$ is the live or direct labour employed for the same production. The equality to 1 derives from our choice of the units in which corn and steel are measured.

You will recall that living labour is a source of surplus value because workers use part of their working day to produce that portion of the social product that returns to them as wage-goods (v), whereas for the rest of the day they produce commodities for the master, which are his surplus or surplus value (s). Marx defines the ratio s/v as the "rate of exploitation", in other words the ratio of the part of the working day that goes to the master to the part that goes to the worker. Assuming a 10-hour working day, if the workers "work for themselves" for 5 hours (producing wage-goods) and for the master for 5 hours (producing the surplus), the resulting rate of exploitation will be $s/v = 5/5 = 1$ (i.e. 100%). This ratio must be the same in the two sectors (for a given working day), namely:

$$\frac{s_c}{v_c} = \frac{s_s}{v_s} \tag{2.7}$$

It has to be the same, otherwise, the workers would migrate to the sector where they are less exploited, i.e. where for a given working day they receive a higher wage. Competition between workers to work in that industry would lead to a decrease in wage in that industry and a levelling of the rate of exploitation. As with communicating vessels, Marx holds that the rate of profit in the two sectors must also be identical. If commodities are exchanged in proportion to their labour values, we determined the rate of profit using relation (2.5), $r = \frac{s}{(c+v)}$ (the surplus value or profits divided by the constant and variable capital advanced). Hence the condition for uniformity of the rate of profit in the two sectors is:

$$r_c = \frac{s_c}{c_c + v_c} = r_s = \frac{s_s}{c_s + v_s} \tag{2.8}$$

If you are lucky enough to have a daughter who is a science nerd (if not, you must trust me), you can check with her that we simultaneously have uniformity of the rates of exploitation (relation 2.7) and of the rates of profit (relation 2.8) only if $\frac{c_c}{v_c} = \frac{c_s}{v_s}$. This ratio, that Marx calls the "organic composition of capital"— i.e. the ratio of the two capital components (constant and variable)—must be the same in both sectors. But this is what we said in words: if commodities are exchanged at their labour values, uniformity of the rate of profit entails that there are no light and heavy sectors: the organic composition of capital must be the same. Since this is impossible, as a true scientist, Marx can only conclude that commodities are not exchanged according to the labour embodied in them.

Now for some numbers. Here is a numerical example of relations (2.6). The numerical values are taken from Garegnani[14]:

$$\begin{cases} p_c = 1 = 0.4 + 0.3 + 0.3 \\ p_s = 1 = 0.6 + 0.2 + 0.2 \end{cases} \tag{2.6'}$$

---

[14] Garegnani (1984).

The rate of profit in the corn sector is $r_c = \dfrac{s_c}{c_c + v_c} = \dfrac{0.3}{0.4 + 0.3} = 3/7$, which is different from that in the steel sector, which comes to 1/4. In the lighter sector (corn), it is higher.

Marx then reasons as follows. If capitalists have to obtain the same rate of profit (r), prices should be calculated by applying the latter to all the capital advanced in each sector (respectively $c_c + v_c$ and $c_s + v_s$). Marx does this with relations (2.9), in which he determines the "prices of production":

$$\begin{cases} p_c = (c_c + v_c)(1 + r) \\ p_s = (c_s + v_s)(1 + r) \end{cases} \tag{2.9}$$

Relations (2.9) "transform" labour values (c_c, c_s, v_c and v_s) into prices (p_c and p_s). However, Marx insists that the rate of profit for the economy continues to be calculated on the basis of relation (2.5) [$s/(c + v)$], where the values of c, v and s for the whole economy are still measured in labour content. The idea that the rate of profit depends on the ratio of the surplus to capital advanced, all measured in labour terms, is thus preserved from the viewpoint of the economy as a whole. The prices of production, calculated with relations (2.9), then have the "democratic" task of making sure the same rate of profit is uniformly applied in the two sectors.

With the above numbers, the general rate of profit calculated with relation (2.5) is

$$r = \frac{s}{(c + v)} = \frac{0.5}{(1 + 0.5)} = \frac{1}{3}$$

where $s = s_c + s_s = 0.3 + 0.2$, etc.

Relations (2.9) become:

$$\begin{cases} p_c = (0.4 + 0.3)\left(1 + \frac{1}{3}\right) = 28/30 \\ p_s = (0.6 + 0.2)\left(1 + \frac{1}{3}\right) = 32/30 \end{cases} \tag{2.9'}$$

Before the "transformation", a unit of corn was exchanged for a unit of steel. Not now! Steel is worth more (32/30 against 28/30 of corn) for a reason. Indeed, the prices of production settle the "unfair" situation in which capitalists in the steel sector obtained a lower rate of profit for labour values.

At this point, Marx perceives a further problem: when capitalists calculate prices of production on the basis of the costs of capital advanced for means of production (c) and for wages (v), they do not calculate these costs at their "labour value". Indeed, in relations (2.9), we see that the quantities c_c, c_s, v_c and v_s are still "labour values". But capitalists do not purchase means of production c_c and c_s (for example) at their "labour value", they buy them at their production price p_c and p_s. With great acumen, Marx then suggests taking this into account and calculating the cost of inputs c_c, c_s, v_c and v_s at their price of production, which amounts to suggesting that relations (2.9) be modified as follows (although he did not attempt to write relations 2.10):

$$\begin{cases} p_c = \left(c_c p_s + v_c p_c\right)\left(1+r\right) \\ p_s = \left(c_s p_s + v_s p_c\right)\left(1+r\right) \end{cases} \qquad (2.10)$$

These equations could be written in this simple form because of two further simplifying assumptions we made to render the problem as simple as possible: constant capital c_c and c_s is multiplied by p_s because we assumed it consists only of steel, and variable capital v_c and v_s is multiplied by p_c because we assumed wages consist of corn.

Marx does not write down these equations, but from his suggestions it seems clear that he believed that since r is determined by relation (2.5) [$s/(c + v)$], relations (2.10) contains as many unknowns (the prices) as equations (one for each good), and the problem is mathematically determinate (as some of you may remember from school, a system of two equations in two unknowns is solvable, i.e. it allows the two unknowns to be determined.).

However, we can detect a further problem.

Call your scientist daughter. If we set the price of one of the two commodities at one, e.g. $p_s = 1$, that is, we take steel as a unit of measure (or numeraire)—somewhat as in primitive economies prices were measured in terms of cows or other goods, or so they say—then relations (2.10) are sufficient to determine the remaining two unknowns p_c and r. So relation (2.5), upon which Marx continued to rely to calculate the rate of profit on the basis of the "labour value" of c, v and s, is no longer needed!

Very well, Prof, but relations (2.10) still contain labour value coefficients c_c, c_s, v_c and v_s, which therefore still have a determinant role... In actual fact, they do not! It is not easy to explain why, but let me try.

Consider c_c. This "coefficient of production" represents the quantity of labour needed to produce the quantity of steel necessary to produce a unit of corn. Now a unit of steel was defined above as containing one unit of labour (e.g. a working year). In the example, $c_c = 0.4$ means that c_c contains 40% of a unit of labour. What changes if I say that $c_c = 0.4$ means that c_c corresponds to 40% of a physical unit of steel? Nothing, because a physical unit of steel was precisely defined as that containing a unit of labour. Consider v_s which equalled 0.2 in the example. This is the quantity of labour contained in the wage-goods (in our case corn) of the workers employed to produce a quantity of steel that embodies a year of work. Now $v_a = 0.2$ means that v_a is both 20% of a unit of labour, and 20% of a physical unit of corn (since a unit of corn is defined as that produced with a unit of labour). So we no longer need to measure the coefficients c_c, c_s, v_c and v_s in "embodied labour"—we could, but a "physical" measure would do as well, so "embodied labour" does not play any essential role. Relations (2.10) that we derived are a simplified form of the equations Sraffa finally published in 1960 after drafting them in the second half of the 1930s (actually Sraffa did not start with Marx's equations; only later did he realise their converging paths).

Prof. but where are wages in relations (2.10)? We already touched on this. Wages are represented by v_c and v_s, the quantity of corn that goes to workers employed in the two sectors, the quantities of wage-corn per unit product. This quantity depends on a technical factor—whether the sector is light or heavy—but also on the hourly wage, measured in corn, of the workers. If we know the wage rate and the production techniques, relations (2.10) suffice to determine the rate of profit and the exchange ratio between the two commodities. With a little patience, we could even demonstrate that wage and rate of profit are in an inverse relation, but that is enough for now.

Further Reading

The two main popular books written by archaeologist Vere Gordon Childe are Childe (1936, 1942). Useful summaries of his theories are Childe (1950, 1957). A portrait of the great archaeologist is in Sherratt (1989). In light of many studies in anthropology and archaeology, the break that Childe and Diamond envisaged between the Neolithic and Urban revolutions and the primitive state of hunter-gatherers must be revised to some extent. In fact, many scholars speak of complex and affluent hunter-gatherer societies, often characterized by strategies aimed at preventing the emergence of élites. The most classic text in this regard is Marshall Sahlins (1972). With the adoption of agriculture in some parts of the world, this primitive Eden was abandoned and part of the population became progressively subjugated to work in favour of an élite, the only true beneficiary of "civilization". So the reasons for this passage are still much debated. A recent example of the study of the origin of social stratification in ancient civilizations conducted on the basis of the surplus approach is by the distinguished Italian archaeologist, foreign associate member of the American National Academy of Sciences, Marcella Frangipane (2018).

Dennis H. Robertson was famous for his delightful quotes from Alice by Lewis Carroll. What does the organization of economic activity through the market allow us to economize? asks Robertson. And he answers (Robertson 1956, p. 154) by quoting Alice: "'Oh, tis love, tis love,' said the Duchess, 'that makes the world go around'. 'Somebody said,' whispered Alice, 'that it's done by everybody minding their own business.' 'Ah well,' replied the Duchess, 'it means much the same thing.'" And so he concludes: "if we economists mind our own business, and do that business well, we can, I believe, contribute mightily to the economizing, that is to the full but thrifty utilization, of that scarce resource Love—which *we* know, just as well as anybody else, to be the most precious thing in the world". In other words, Robertson argues that by preaching economic organization based primarily on self-interest rather than altruism, economics encourages society not to dissipate its scarce endowment of virtue. Consequently, the more the economy relies on love, the more it will waste it.

In a recent book, Roberto Marchionatti and Mario Cedrini (2017) challenge this logic by defending an economy based on giving and reciprocity. As I already said, anthropology and archaeology studies suggest that most hunter-gatherer communities were probably egalitarian, not due to inherently good human nature, but through social institutions aimed at suppressing hierarchical behaviour. The distinguished archaeologist Bruce Trigger (2003) wonders whether this is possible or even desirable in more complex societies. Regarding the debate in archaeology and anthropology on the origin of inequality, start with Ames (2013). Marchionatti and Cedrini refer, among others, to Karl Polanyi. Though acute, the latter rejected the surplus approach. I discuss this critically in Cesaratto and Di Bucchianico (2020) where it is argued that study of the different economic formations—from the most ancient, through feudalism, to capitalism—concerns how institutions have organized production and distribution of the surplus.

After the First World War, which ended the era of classical liberalism, economic nationalism took hold again and studies on mercantilism flourished, to which Keynes also dedicated sympathetic pages of his opus magnum, the *General Theory* (Keynes 1936). He relied on the classic treatise by Eli Heckscher (1935). Charles Kindleberger, a magnificent example of political economist, set out his thesis on the need for an imperial hegemon to act as a stabilizer of the global economy in Kindleberger (1973). This stabilising role relates in particular to supporting global demand through the expansion of its internal market, so that imperial power acts as "buyer of last resort".

The "Ricardian vice" is examined by Heinz Kurz (2016). The fundamentals of classical theory are discussed in Garegnani (1984). The wage theory of classical economists is well illustrated by Antonella Stirati (1994). I also recommend careful study of the already mentioned booklet by Krishna Bharadwaj (1986). For a development of Sraffa's suggestion regarding the influence of the interest rate pursued by the central bank on the distribution of income, see Massimo Pivetti (1991).

An introduction to different aspects of Sraffa's work can be found in Roncaglia (2009). The events leading up to award of the prestigious Swedish gold medal in 1961 are narrated by Arthmar and McLure (2016). Myrdal was later awarded the so-called "Nobel Prize" for economics of the Sveriges Riksbank, the Swedish central bank, one of the few awarded to a non-conformist economist. Nevertheless, Myrdal was in favour of abolition of the prize, as was the ultraliberalist Friedrich Von Hayek (1899–1992). On the spurious nature of the "Nobel Prize" for economics see Henderson (2005).

Why Marx's labour theory of value is defended by some orthodox Marxists on the basis of elementary errors is well explained by Gary Mongiovi (2002). For a Sraffian criticism of the Law of the tendency of the rate of profit to fall, see Steedman (1977, Chap. 9). I thank Stefano Di Bucchianico for suggestions on some recent Marxist interpretations of the crisis, based on the Law of the tendency of the profit rate to fall.

The question whether or not Sraffa achieved his results independently of Marx is a sensitive political question. Garegnani and Kurz use Sraffa's unpublished works to demonstrate that far from being inspired by Marx's labour theory of value, he initially saw this theory as a corruption of the more solid surplus approach, as found in Petty and the physiocrats (and in Ricardo *land surveyor*). A critical exposition of the different points of view with references can be found in Kurz (2012). The events of the "salary as an independent variable" in the hot years of the workers' struggles are evoked by Fernando Vianello (2004, pp. 510–12).

Sraffa, one of the greatest intellectuals of the previous century, was obviously in contact with his peers. Andrea Ginzburg (2014, 2016) and Amartya Sen (2003) provide interesting pictures of his relationship with Gramsci and Wittgenstein, respectively. The friendship with Gramsci occurred against the dramatic political and human events of the period. Gramsci died suspecting that the Italian Communist Party had deliberately let him languish in prison. Close to the Communist leader to the end, Sraffa tried to dissuade him from this idea, and after his death there followed a dramatic break between the economist and Tania Schucht, Gramsci's sister-in-law. At the centre is the story of a letter that Ruggero Grieco, a high communist leader in exile, wrote to Gramsci in 1928, a letter that put him in bad light before the fascist court. Various charlatans accused Sraffa of connivance with the alleged Communist strategy of isolating Gramsci in prison. A more balanced reconstruction of this dramatic and exciting story is by Giancarlo De Vivo (2017). Regarding the letter and more generally the relationship between Sraffa and Gramsci, see also Nerio Naldi (2012, 2020).

On the role of unemployment as a disciplinary tool, it is essential to read the essay by Michal Kalecki (1943), where the Polish economist (1899–1970) explains why capitalism is incompatible with full employment: capitalism could achieve it, but it would make the working class too strong. And if it did so by expanding public spending, it would prefer military spending, because social spending could make the working classes aware that modern society can afford generalized welfare. Pure economic poetry.

References

Ames, K. M. (2013). Complex hunter-gatherers. In C. Smith (Ed.), *Encyclopedia of global archaeology*. New York: Springer Science+Business Media.

Arthmar, R., & McLure, M. (2016). *Sraffa, Myrdal and the 1961 Soderstrom gold medal*. Business School, University of Western Australia, Working Paper No. 16.18.

Bharadwaj, K. (1986). *Classical political economy and the rise to dominance of supply and demand theories* (2nd ed.). Calcutta: University Press India (1st ed. Orient Longman, 1978).

Braverman, H. (1974). *Labor and monopoly capital: The degradation of work in the twentieth century*. New York: Monthly Review Press.

Cesaratto, S., & Di Bucchianico, S. (2020). The surplus approach, Polanyi and institutions in economic anthropology and archaeology. Quaderni DEPS, N. 828 (forthcoming in *Annals of the Fondazione Luigi Einaudi*, special issue "Marshall Sahlins's Stone Age Economics, a Semicentenary Estimate").

Childe, G. C. (1936). *Man makes himself.* London: Watt.

Childe, G. C. (1942). *What happened in history.* London: Pelican Book.

Childe, G. C. (1950). The urban revolution. *The Town Planning Review, 21*(1), 3–17.

Childe, G. C. (1957). The bronze age. *Past & Present, 12,* 2–15.

De Vivo, G. (2017). *Nella bufera del Novecento. Antonio Gramsci e Piero Sraffa tra lotta politica e teoria critica.* Rome: Castelvecchi.

Diamond, J. (1997). *Guns, germs, and steel: The fates of human societies.* New York: Norton & Company.

Frangipane, M. (2018). From a subsistence economy to the production of wealth in ancient formative societies: A political economy perspective. *Economia Politica, 35*(3), 677–689.

Furniss, E. (1920). *The position of the laborer in a system of nationalism: A study in the labor theories of the later English mercantilists.* Boston: Houghton Mifflin Company.

Garegnani, P. (1984). Value and distribution in the classical economists and Marx. *Oxford Economic Papers, 36*(2), 291–325.

Ginzburg, A. (2014). *Two translators: Gramsci and Sraffa.* Centro Sraffa Working Papers, No. 1.

Ginzburg, A. (2016). Sraffa and social analysis: Some methodological aspects. *Situations, 6*(1/2), 151–185.

Heckscher, E. F. (1935). *Mercantilism.* London: George Allen and Unwin (2nd ed. 1955), 2 volumes.

Henderson, H. (2005, February). L'imposture. *Le Monde diplomatique.*

Kalecki, M. (1943). Political aspects of full employment. *The Political Quarterly, 14*(4).

Keynes, J. M. (1936). *The general theory of employment, interest, and money.* London: Macmillan.

Kindleberger, C. (1973). *The world in depression: 1929–1939.* Berkeley: University of California Press.

Kurz, H. (2012). Don't treat too ill my Piero! Interpreting Sraffa's papers. *Cambridge Journal of Economics, 36*(6), 1535–1569.

Kurz, H. (2016). Is there a "Ricardian vice"? And what is its relationship with economic policy ad "vice"? *Journal of Evolutionary Economics, 27*(1), 91–114.

Marchionatti, R., & Cedrini, M. (2017). *Economics as social science: Economics imperialism and the challenge of interdisciplinarity.* Abingdon: Routledge.

Mongiovi, G. (2002). Vulgar economy in Marxian garb: A critique of temporal single system Marxism. *Review of Radical Political Economics, 34*(4), 393–416.

Naldi, N. (2012). Two notes on Piero Sraffa and Antonio Gramsci. *Cambridge Journal of Economics, 36*(6), 1401–1415.

Naldi, N. (2020). Antonio Gramsci's letters that Piero Sraffa did not forward to the Italian Communist Party. In A. Sinha (Ed.), *A reflection on Sraffa's revolution in economic theory.* London: Palgrave Macmillan.

Pivetti, M. (1991). *An essay on money and distribution.* London: Macmillan.

Robertson, D. H. (1956). What does the economist economize? In D. H. Robertson (Ed.), *Economic commentaries.* London: Staples Press Limited.

Roncaglia, A. (2009). *Piero Sraffa*. Houndmills: Palgrave Macmillan.

Sahlins, M. (1972). *Stone age economics*. New York: de Gruyter.

Sen, A. (2003). Sraffa, Wittgenstein, and Gramsci. *Journal of Economic Literature, 41*(4), 1240–1255.

Sherratt, A. (1989). V. Gordon Childe: Archaeology and intellectual history. *Past & Present, 125*(Nov.), 151–185.

Smith, A. (1776). *An inquiry into the nature and causes of the wealth of nations*. Edited by R. H. Campbell & A. S. Skinner. Indianapolis: Liberty Classics.

Sraffa, P. (1960). *Production of commodities by means of commodities*. Cambridge: Cambridge University Press.

Steedman, I. (1977). *Marx after Sraffa*. London: New Left Books.

Stirati, A. (1994). *The theory of wages in classical economics*. Aldershot: Edward Elgar.

Trigger, B. (2003). All people are [not] good. *Anthropologica, 45*(1), 39–44.

Turgot, A. R. J. (2011). *The Turgot collection* (D. Gordon, Ed.). Auburn: Mises Institute.

Varoufakis, Y. (2011). *The Global Minotaur: America, Europe and the future of the global economy*. London: Zed Books.

Vianello, F. (2004). La Facoltà di Economia e Commercio di Modena nella prima fase della sua vita. Storia di un gruppo di economisti. In A. Graziani & G. Garofalo (Eds.), *La formazione degli economisti in Italia (1950-1975)* (pp. 481–534). Bologna: Il Mulino.

3

Marginal Economics

Abstract This chapter introduces mainstream economics. Marginal (or marginalist) theory is based on a harmonic view of income distribution, unlike the conflictual approach of classical theory. According to marginal theory, every "factor of production" (labour, "capital" and land) is rewarded in proportion to its presumed contribution to production. According to the surplus approach, capital exploits labour, whereas in marginalist theory no one exploits anyone. We also examine the marginalist belief that in the absence of obstacles, the free market leads to full employment of labour and of the other "factors of production".

We then consider marginalist monetary analysis. This is particularly important because it forms the basis of the European treaties for the currency union. According to marginalist monetary analysis, if the markets for production factors and goods are flexible enough, the economy tends towards full employment. Monetary policy is therefore of no help for achieving full employment but is only concerned with price stability. Keynes was critical of this view. However, he did not have enough analytical tools to undermine it definitively. Thanks to the results of the "two Cambridges controversy" we have such instruments today. The chapter explains in an introductory way where the analytical problems of marginalism lie.

© Springer Nature Switzerland AG 2020
S. Cesaratto, *Heterodox Challenges in Economics*,
https://doi.org/10.1007/978-3-030-54448-5_3

3.1   The Journey of the Critical Economic Theory

The title of this chapter, Marginal Economics, evokes a famous Italian book of poems from the gloomy second half of the 1970s, *Dal fondo—La poesia dei marginali* (*From the bottom—The poetry of the marginalized*).[1] At that time, in Italy and elsewhere, the hopes of a radical change born in the 1960s were fading (it was called *desencanto* or disenchantment in Spain, *riflusso* or reflux in Italy). By marginal economics, however, I am not referring to poetic "alternative economies" (alternative to the market economy), but to mainstream economic doctrine, the correct name of which is not "neoclassical", but, as we shall see, "marginalist" or "marginal".

In distant 1973, two distinguished Sraffian economists, Andrea Ginzburg and Fernando Vianello, began a (then) influential article on Marxism and economics with the following optimistic statement: "In our opinion, there is no doubt that the economic theory that has reigned practically unchallenged for almost a century is now in deep crisis."[2] Unfortunately, at the same time, a monetarist counter-revolution was incubating in US universities, destined to sweep aside Keynesian theory which had held sway since the end of World War 2. It would also prepare the way for Reagan and Thatcher at the end of the decade. The climate in Italy was still quite different. With events like the foundation of the heterodox Faculty of Economics at Modena University and the "150 hours" (time available for workers wishing to study, met by many universities with courses ad hoc), criticism of political economy, profoundly influenced by the work of Sraffa, merged with the cream of worker militancy and union claims. Unfortunately, also in Italy, things were soon about to go in a very different direction.

The intellectual demand of the worker movement for an alternative to mainstream economic theory clearly contributed to the formidable impact of Sraffa's work in the halcyon years of the worker and student movements, at least in Italy. At a more intellectual level, a central role was taken by the echo of the shock to economic theory occasioned by the famous Cambridge controversy on capital theory. To hazard a metaphor, this controversy was the Vietnamese front in the political economy battle of ideas. Italian academia, initially cool to the Keynesian revolution—with the exception of Federico Caffè (1914–1987), Paolo Sylos Labini (1920–2005) and a few others—was for several years convinced by Sraffa's lesson, the effect of which also spread

---

[1] Bordini and Veneziani (1978).
[2] Ginzburg and Vianello (1973).

abroad. The example of a distinguished Italian economist, Luigi Spaventa (1934–2013), is emblematic of how things went: initially a fervent follower of Sraffa, he was gradually convinced by the monetarist counter-revolution and regretted the 1960s and 1970s as years the profession had not spent on more "serious" economic research.

As often said, the Sraffians won the (analytical) war, but (in practice) lost the peace. Today, the situation is in many ways discouraging. Both critical economists and subjects are marginalised, if not excluded, from universities all around the world. In the 1980s, the number of young people interested in the study of critical theory was already declining. High unemployment not only tamed worker insubordination, as we have learned from Kalecki (see the Further Reading, Chap. 2), but also sedated youthful rebellion. At university, culture, let alone critical thought, has become a luxury, replaced in countries like Italy and Germany by so-called "short degrees", possibly with mainstream orientation, to compete in an increasingly difficult labour market. Despite this, the flame of critical theory continues to burn and many brave young people continue to show a desire for something different, even if it has become difficult to offer them nonconformist training and above all an academic future.

Considering the devastating economic crisis begun in 2008, this may seem paradoxical. On one hand, the crisis was certainly due to policy errors, especially in Europe, backed by faulty theories; on the other hand, it brought out the basic difficulties of capitalism, such as the spectre of stagnation, inequality and the environmental disaster. Although both aspects were denounced, even by conventional economists, mainstream theory emerged unscathed from the crisis and even the most critical voices on austerity policy, such as Paul Krugman and Joseph Stiglitz, are careful not to criticise the basics of the doctrine that they themselves helped to consolidate in their textbooks.

The rise and fall of heterodox economic theory has also been due to the fact that the heterodox critics of mainstream theory have not always been equal to the challenge. With hindsight, the high season of critical economics was too brief, in Italy and elsewhere, to build a sufficient body of studies, among which the filter of time would have selected the most rigorous.

If this picture is not reassuring, a positive aspect is that in the last years there has been a considerable upsurge in public interest, especially by young people, towards non-orthodox economic topics. This interest manifests above all in social networks, blogs and so forth. In Italy, it is closely linked to impatience with European economic policy. The difference with respect to the 1970s is that then one moved, albeit innovatively, in the traditional framework of ideology and organisation of the workers' movement, which gave body and weight to intellectual communication. Now the situation is more fluid and information is fragmented and shallow, in line with the speed of social networks, at times guided by gurus propounding magical thinking.

This chapter takes us deeper into mainstream theory, which re-emerged in the 1970s after being briefly eclipsed by historical circumstances (the Soviet Union's challenge) that favoured a transient hegemony of Keynesian theory. As we shall see, this mainstream theory is neither new nor recent. We have already used the metaphor of the goldfish living happily in its glass bowl: its world always seems new because the fish forgets from one turn of the bowl to the next. The history of economic thought has long been designated a super-fluous discipline in the faculties of economics: the goldfish has thus been lobotomised. You never know!

3.2   Neo-classical, in Fact Anti-classical

While passing themselves off as cutting-edge scientists, conventional econo-mists embrace a theory that emerged in about 1870, with the so-called mar-ginal revolution. This theory is based on the idea that the economy is made up of individuals in the double role of owners of "factors of production" (labour, "capital" and land) and consumers.

As producers, which is the aspect that most interests us, they receive an income (wage, profit or rent) in proportion to the contribution—the so-called "marginal product"—of the production factor they respectively own (labour, "capital" or land) to production. This contribution can be calculated by "mar-ginal calculus" (differential calculus or derivatives for those who studied mathematics); hence the name *marginal theory*. This label is more correct than the more common *neo-classical theory*, which evokes a non-existent continuity with classical theory. Indeed, marginalism arose as a reaction to the implica-tions of the theory of Ricardo, continued by Marx. Let us now look at its arguments.

Prof, before you begin, why did you write capital in inverted commas? I should always do so when it comes to the marginalist notion of capital. It is the Achille's heel of marginalism. In marginalist analysis the "quantity of capital" must be known from the outset, together with the quantities of labour and land. But this is possible—at least at an abstract level—for labour and land that can be measured in physical terms, enabling us to say: "in economy X there are Y units of labour and Z units of land". What about capital? The "capital" consists of many physical items (ploughs, hoes, computers…) that can only be summed if prices are known.

Then the problem can be solved! No, prices are what we want to determine. It is a vicious circle: if prices are not known we cannot measure the quantity of capital, but if we do not know the quantity of capital we cannot determine prices. More about this later.

Prof, but the title of Marx's main work was "Capital", like the title of Picketty's book denouncing inequality... Well, Picketty's title is a commercial stunt. The book is interesting but we are light years from Marx's depth. In the latter, "Capital" indicates the means of production owned by capitalists; capital stands as a disturbing monolith in front of the workers forced to serve it. Capital, therefore, indicates a "social order". In more concrete terms, the value of the means of production is calculated in Marx like that of any other commodity (like steel in relations 2.10).

3.3 Useless Curves, in Fact Marginal

Many of you will be accustomed to thinking of economists as obsessed with the concepts of supply and demand. The more sophisticated think of economics as all about supply and demand *curves*. This is not exactly true. Classical economists talk about supply and demand, but only marginalists are concerned with supply and demand curves.

The best known and apparently intuitive of these curves is the demand curve for goods: if price falls, demand increases. For marginalists, the demand for a good can in fact be represented as a decreasing curve in Cartesian space with price on the vertical axis and the quantity demanded on the horizontal axis. The demand curve is decreasing because the more a good is consumed, the lower the utility or well-being obtained by an extra unit of the good. This means that we are willing to consume more of a certain good, but only if we pay less and less for the extra unit. Thus, the demand curve of the good represents our willingness to pay more for the first sandwich, a little less for the second, even less for the third and so forth. We will only eat the tenth sandwich if it is free—somewhat as we do when we overeat at a buffet. Summing up, the decreasing demand curve of a good represents the willingness of a consumer to buy a certain good. If she has already consumed a lot of it, her willingness to pay will be low.

But incidentally, Prof, how did classical economists analyse the demand for consumer goods? More than relative prices (how much one good costs compared to another), the classical surplus approach looks at consumption choices through the lenses of income distribution among the social classes, local conditions influencing the cost of production of the goods composing the basic food-basket (the classical "necessities"), the general level of development and social conditioning. The American institutionalist economist Thorstein Veblen (1857–1929) attached great importance to the latter. Even marginalist theory admits that the level of income influences consumption choices (see next box), but attention is more on the formal properties of the analysis.

Comida marginale. As we said, marginalists do actually consider the role of income in determining demand for a certain good (technically, the consumer's income determines the position of the demand curve in Cartesian space), but this causes them some headaches. Let us consider the case of a poor Mexican household that spends its entire income of 1000 pesos per month on maize and beans, its basic meal. If the price of maize and beans halves due to a technological innovation, our household will have 500 pesos left over each month, provided its consumption choices do not change. The nominal income (1000 pesos) remains the same, but the real income, the purchasing power of the 1000 pesos, doubles (real income increased by 100%). Having access to other consumer goods, such as chickens and eggs, the household will perhaps reduce its consumption of maize and beans to 400 pesos (from 500 pesos) and spend 400 pesos on chicken and eggs and the remaining 200 pesos on new clothes. In this example, the demand for maize and beans falls as a result of the fall in their price, not rising as one would expect based on the marginalist demand curve. If the demand for a consumption good increases less than proportionally to an increase in real income—for example, it increases by 10% while real income increases by 100%—the good is called "inferior". If demand falls when prices fall (like maize and beans in the example), they are called Giffen goods. For Giffen goods, the demand curve is "perverse": it has an increasing and not a decreasing slope.

Imitating the decreasing demand curve for goods, the early marginalists reasoned in the same way regarding demand curves for "production factors" (typically labour, "capital" and land). When a firm with a certain capital, e.g. certain equipment, begins to demand labour, it is willing to pay a high wage—as in the case of the first sandwich, the first dose of work has a very high utility (or, technically, a high marginal productivity). However, as it gradually hires extra workers, the labour becomes abundant with respect to capital and relatively less useful, in a certain sense, so the firm is only willing to take on extra workers at lower wages. The labour demand curve expresses the willingness of firms to hire additional labour: this willingness is very high when the firm hires little labour and the relative contribution of the initial doses to production is high, and low when it hires much labour and the relative contribution of further doses to production is low—like the tenth sandwich that we eat if it is free. In 1925, Sraffa observed: "Is it not strange that two such heterogeneous things as human nature and industrial technology should have such similar results?" [i.e. diminishing marginal utility in consumption and diminishing returns in production].[3]

In general, therefore, the more we use of a factor of production (e.g. labour) for a given availability of other factors (e.g. capital), the less the productive contributions of the extra (or marginal) units of the variable factor (in this case labour) and the lower the willingness to pay for it.

A similar story can be told for "capital". Let us suppose (Ricardian vice) that we form a cooperative with ten of our friends in order to start a new activity (a start-up, to be in fashion). We need capital to buy equipment. In the marginalist world, we turn to savers: we want to spend more of our incomes in order to invest, while savers spend less of their incomes to hoard. What a great idea to meet and for us to invest their saving productively in the firm! In this Legoland situation, the banks intermediate saving by collecting and transferring it to investors. The latter are committed to paying interest and to paying back the loan at term.

> This view of banks as intermediating saving collected as deposits is known as "loanable funds theory". I'm sure that some of you are already protesting that the bank system does not work in this way and that banks create money when they lend. I know that, and even some marginalists and the Buba (affectionate name for the Bundesbank in Germany) say so. But more about this later, especially in Chap. 5 where we talk about money.

Returning to our cooperative, how much capital, i.e. saving, will it apply for? The story is somewhat similar to that regarding labour. When we have little capital to buy equipment, we are willing to pay quite a lot to obtain it because it is useful for our production. We are therefore willing to pay a good interest rate to the banks. However, when we have already borrowed a good deal of capital, and have a good deal of equipment, we are only willing to buy more if the interest rate is low. Already having much capital, adding more does not greatly increment our production, especially since there are only ten of us and extra equipment is likely to remain idle. Therefore the demand for "capital" is decreasing with respect to the interest rate, like the demand for labour (with respect to the wage rate) and for sandwiches (with respect to their price): it expresses our willingness to get into debt with the banks, which is high when our capital is scarce (we are ready to pay a high interest rate) and low when it is abundant (we only borrow more at very low interest rates). The

---

[3] Quoted by Tony Aspromourgos (2019, p. 32).

principle remains the same: when something is relatively scarce, it is very useful and we are willing to pay a lot for it; when it is relatively abundant, it is relatively less useful and our willingness to pay decreases.

Let us concentrate for a moment on saving as a source of capital: according to this view, the community can invest, i.e. produce and install new equipment (new capital) only if someone has saved, in other words has refrained from purchasing consumer goods which are therefore not produced, thus leaving resources free to produce new capital goods. Investment implies lower consumption.

Let me be clear that in order to increase investment, consumption must be reduced, because according to marginalists, the economy is, on average, in full employment. In other words, according to marginal theory, economic resources—such as labour and plant (capital)—are fully employed, and if we want to increase the share that goes to investment we have to decrease the share that goes to consumption. So if we produce more lathes we have to produce fewer brioches. This also has moral and political content: saving makes the economy grow because it enables an increase in capital goods. A little social injustice is therefore welcome because, as we all know, the working class knows little about the virtues of parsimony.

In Chap. 4, we shall see how Keynes overturned this concept, showing that once we admit that on average full employment of labour and plant does not happen under capitalism, consumption and investment can increase at the same time.

3.4   Lots of Dangerous Curves

We looked at demand curves for goods and "factors of production". What about supply curves?

Let us begin with supply curves for goods. Almost anyone knows that these are increasing: the higher the sales price, the greater the quantity of a commodity offered. Intuitively, such a supply curve is backed by the idea that by increasing production of a good, costs of production rise, so it has to be sold at a higher price. A simple way to explain this is as follows. Let us imagine two commodities, corn and cloth (the very commodities used by Ricardo: economists haven't much imagination). They are produced with the factors labour and "capital", and let us postulate that more capital is used per unit of labour to produce cloth than to produce corn. Let us also suppose that in our economy the quantities of labour and "capital" are given and fully employed.

Slow down, Prof, I need to get this straight. You assume two goods, one of which (corn) is more "labour intensive" (tends to use relatively more labour than capital) and the other (cloth) is more "capital intensive" (tends to use relatively more capital than labour); you also assume that "production factors" (capital and labour) are fully employed. Yes, precisely. Now let us imagine that consumer preferences change: for example, tighter jeans become fashionable so people diet avoiding corn, and demand more cloth to make jeans. Since the production of cloth requires relatively more capital than corn, the overall demand for capital increases and with it the price of capital. Since capital is now more costly, and is a cost of production for cloth producers, the price of cloth will increase.

Prof, if I understand correctly, the idea is that commodities are produced with different proportions of "factors of production", so if production of a certain good increases, the demand and the price of the more intensely used "production factor" for that good will also increase, and that will increase the cost of production of that commodity and hence its sales price. That's right. The reasoning seems logical… well, not too logical. A simple objection is that, as we shall see, it is not correct to assume full employment of "factors". If there were unemployed capital in our example, cloth production could be expanded without increasing the price of capital and hence of cloth. Then the supply curve would be horizontal at least up to full employment.

So Prof, if costs are independent of the quantity produced, demand would be useless for determining prices! In other words, however the demand and production of a commodity change, its cost and therefore its price remain the same. Indeed. This is why marginalists try to have increasing cost curves. In the metaphor of Alfred Marshall, one of the founders of marginalism, supply and demand are like the two scissor blades and it is impossible to say which is more important in determining price.

(In two memorable articles published in 1925 in Italian and in 1926 in the *Economic Journal*, then directed by Keynes, Sraffa had already begun to point out the mess Marshall had got himself into to demonstrate this theory).

But Prof, once full employment is reached, the marginalists are right! Even with full employment, firms have unused margins of capacity that they keep in case of sudden peaks in demand (otherwise their customers would turn to their competitors). This gives them time to increase plant if the increase in demand persists, and they can continue supplying their customers without any price increase. They have to do this, otherwise a competitor will do it, excluding them from the market.

But why are marginalists so attached to the "scissors"? Why do they want to assign such a decisive role to the demand for goods? Good question! I suppose it has to do with the centrality of the consumer: he is the protagonist of marginalism, not subversive concepts like the distribution conflict, dear to the classical school. In the example of jeans, consumer tastes influence the distribution of income, and this is a way to reaffirm the centrality of the consumer.

Somewhat ideological on their part… You said it! When I was studying for the exam on classical theory with friends, a course taught by Pierangelo Garegnani (Sraffa's favourite pupil, remember?), my mother came to scold us: "That will be enough of politics (workers, capitalists, exploitation, social conflict…). You are meant to be studying!" It was not easy to convince her that this was political economy … genuine political economy.

But let us move now from the supply curves for commodities to the supply curves of "production factors".

Like the former, the supply curves of "inputs" are also generally held to have a positive slope: so if wages rise, more workers offer their services or are willing to work longer; similarly if the interest rate rises, households offer more saving (recall that, according to marginal theory, saving is the ultimate source of capital). The idea behind increasing factor supply curves is that more supply involves greater sacrifice. For example, every extra hour of work costs us increasing "disutility" (negative utility) in terms of extra fatigue; and every extra unit of saving costs us increasing sacrifice of present consumption.

It seems plausible, doesn't it? But if you think about it, some doubts arise. Young people in most of Italy and immigrants all over the world would work for almost any wage, provided it was at least positive and more than what she would get from begging (or even a little less because begging isn't exactly dignified). The labour supply is actually very rigid (technically close to a vertical line, see Fig. 3.1) and fundamentally independent of wage: one works to survive, accepting any wage.

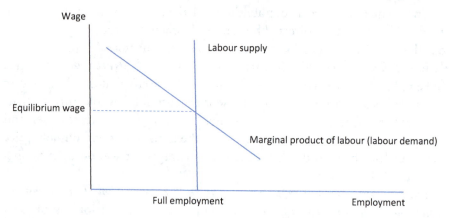

Fig. 3.1 The labour market according to marginal theory

Regarding saving, I know what you want to tell me: at the end of the month you don't decide how much to save on the basis of interest on deposits or bonds. If you are well-off you will save even if Christine Lagarde (the President of the ECB after Mario Draghi) keeps interest rates below zero; if you are a young temporary worker you will probably often have to borrow from your parents (i.e. you have negative saving). Saving decisions, therefore, do not depend much on the interest rate but on income, as Keynes would later explain. So we also plot the "capital" (saving) supply function as vertical. These curves are not so difficult to understand, are they?

In the early 1920s, young Sraffa was disconcerted by the mass of psycho-moral concepts at the basis of marginal theory, such as utility, disutility and sacrifice. That theory showed a subjectivism and individualism very far from the materialism of the surplus approach.

Petty the cynic. The image of human society that we have from marginalism is that of a robot (*Homo economicus*) that reacts to economic incentives, decides, for example, to work more or less or to save more or less on the basis of a balance between sacrifice and pleasure: a completely subjective view that the first marginalists, not by chance, counterposed to the school of Ricardo. For a contrast with marginalist subjectivity, read the following passages from Petty about his method:

> The method is not very usual for instead of using only Comparative and Superlative Words and Intellectual Arguments, I have taken the course to express myself in terms of Number, Weight or Measure, to use only Arguments of Sense and to consider only such causes as have Visible Foundations in Nature; leaving those that depend upon the mutable Minds, Opinions, Appetites, and Passions of particular Men to the Consideration of others.[4]

The admiration of Marx and Sraffa for Petty is understandable. But beware: the pseudo-economists from social forums criticise marginalists because they depict humanity as exclusively egotistical, ignoring the existence of generosity, altruism and so forth. In this way, we merely replace one subjectivity with another. The question is to study the objective determinants of individual and social behaviour on the basis of the historically prevalent material circumstances.

---

[4] Bharadwaj (1986, p. 23).

3.5   To Each His Own

Summing up, like scissor blades, the supply and demand functions of commodities and "production factors", respectively, determine their prices. Now let us concentrate on the markets for production factors, which are the most relevant markets for economic and political issues. Let us look in particular at two key markets, those for labour and capital (saving).

In the labour market, a labour demand curve, decreasing because labour becomes less useful when more is employed relative to the other "factors of production", intersects a vertical line representing the labour supply (Fig. 3.1). At the point of intersection, labour supply and labour demand are equal or, in other words, the point identifies the wage at which firms' demand for labour is equal to the supply of labour. At that point, the wage precisely matches the utility of labour in production, that is, its contribution to production: to each his own. It also precisely compensates the sacrifice (disutility) a worker incurs in offering that amount of work. That wage is said to be "natural". If the supply of labour increases (the vertical line moves to the right), competition between workers causes wages to fall and companies employ more workers. The fall in wages is justified by the fact that, since labour is now more abundant, it is, so to speak, also less valuable.

What we must underline is that if the wage rate is flexible, there is always full employment, that is, the whole supply of labour finds employment. Years ago the American magazine *Time* defined Fig. 3.1 the most important graph of political economy, with good reason.

Figure 3.1 enables us to understand why conformist economists support neoliberal politicians in their request for a more flexible labour market.

Labour market flexibility basically means freedom for firms to hire and fire workers. Barriers to the dismissal of workers—often called rigidities of the labour market—mean that the so-called insiders, those who have a job, can easily strike and get higher wages, higher than the natural wage. The insiders will certainly be better off, but part of the labour force (the outsiders) will remain unemployed (Fig. 3.2). Thus marginal theory leads us to conclude that the price of higher wages is higher unemployment. If, as in Fig. 3.2, workers enjoy excessively high union wages, the demand for their services will fall to U. The interval U-FE will be made up of involuntary unemployed, namely workers who would accept employment at the natural wage, but cannot do so because the unions and the laws protecting them prevent the union wage from falling. These graphs underlie the mainstream thesis that labour market flexibility—namely abolition of union protection and of impediments on laying workers off—leads to full employment.

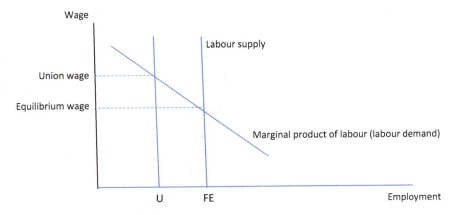

Fig. 3.2 Wages and employment according to marginal theory

Suppose that under a rule of labour market rigidity unemployed workers knock on the doors of firms, offering to work for a wage lower than union pay. The firms' likely reply is that they would willingly employ them, but that labour protection laws prevent them from laying workers off without "good reason". If the labour protection laws are abolished and firms are again completely free to hire and fire, they could say to their employees (the insiders): "Outside there are unemployed workers offering to work at a lower wage. Either accept a lower wage or we fire you". What would you do? The law is no longer on your side! The interest of the situation is that once you have been bribed to work for less, everyone works—all insiders now! The question has often been framed in the Italian political discourse as "now you and your son both work". It was your fault, and that of the trade union and the labour protection laws, that your son was at the factory gate.

There was a militant song that I sang when I was young (and militant), which went more or less: "O dear wife, tonight please tell our son to go to bed, because the things I have to tell you are things he must not hear. Just this morning at work, with the smile of the supervisor, I was given notice: they fired me without mercy", and this happened because I defended our rights, the union, our wages, freedom and so forth. But the ending of the song is not correct: "O dear wife, I was wrong, tell our son to come and learn the price of freedom". The correct ending is that if Dad stopped being a militant, he and his son would both work. End of story? No, we will have more to say in defence of Ivan Della Mea (1940–2009), a great Italian emulator of Woody Guthrie.

Let us now consider the other production factor, "capital". In the capital market (also called the saving market), we have the demand function, which

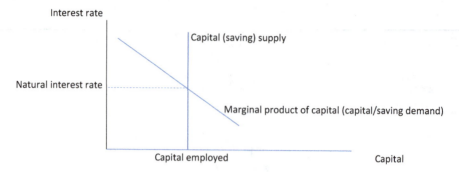

Fig. 3.3 The capital (saving) market

expresses the willingness of firms to pay for successive doses of capital, and the supply of capital represented by the vertical line (Fig. 3.3). There is an equilibrium interest rate that the great marginalist economist Knut Wicksell termed *natural interest rate*, at which capital (saving) supply and demand balance. If the actual interest rate were higher than the natural interest rate, firms would demand less capital but savers, or if you wish the banks where they keep their savings, would compete to lend all their savings, lowering the price at which they offer loans. Thus the interest rate would fall until equilibrium between supply and demand of capital (or saving) is restored. The remuneration of capital (or saving) depends on its relative scarcity: if the "factor capital" becomes scarcer (the vertical line shifts to the left), the equilibrium rate of interest rises; if capital becomes more abundant (the line shifts to the right), the equilibrium rate of interest falls. To each his own also in this case. As you can see, in this theory the distribution of income depends on the relative scarcity of factors. There is no exploitation here: each "factor" receives in proportion to its contribution to production and to the sacrifice of its owner in offering its services. According to this theory, if labour, for example, becomes scarcer than capital because of an epidemic, the distribution of the cake moves in favour of the workers.

But Prof, this would also happen under classical economic theory! Yes, you are right, but in that case because labour shortages would strengthen the bargaining power of workers. Instead for the marginalists, it is a technical fact: the more a factor is scarce, the more it is precious in production and the higher the remuneration due to it. Moreover, while in classical economic theory there is no mechanical relationship between income distribution and employment, in marginal theory there is a well-defined natural income distribution associated with full employment of labour and capital.

But Prof, even in the surplus approach, higher wages can lead to an increase in unemployment! True, but because capitalists are reacting to a fall in the profit rate by investing less or by pressuring governments and central banks to implement policies that increase unemployment so that wages fall. During the golden age of capitalism (1950–1979), while the Soviet challenge persisted, capitalists accepted high wages and full employment. It's a political question.

> Let us refresh our ideas about the relation between capital and saving. Let us consider a bath containing 50 L of water. This water is a *stock*: its quantity is independent of time.
> *But Prof, water evaporates with time...* True, and perhaps the plug leaks a little. If the water decreases by 10 L per day, to maintain a constant level we have to add 10 L of water per day from the tap. The tap water, and the water lost, are *flows*, defined per unit of time (10 L per day). If, however, more than 10 L come out of the tap, the water level rises. Let us get out of metaphor: capital is a stock, like the amount of water in the bath at a given time. Like water, capital "evaporates" in time due to physical wear (and technological obsolescence). Gross investment is like tap water: it is a flow that compensates for losses and may increase the stock of capital. Investment that increase capital is known as net investment, a part of gross investment. So gross investment = replacements + net investment. So far we have definitions. According to marginal theory, saving is the ultimate source of the flow of investment. According to Keynesian theory, we shall see, saving does not precede but is a consequence of investment, and banks create credit out of nothing to finance investment.

If we consider two markets at the same time: the labour and the "capital" market, what the marginalists call general economic equilibrium, the law "to each his own", prevails in a big way: in an economy with abundant labour and little capital, wages are low and the interest rate high; vice versa, in economies with abundant capital and little labour, the interest rate is low and wages high. In other words, the distribution of income depends on the relative scarcity of production factors: the scarcer a production factor with respect to the others, the higher its remuneration (and the lower the remuneration of the other factors).

It should also be noted that the techniques used in the economy adjust in such a way that the entire supply of each factor is used at its equilibrium price. If, for example, people saved more and thus offered more capital, the banks, having raised more savings, would offer it at a lower interest rate. Companies would, therefore, be encouraged to adopt production techniques that use more capital in relation to labour. If, on the other hand, there were a flow of immigrants, if the labour market is flexible, the equilibrium wage would decrease and companies would adopt more labour-intensive techniques, hiring immigrants.

General economic equilibrium is completed by also considering the market of products, where the intersection between the curves of supply and demand at the equilibrium price is such that the utility consumers receive from consuming a certain good is equal to the sacrifice (disutility of labour and sacrifices of savers) needed to produce it. As we have seen, changes in consumer tastes for or against certain goods are not without effects on distribution. If, for example, the demand for certain goods produced with much labour and little capital (highly labour intensive) increases with respect to those using relatively more capital than labour (low labour intensity), the increased demand for labour increases wages with respect to profits. If you think about this, the greater demand for labour means that labour has become scarcer (or more wanted) than capital.

Marginalism with a human face. More "democratic" versions of marginal theory, so-called "welfare economics" admit that marginal calculus can lead to a "natural" or "equilibrium" distribution of income blatantly biased in favour of capitalists, or in any case in favour of those with an initial advantage. This is true of those who have access to better education, both at home and at school, and can equip themselves with more "human capital" than those from disadvantaged social backgrounds. The suggestion of welfare economics is therefore to correct the "initial endowments" of factors so as to make starting conditions more even. This can be done, for instance, through inheritance tax that decreases the capital endowment in the hands of the offspring of capitalists, the revenue from which can be used to improve the education of working class children so as to increase their "human capital". This amounts to setting more even conditions for the 400-m hurdles, ensuring that some competitors do not compete without hurdles and start with a 100-m advantage. These are interesting corrections but they do not change the basic features of mainstream theory and its analytical flaws.

3.6   The Best of All Worlds Is Possible

Marginal theory has two strong implications: there is only one natural distribution of income (to each his own) and when this distribution prevails there is full employment.

The first implication is based on the fact that since factors receive an income according to their respective contribution to production, no "factor" exploits another and each receives what is "right". In this way, the "marginal revolution" claims to have struck and sunk the theory of Marx (and Ricardo) on exploitation.

The second crucial implication of marginal theory is that if factors of production accept their "natural" remuneration, they are fully employed, as we saw in the case of labour (Fig. 3.1). Once production has been completed using factors fully and remunerating them according to the marginal rule, marginal theory says that all incomes are spent buying the production. In this way, all products are sold. Firms are content and in the next period they confirm full employment of factors. Marginal theory, therefore, believes in Say's Law (or the law of markets), according to which the whole production finds a market because it generates incomes and expenditure having the same value as the production ("supply creates its own demand").

But Prof, what about the fact that part of income is saved? Marginalists admit that part of income is not consumed but saved (i.e. it is not translated directly into demand). But this is not a problem; to the contrary, saving is the source of the production factor "capital" (recall the metaphor of a previous box: saving is the flow of water from the tap and capital is the stock of water in the tank).

As you will remember, in Fig. 3.3 we represented the capital demand curve. Taking advantage of the close kinship between capital and saving, we can then represent by analogy the saving demand curve as a decreasing function of the interest rate. The lower the interest rate, the higher the demand for saving by companies to make investment. The saving demand curve is in this sense also commonly called the "investment function". Again by analogy, we can think also of a "saving supply function" that we draw, for the reasons already explained above, as a vertical line. Once we put together supply and demand for saving, their intersection will normally determine an interest rate at which firms absorb all the savings supplied by households and lent through the banks. So what households do not spend on consumer goods, they loan to firms, who use it to purchase investment goods, so that in the end all the production finds an outlet either as consumption or as investment goods. Saving is therefore a positive act that enables the economy to increase its productive capacity.

Spartacus and Menenius Agrippa. Let us compare the two theories, the theory of surplus value seen in Chap. 2 and marginal theory. It is clear from both that a higher wage means a lower rate of profit (or rate of interest, which we consider synonymous here). However, the marginalists have a single equilibrium distribution, dictated by the relative scarcity of "factors of production", whereas according to the classical school and Marx there are many possible outcomes of the distribution problem. For the former, the natural distribution is dictated by "technical" factors, for the latter by socio-political factors. The concept of "capital", too, is different in the two approaches. For marginalists "capital" is a fruit of saving and contributes to production to a mathematically definable extent (the marginal product of capital). "Capital" is a pool of savings, an ectoplasm preceding production whose value is known before prices are determined: it is a "factor of production" together with land and labour. For the classical school, capital consists of commodities produced and used as means of production, the value of which is determined at the same time as that of all the other commodities. The class of capitalists pockets the surplus as owners of the means of production. Bread is produced by a baker (labour) aided by an oven (capital): according to marginalists, it is possible to pinpoint the respective contributions of the oven and the baker to production, and therefore the corresponding "natural" profit and wage rates. For the classical school, the amount of bread going to the owners of the oven (capital) and the amount going to the baker (labour) depends on power relations, and the fact that capitalists have a right to a share of the net product depends solely on their rights of ownership of the means of production (the oven). In other words, it is a question of "social order".

The marginalists also see harmony between capital and labour, which as in the *fable* of Menenius Agrippa, cooperate towards production. Again with reference to Roman times, the *historical episode* of Spartacus better represents the point of view of classical economists. In the classical approach, there may also be cooperation but it is a *compromise* between two antagonistic social classes. As we have already seen, one of the fathers of the Scandinavian social-democratic compromise, Gunnar Myrdal, was actually inspired by Ricardo's class-conflict views on the distribution of income.

According to the marginalists, wage level is inversely linked to employment level, whereas the classical school does not contemplate any such relationship. Indeed, in the classical approach, the relation between levels of occupation and distribution is more complex and often the opposite of that of marginal theory. As I said, in the "golden era" of capitalism (1950–1979), high wages were associated with full employment, whereas in many instances (including in the eurozone crisis), lower wages have been associated with high unemployment. Unemployment is also seen by the classical school as instrumental to working class docility (the industrial reserve army encountered in Marx).

3.7 The Marginal Role of Money

The last aspect of marginal theory to underline regards the role of money. As already explained, in marginal theory the level of production is irrevocably fixed in the real part of the economic system on the basis of the functions of supply and demand for productive factors. To consolidate these ideas, marginalists often use the production function, $Y = F(K, L)$: in words, the level of production (Y) depends on (is a function of) the quantities of capital (K) and labour (L) used in the economy. K and L are what we determined in Figs. 3.1 and 3.3, together with the wage rate w and the rate of interest i. If K, L, w and i are known, we can calculate $Y (= wL + iK)$. This is the real part of the economic system: it is where the pie Y and the slices that go to wages (wL)

and *profits (iK)* are determined. The size of the pie is such that if markets are "flexible", all labour and capital is employed.

In this framework, money plays the mere role of facilitating exchange, in place of barter. Springing from this role, the level of prices is determined in the monetary part of the economic system. Let us take a second to anticipate some elements of monetary analysis that will be developed in Chap. 5. These will also be important for understanding, for example, the task and role of the European Central Bank (ECB) in Europe in Chap. 7.

We saw that the role of commercial banks, according to marginal theory, is to mediate between savers (depositors) and creditors—the latter are firms seeking loans to purchase capital goods or households seeking housing loans or making instalment purchases (for example, when you buy a car on instalments, there is a bank behind the credit offered by the car salon). The theory according to which banks mediate saving is often called the "theory of loanable funds". Contrary to this theory, in the real world when banks grant credit they are not bound by the deposits they hold, as we shall see in more detail in Chap. 5. If you go to the bank to ask for a loan, the official will inspect your paycheck and credentials, and if you are a reliable customer, grants the loan with a stroke of the pen (now through the computer keyboard), without checking whether that morning anyone deposited new "loanable funds". In other words, the bank official creates a deposit in your favour from which you can draw the sums required for your payments. Many of you will have taken out a real estate loan to buy a house: what did the bank do? It credited the sum requested to your cheque account, or if you did not have one at the lending bank, the latter asked you to open a current account with them. The official certainly did not call the cashier to ask if sufficient funds had been banked that morning for the loan. This is the endogeneity of money that we mentioned in a previous box: banks create bank money, namely deposits that circulate via cheques, bank transfers or card payments, like when you used the bank credit to pay whoever sold you the house with bank transfer. Well then, the most clever marginalists agree with this story, with one warning: since commercial banks have the power to create money, they should be kept under strict control because too much credit to finance additional expenditure could cause inflation. This control is exercised by the central bank by adjusting the rate of interest (we shall see how in Chap. 7).

More specifically, according to marginalists, the task of the central bank is to ensure that the natural rate of interest prevails. Yes, as in Fig. 3.3 where the supply and demand for saving are in equilibrium. Let us recall that according to marginal theory, at that rate there is full employment in the economy. In other words, at that rate savers' abstention from spending is precisely compensated by the spending decisions of investors or of households who want to spend more than their incomes.

In this way, fewer consumer goods are produced and correspondingly more capital goods are produced for firms, or the consumer goods that thrifty households refrained from purchasing are bought by other households obtaining consumer credit for instalment purchases. At the natural rate of interest, the amount of credit created by banks matches the supply of saving resulting from the full employment income, saving which at that interest rate is fully employed in investment by firms (or in consumer credit), ensuring that the economy maintains full employment.

What would happen if the central bank fixed a lower-than-natural interest rate? According to marginal theory, at a lower interest rate investors and households would ask banks for loans exceeding the supply of savings. In other words, the money that households of savers do not spend is less than what firms want to invest and what other households want to spend over and above their income. Overall expenditure and demand increase, and since with the flexibility of markets we have full employment, the higher demand cannot be met by higher production and the result is inflation. In a nutshell, according to this theory, if the market interest rate is below the natural interest rate, too much money is created (as deposits created for loan applicants) and this causes inflation. However, nothing changes in the real economy. We can create all the money we like and only prices will rise, not production. The level of prices depends on the quantity of money. Once it has set the rate of interest at its natural level, the central bank only has to ensure that the quantity of money increases in line with the real product, so that it does not become scarce, which would lead to the opposite problem of deflation or lower prices.

According to marginalist theory, the economy is therefore dualistic: on the real side, the demand and supply of "production factors" determines output and its distribution among the factors; on the monetary side, monetary policy must follow the rule of fixing the interest rate at its natural level, thus making the quantity of money grow in line with the growth of production. Any attempt to violate the monetary rule causes inflation (or deflation).

But this is the EMU professor! Full employment entrusted to the flexibility of the markets and price stability entrusted to the central bank which obeys strict rules. Exactly. You can call it monetarism, the doctrine associated with the name of Milton Friedman (1912–2006). But even Friedman was critical of the EMU. Not surprisingly, especially during Mario Draghi's mandate (2011–2019), the ECB has not followed strict rules, as we shall see in Chap. 7.

But Prof, how does the central bank know the natural rate of interest? Good point. Actually Fig. 3.3 is only found in the textbooks that maybe your college made you study, and in fact the central bank does not know the natural rate. However, it argues in this manner: if inflation is above a certain reference level, for example, above the famous 2% of the ECB, it means that the central bank is keeping the policy rate of interest too low and is therefore creating "too much money". It must therefore increase the interest rate until inflation settles at the desired level. Vice versa, if the rate of inflation is too low (*subdued* is the word used in ECB documents) or prices are falling and unemployment is high, which amounts to deflation, the policy interest rate must be lowered, even to zero, as the ECB did recently in order to stimulate borrowing and spending. These are the rules of conduct followed by central banks.

But Professor, you do not believe very much in the natural interest rate, so how effective can rules based on this very concept be? A good question! The central banks do indeed pursue a certain rate of inflation, below but close to 2% in the case of the ECB. Since the inflation rate is basically dependent on the trend in monetary wages, keeping inflation under control means keeping wages under control. The central bank is very effective at regulating wages by threatening an increase in the interest rate, which could have negative effects on employment. However, this cannot be written in textbooks—a "too sensational metallic problem" to paraphrase Oscar Wilde—so in the next section we will see the fairytale that is told in the manuals. However, the central bank is less good at combatting deflation, the situation where prices are falling and unemployment is too high.

And why is that? You make me anticipate too much! The problem is that if the economy has been suffering a financial crisis, firms and households will be reluctant to borrow in order to spend—they are still trying to figure how to pay their debts—and anyway, the interest rate has no tangible effects on firms' decisions to invest. You can lead a horse to water but you cannot make him drink. This is the battle that Draghi faced in Europe, and Lagarde is now facing. Fiscal policy should be used, but it is still regarded with suspicion in Berlin. More about this in Chaps. 6 and 7.

Anyway, to get back to your initial question, central banks use the simple rule: "raise interest rates when inflation increases, lower them when it decreases," regardless of the story of the natural interest rate (which is useful at most for the most gullible students), for another more concrete reason: to steer the economy into a *aurea mediocritas* with moderate inflation and unemployment. The period in which the recipe seemed to work, until its collapse with the great financial crisis of 2008, was in fact called "the great moderation".

To recapitulate, according to mainstream theory, an excessively expansive monetary stance, which induces banks to stimulate demand for credit through an effective interest rate lower than the natural interest rate, would only increase prices (inflation) because the economy already has full employment of labour and plant (capital). This is the essence of "monetarism" which has dominated economic thinking since the 1970s, and it is why since the 1980s monetary policy has been in the hands of "independent" central banks, the only task of which was to keep inflation as low as possible. If central banks, possibly spurred by politicians, sought to increase employment by monetary expansion, stimulating demand with low rates of interest, they would only cause damage (i.e. inflation). As we have noticed, the statute of the ECB is based on such monetary theory. If the economy is not at full employment (if there are involuntary unemployed workers), according to monetary theory this is not the fault of central banks but of the rigidity of the labour market, which is where action is needed: measures to make it more flexible. Of course, once involuntary unemployment has been eliminated under the lash of flexibility, there are still the voluntary unemployed. These are adults who do not work by choice because they are too choosy—too fussy for current labour market conditions—to use the unhappy expression of a former Italian Minister of Labour under Mario Monti's government (yes, the one imposed in 2011 by the European institutions with the approval of the Italian President of the Republic). Some deconstruction of this theory is in order.

3.8   Friedman's Tale

From what we saw above, according to mainstream theory, if inflation is zero, or more plausibly slightly positive and constant—as in the ECB's famous "below but close to 2%"—we will have the best of all possible worlds. This rate of inflation would indicate that banks are not creating too much or too little credit for firms, or that firms are investing exactly as much as households wish to save. This means that the central bank is correctly guessing the natural rate of interest, the one that balances saving and investment decisions. At this rate, the Smith family refrains from buying a second car and puts the money away "for a rainy day" and at the same time that car (otherwise unsold) is bought as a company car by the firm Jones & Co. through the corner bank that uses the Smith's saving to finance purchase of the company car. Or the son of another family, who has just found employment, buys a new car with an advance from the corner bank. An idyllic picture!

Then if Smith's daughter is involuntarily unemployed (she is willing to work at the equilibrium wage) and cannot find work, it is the fault of her father and his union, as we said. If union protection is abolished, the idyllic picture recomposes itself, even Smith's daughter works and there are no involuntary unemployed. True, there are some unemployed adults, our choosy friends (that one imagines to be chic women and young dandies sitting in elegant cafes), people unwilling to work for the equilibrium wage but demanding a higher wage. These people are defined as voluntary unemployed (not working by choice). In this Panglossian picture (the best of all possible worlds...) conventional economists say that unemployment is at its natural level.

And here begins the tale of the ineffectiveness of monetary policy, a tale I am ashamed to tell my students—and I ask how far the study of economics has degenerated, since thousands of my "colleagues" shamelessly tell it to their students and the students unfortunately do not rebel. It is a tale told by Milton Friedman, the already mentioned founder of monetarism. Let us begin with an idyllic situation where the interest rate is at its natural level, Jones & Co. invest as much as the Smiths save, the current wage is at equilibrium level and therefore unemployment is at is natural rate too. The government decides to increase employment above its natural level, for example, to elicit a booming economy and improve its image prior to the next election. It does so by ordering the central bank (which is not independent) to decrease the rate of interest below its natural level. Thus it happens that Jones & Co. invest more than the Smiths want to save. In the example, it orders two company cars instead of one. Demand pushes supply and firms try to produce more. To do so they have to hire new workers. But attention! The economy was at its natural level of unemployment, at which there are indeed unemployed workers, but only voluntary ones, the choosy who would only work for wages higher than those currently prevailing. Firms, wishing to meet the greater demand stimulated by low interest rates, offer higher nominal wages. They do so knowing that they can pass the higher wages on to higher prices. The voluntary unemployed are however somewhat stupid (or have drunk too many spritz at the cafe)—more elegantly it is said that they suffer from "monetary illusion"—i.e. they see an increase in the nominal wages offered and decide to work, but they do not realise that prices are increasing too. In other words, they do not realise that the real wage—the wage measured in purchasing power—is not increasing: the nominal wage packets increase by 10%, but so do prices. So albeit at the cost of higher inflation, the government succeeds in increasing employment and as the tale goes, cuts a fine figure with voters and wins the elections. However, with time, the ex-voluntary unemployed, who now work believing to do so for a higher real wage, wake up to the trick and realise that they are working for a real wage which is lower than the one for which they previously refused to get out of bed in the morning (in the marginalist language of incentives: the utility of the real wage is less than the disutility of getting up). And so they withdraw from the labour market. The government could try to deceive them again by further stimulating the economy through even more expansive monetary policy and thus generating additional inflation, but eventually they will again realise that prices and nominal wages increase as a consequence, until in the long period they learn not to fall into the trap. Thus employment returns to its original level, while in the meantime the government has won the elections again. The only effect of expansive monetary policy has been higher prices (or worse, stably higher inflation). No gain on one hand, and possibly damage on the other. Monetary policy does not have real effects in the long period, but only nominal effects, i.e. effects on price levels. As I said, the economic system is dichotomised: product and employment are determined in the real part; price levels (or the rate of inflation) are determined in the monetary part.

The precept is therefore to relieve governments of monetary policy and assign it to independent central banks whose only task is to keep the rate of inflation stable at a low and constant level. In certain reprehensible countries, where central bankers are allowed to heed the sirens of politics or are sensitive to the social costs of controlling inflation, it is even better to place control of monetary policy in the hands of a foreign central bank. This is known as "tying one's own hands", after the appropriate definition of two champions of conformism Francesco Giavazzi and Marco Pagano (two internationally well-known Italian economists). This is what countries do when they adopt a currency board, as in the case of Argentina in 1991, or when they adopt a foreign currency and a foreign central bank, as in the case of Italy in 1999 with the euro.

3.9   Tug-of-War

Friedman's tale sounds strange to heterodox ears. Indeed, as we shall see, Keynes's and Sraffa's criticisms lead us to think that laissez-faire will not bring the economy to full employment, not even with labour market flexibility. And if the economy does not have full employment, expansive monetary policy will be helpful for restoring it: it will have real effects. It will also affect the price levels, but for reasons that are quite different from those of Friedman's tale.

For heterodox economists, inflation is a tug-of-war, the expression used by the great political economist Albert Hirschman (1915–2012). When the industrial reserve army decreases and the contractual power of workers increases, nominal wages tend to increase, followed by an increase in prices, and so forth. But as long as the tug-of-war lasts, the workers have a chance of winning. Persistent inflation indicates that workers are trying to defend themselves against price increases by obtaining nominal wage increases aimed at defending the real wage: they are taking their chance. Employers, however, have an additional weapon: getting conniving governments and central banks to impose restrictive fiscal and monetary policies. These policies, justified to defeat evil inflation, cause some workers to lose their jobs and they are out of the game. It is easy to guess the outcome. Weakened and betrayed, workers relent and the tug-of-war comes to a sudden end with the victory of the "bosses".

Once I saw a Spanish cartoon in which a beefy worker, visibly battered and bruised, is playing cards with his workmates, who ask him: "How is it that the boss got the better of you, you being so much stronger?", "An economist had me in an armlock", he replies. Being an economist is an ugly job.

If we revisit Friedman's tale in this light, we discover that:

- there is nothing "natural" about the natural rate of unemployment: it is simply that rate at which the industrial reserve army is sufficiently large for workers to behave themselves and therefore for inflation to be low and constant. It is not true that there are only voluntary unemployed at the natural unemployment rate: there are generally also involuntary unemployed. Certainly, if employment is increased by expansive monetary (and fiscal) policy, inflation will rise, but not because voluntary unemployed have to be tricked as told by Friedman and textbooks, but simply because a tug-of-war ensues: in militant language, the *class struggle*.
- nor is there anything natural about the natural rate of interest: it is just the rate that helps keep unemployment high enough (therefore at its "natural" rate) to prevent a tug-of-war.

In short, the idea of handing over monetary policy to a (politically) independent central bank, preferably foreign, means giving the dirty work of controlling social conflict to an ad hoc authority, so that politicians can wash their hands of it. In simple terms, an independent central bank is not just the watchdog of inflation, but the guard dog against worker militancy.

Finally, let us compare the two theories, marginalist and classical, on inflation and unemployment. By assuming that labour market flexibility leads to full employment, marginalists think they can deny the existence of involuntary unemployment: there are only voluntary unemployed workers, those who do not work because they want a real wage higher than the equilibrium wage.

Via inflation, monetary policy can deceive them into thinking that the economy is paying them more and induce them to work, but in the long run they wake up to the trick. For heterodox theorists, on the other hand, even with flexibility of the labour market, laissez-faire is generally accompanied by involuntary unemployment, with some people more than willing to work at the current real wage (or even for a lower wage) but who do not find jobs. Certainly, monetary policy can generate inflation, but only because by stimulating the economy it triggers a tug-of-war, not because it is trying to deceive anybody.

Now we have to see who is right: those embracing the conventional view that labour market flexibility eliminates involuntary unemployment or those embracing the non-orthodox view that even with labour market flexibility, there is involuntary unemployment. We have to delve deeply, beyond the generic cry of "mainstream neoliberalism", a mantra we shall leave to social forum economists. The conventional thesis has been challenged on two main fronts: by Keynes, which we see in more detail in Chap. 4, and by Sraffa.

Let us return to the different meaning of the term *natural* in classical and marginal theory (see box in Sect. 2.7). In the former, the adjective indicates that economics is concerned with equilibria determined by knowable social laws. The term has no ethical or moral connotations. In marginal theory, the term *natural* has a stronger meaning indicating that if allowed to operate, the great book of nature written by a benign divinity (called laissez-faire) leads to "natural equilibria", which according to the definition of Pareto, cannot be improved without damaging someone. Political subjectivity aimed at correcting these outcomes is therefore condemned as undue interference with the great book of nature. On the other hand, the classical surplus approach regards the subjectivity of social forces in changing outcomes as part of the natural forces at play.

3.10   The Two Challenges to Marginalism

3.10.1   The Unfinished Keynesian Revolution

A first challenge to marginal theory came from Keynes, partly prompted by the evident failure of mainstream theory when faced with the economic crisis of the 1930s. Keynes did not dispute the mainstays of traditional theory and this led to his *General Theory* being considered by conventional economists to be a special case of mainstream theory—a *Particular Theory of the Crisis*, so to speak—not exactly what Keynes had in mind!

Keynes criticises the idea we saw above that a market economy cannot suffer from problems of demand. His target was Say's law. He considers firms' investment a particularly unstable component of aggregate demand that on average does not completely absorb the supply of saving of households at full employment. He goes even further: entrepreneurs' investment decisions are the starter of the economy (and if insufficient, they must be supplemented by government spending). These expenditure decisions generate income that is partly consumed and partly saved through a process known as the income multiplier. Unlike the marginalists, he maintained that investment generates saving and not vice versa. This inversion of the relation between investment and saving is the analytical heart of the Keynesian revolution. Morally, it is also significantly transgressive: from a macroeconomic viewpoint, saving is a damaging activity. An increase in saving for a given level of investment causes a fall in income and employment. Besides being immoral, it is therefore also stupid to lower real wages in order to increase saving. Keynes calls the fall of income as a result of the attempt of people to save more the "saving paradox". In simple terms: a given investment level, generating demand, sets in motion the process of producing income, from which saving is derived; if people want to save a greater share of their income—say 20% instead of 10%—then less income is needed to generate an amount of saving equal to the given level of investment. Too condensed? We shall come back to this in Chap. 4.

From the viewpoint of economic policy, the heart of the Keynesian revolution lies in the role assigned to budget policy and to monetary policy in maintaining full employment. Indeed, if private investment is insufficient, the only way to support expenditure and production is to resort to greater public spending and expansive monetary policies. Through low-interest rates, monetary policy makes deficit spending relatively inexpensive for the state and encourages private spending.

It is said that German mainstream economists are divided between those who have not read Keynes and those who have not understood him. These economists bring to mind the *Fable of the Bees* by Bernard Mandeville (1670–1733). In that poem, Mandeville recounts how a state fell into ruin as a result of the moralization of customs, explaining how saving, perhaps praiseworthy privately, is pernicious at community level. The poem, to which Keynes dedicates several pages of the *General Theory*, was condemned as socially harmful: "No wonder—Keynes bitterly concluded—that such wicked sentiments called down the opprobrium of two centuries of moralists and economists who felt much more virtuous in possession of their austere doctrine that no sound remedy for unemployment was discoverable except in the utmost of thrift and economy both by the individual and by the state".[5] Curiously, Keynes says in the preface to the German edition of the *General Theory* that he expected better reception in Germany than in his own country. This was not because Keynes sympathized with Nazism—as his adversaries still hasten to absurdly suggest—but because most German economists (like American ones) had until then remained relatively immune from marginalism. A bit like I do with you, Keynes urged them to adopt a theory, *his own* obviously: "Can I persuade German economists that [my] methods of formal analysis have something important to contribute to the interpretation of contemporary events and to the moulding of contemporary policy? After all, it is German to like a theory".[6] Then things went differently. In Germany, as in Italy, liberal economists have played dirty by identifying public intervention with dictatorship. This does not mean that Nazi Germany did not obnoxiously use Keynesian policies in military rearmament. These policies, adopted in Germany as in the liberal countries, led the world economy out of crisis. Unfortunately, the armaments did not remain unused for long. This of course was not a consequence of Keynesianism, but of the political deformations of capitalism. In Chap. 2 (Further Reading), we quoted Kalecki who argued that capitalists prefer military spending to welfare spending.

Now let us see Sraffa's criticism.

3.10.2   The Return to Classical Theory and the Capital Controversy

Besides rediscovering the surplus approach and working towards a solution of the problems encountered by Ricardo and Marx, in *Production of commodities by means of commodities*, Sraffa also shed light on the difficulties of the marginal theory of capital. Let us look at these briefly. Certain more evident problems were already known to the founders of that theory and here we give an intuitive explanation.

As we have said, marginalism starts from the quantity of "production factors" possessed by economic subjects. We said that the scarcer a factor with respect to the others, the more its contribution to production is valuable and the higher its remuneration. Let us look at the economy as a whole.

Some of these factors can be measured as physical quantities. Work of a certain quality, for example, can be measured in hours of labour, and the quantity of land having certain characteristics can be measured in hectares (work or land of different qualities can be treated as different factors of

[5] Keynes (1936, p. 362).

[6] Keynes's introduction to the German edition of the *General Theory* is available at http://gutenberg.net.au/ebooks03/0300071h/gerpref.html. Accessed 27 February 2020.

production. This is not true of the stock of capital. It consists of different types of equipment: ploughs, tractors, machinery and thousands of other commodities. The stock of "capital" is therefore measurable only as a value, multiplying the quantity of each capital good by its price and summing the total, just as they taught us to calculate the shopping list in first class of primary school.

The problem is that we do not yet know the prices of the goods. In other words, to determine prices and distribution, we need to know the value of the stock of capital, but to know the value of the stock of capital we should already know the prices and distribution: a vicious circle.

Then how can we claim that the distribution between wages and profits is based on the relative scarcity of capital and labour when "capital" is a mysterious ectoplasm that we presume measurable independently of prices and distribution?

Prof, another vicious circle! Yes, absolutely. Except that this one cannot be solved. Or rather, it can be solved following Sraffa, who determines the price of the means of production together with that of all the other commodities. We saw this in relations (2.10) of Chap. 2, where the price of capital advanced as corn and steel was a result of our analysis, not known at the outset. But this means that a "production factor" called "capital", the value of which is known before and independently of prices, simply does not exist. The first marginalists tackle the problem openly and in so doing were more honest than their modern imitators, who sweep the question under the mat. Few economists who received their doctorates after 1980 have taken the trouble to understand the difficulties of the marginal theory of capital, and wrongly presume that they were resolved in a way that left the fundamentals of mainstream economics intact.

Some of you will remember the similar situation of the labour theory of value of Ricardo and Marx. Curiously, the first marginalists also sought to measure the stock of capital in terms of the hours of labour needed directly or indirectly to produce it. They encountered problems similar to those met by Ricardo and Marx. It is funny that the labour theory of value and the neoclassical theory of capital both function on the same hypothesis: that there is only one commodity in the world!

Sraffa brought other problems to light, especially the complex phenomenon of the "re-switching of techniques", too complicated to deal with in the present book. However, we can recall that the main implication of Sraffa's criticism concerns the impossibility of tracing a decreasing capital demand function as in Fig. 3.3. In other words, while according to marginal theory firms demand more capital when interest rates are low because they are stimulated to adopt techniques that use more capital (now cheaper) than labour, Sraffa demonstrates that this does not necessarily happen. In other words, lower interest rates could make the demand for capital fall rather than rise. Symmetrically, not even a decreasing labour demand curve (Figs. 3.1 and 3.2) can be traced. If you remember, the labour demand curve tells us about the willingness of firms to pay additional doses of labour; this willingness decreases when labour becomes more abundant (less "precious") than existing capital. But how do we measure this "existing capital"? Sraffa shows that when we move along the labour demand curve by lowering wages, the value of capital may rise, then fall and then rise again.

So Prof, the value of the stock of capital that ought to be "known" when studying the labour demand curve is not known at all and cannot be considered "given". That's right.

In the imagination of the typical marginalist (your economics lecturer or the one invited on TV shows), when wages and employment are supposed to vary along the labour demand curve, the value of the capital stock should remain the same, although its physical form should change to adapt to the different quantities of labour theoretically employed. For example, when little labour is employed, the capital consists of mechanised ploughs; when labour increases, it consists of ploughs drawn by horses; when labour is abundant, it is composed of hoes and spades: all these changes while maintaining the same value. This is impossible: when wages change, the value of capital changes as well (assuming it can be given an initial value without knowing prices).

So the marginalist curve of labour demand is a fake? Absolutely yes. We avenged Ivan della Mea (you remember, the Italian protest singer).

Those who think that Sraffa was a maverick may note that Sraffa's results were the subject of the famous "Cambridge capital debate" in the 1970s between the University of Cambridge (UK) and the Massachusetts Institute of Technology (MIT), probably the most important theoretical dispute in economic history. Cambridge in England boasted the cream of Keynes's followers, as well as Sraffa who had attracted the best young Italian economists (including Pierangelo Garegnani and Luigi Pasinetti), while Cambridge in America had the top American economists (Franco Modigliani, Robert Solow and James Tobin), led by Paul Samuelson (1915–2009). Samuelson in the end admitted that the English Cambridge (but we should say Italian) was right. Despite this, now almost nobody talks about the problem of capital. If you can't beat them, ignore them! Samuelson and Garegnani, however, continued discussion into their final years of life.

An Ectoplasm of No Value. *But Prof, in the case of capital, wouldn't it be legitimate to treat each physical capital good (ploughs, tractors, lathes...) as a separate factor, thus avoiding summing their values?* The option of regarding capital goods as a collection of productive factors defined in a physical form was effectively undertaken by one of the great fathers of marginal theory, Léon Walras (1834–1910).

In principle, it is possible to take the capital stock as a collection of physical capital goods, but we would violate the postulate of the *tendency of the rate of profit to become uniform* on the various capital goods: ploughs would have a certain rate of profit, tractors another and lathes yet another. This is illegitimate (or rather, it was considered illegitimate by classical economists and by most of the founding fathers of marginal theory). Indeed, while it is legitimate to suppose that the wages of workers with different qualifications differ, the different capital goods all originate from saving (or perhaps it would be better to say from the creation ex nihilo of credit by banks), i.e. they have the same "substance", and therefore must have the same remuneration, irrespective of the physical form in which they are invested. The remuneration of capital must be the same whatever the physical form in which it is invested (whether in ploughs, tractors or lathes). This principle underlies the mechanism of Adam Smith's "invisible hand" that we saw in the Chap. 2. As we have seen, the early marginalists thought of capital as an ectoplasm arising from saving (they spoke of capital as a "saving fund"), the value of which they assumed as known before determining prices. This ectoplasm then took specific physical forms, depending on the quantity of labour and other "production factors" used in production, in such a way as to ensure a uniform rate of profit. Unfortunately, without already knowing prices and distribution, the ectoplasm cannot be given a value. But without giving the ectoplasm a value, we cannot know prices or distribution.

To be more precise, the tendency of rates of profit to be uniform will also persist with capital measured in physical form. However, the Walrasian theory is unable to tell us where the invisible hand will lead us since it is unable to determine a long-run equilibrium (a centre of gravitation) characterised by a uniform rate of profit. So if we wish to study the effects of a change in the economy—like a policy measure, e.g. a new tax or a different rate of interest, or an innovation—we are unable to get an answer from this theory. Note that this is what science is about: to tell us where we end up if, starting from an initial state, we introduce a change. We indeed presume that after a change, the *real economy* gravitates towards some new long-period equilibrium (possibly without ever completely reaching it, since in the meantime there are further changes, e.g. due to further technical progress). In the model of Walras, the economy persistently wanders in search of an equilibrium that the theory is unable to indicate, or gets lost among ephemeral short-period equilibria. Thus economic science loses its predictive value and proves to be useless. It is like getting a drunk to take you to a hotel at night in an unknown city. Notably, Vilfredo Pareto (1848–1923), who succeeded Walras in the chair of economics in Lausanne, completely avoided the problem of capital, removing it from his lectures.

These problems of capital theory were brought back into view, independently of Sraffa, by the doctoral thesis of Pierangelo Garegnani in Cambridge. Today, marginalist economists are referring to the Walrasian approach, considering it immune from the problems of capital, since capital as an ectoplasm does not appear. They do not realize, however, that they rely on a version of their theory that provides no guidance for the understanding of what happens in the real world, so much so that for economic policy problems they use the other version, the one with the ectoplasm.

3.11   Where Are We Headed?

Garegnani and others have drawn important implications from the capital debate, two in particular:

(a) the "harmonic" determination of the distribution of income by "neoclassical" theory is wrong, and this justifies a return to the "conflictual" approach of classical theory;
(b) it is not true that there are no systematic aggregate demand problems, as maintained by neoclassical theory. The reason is that flexibility of the rate of interest is not sufficient to ensure that the entire supply of saving at full employment is absorbed by investment (Fig. 3.3 is wrong: there is no such thing as the natural rate of interest). This conclusion makes it possible to save the main conclusions of Keynes's theory from being reabsorbed into marginal theory.

Despite the initial outcry, the contents and outcomes of the capital debate have been progressively removed from university curricula in the United States and in Europe, including Italy. So students of economics in the last 20 years are unlikely to know anything about it. "Sraffa who?" is a well-known tactic to annihilate adversaries. However, for several years Sraffa's results strengthened heterodox lines of research, obviously in a progressive social climate that encouraged alternative analyses. Sraffa's criticism of mainstream theory was strong because it was analytical rather than ideological. Despite the increasing difficulties described at the beginning of this lecture, critical work continues today, for example, with regard to the extension of Keynes to problems of economic growth. Nor has critical work on the theory of capital ceased, while that on monetary theory, a line of research cultivated by several heterodox schools such as the "monetary circuit" school founded in Italy by the late Augusto Graziani, continues.

Further Reading

On Luigi Spaventa and the debate among Italian left-wing economists, see Bini (2013) and Lunghini (1981). See Bharadwaj (1986) for a comparison of the objective analysis of classical economists and the subjective analysis of marginalists. A decent marginalist textbook is Frank and Cartwright (2016). On Veblen and the studies he inspired regarding consumption as an ostentation of wealth, see Attilio Trezzini (2016). The Bundesbank acknowledges that banks create credit without having to collect savings (in the form of deposits) in Deutsche Bundesbank (2017). What a shock for the German public: banks lend what they don't have, and with Buba's blessing! We will come back to the subject in Chap. 5.

A critique of marginalist welfare economics and an alternative explanation of the origins of the welfare state based on the surplus approach can be found in Cesaratto (2007). A clear introduction to the unfortunately very complicated debates on capital theory has been written by Andres Lazzarini (2011). The beginning of the controversy over capital theory is often identified with Joan Robinson, a pupil of Keynes and heroine of many heterodox economists. Her contributions to the controversy seem rather marginal and misleading, as Lazzarini shows. On the figure of Garegnani, see Roberto Ciccone (2012). Paul Samuelson, who held Sraffa and Garegnani in high esteem, continued discussions with the latter until his death in 2009, see Heinz Kurz (2013). Garegnani's doctoral thesis was published in Italian (Garegnani 1960). An English translation has been ready for years as part of a collection of papers prepared by Garegnani himself and is now languishing with an important publisher who for mysterious reasons—or maybe not so mysterious—does not publish it. By Luigi Pasinetti, the other great Sraffian protagonist of the debate on the theory of capital, see Pasinetti (2000). A fine article on the implications for economic policy of criticism of capital theory, explaining the importance of the method of long-term equilibrium (or positions), is by the Argentine economist Ariel Dvoskin (2016). This contribution shows that if contemporary marginalism wants to keep its predictive power, it must resort to its traditional version, the one with the ectoplasm, and not rely on the Walrasian approach. But this exposes it to the capital theory criticism. Modern marginalism is thus caught between error and irrelevance (see also Dvoskin and Petri 2017).

Economics students should also note that criticism of the marginalist theory of capital has had a devastating effect on two central models in their economics studies: Robert Solow's neoclassical growth model, and the Heckscher-Ohlin model of international trade. For criticism of the first model see again Pasinetti (2000); for the second see Steedman (1979) and Cesaratto (2013).

On Augusto Graziani's "monetary circuit theory", of which the late Neapolitan economist was a leading exponent see, for example, Graziani (1990). This theory has the merit of having contributed to spread the idea of "endogenous money", but it meets various difficulties—see Cesaratto (2017) and Cesaratto and Di Bucchianico (2020) for a critical discussion.

References

Aspromourgos, T. (2019). What is supply-and-demand? The Marshallian cross versus classical economics. *Review of Political Economy, 31*(1), 26–41.

Bharadwaj, K. (1986). *Classical political economy and the rise to dominance of supply and demand theories* (2nd ed.). Calcutta: University Press India (1st. ed. Orient Longman, 1978).

Bini, P. (2013). Violare gli equilibri. Gli economisti italiani di sinistra nella crisi degli anni Settanta del Novecento. *Rivista di Politica Economica, 2013*(1), 75–112.

Bordini, C., & Veneziani, C. A. (Eds.). (1978). *Dal fondo – La poesia dei marginali.* Roma: Savelli.

Cesaratto, S. (2007). The classical surplus' approach and the theory of the welfare state and public pensions. In G. Chiodi & L. Ditta (Eds.), *Sraffa or an alternative economics*. Basingstoke: Palgrave Macmillan.

Cesaratto, S. (2013). Harmonic and conflict views in international economic relations: A Sraffian view. In E. S. Levrero, A. Palumbo, & A. Stirati (Eds.), *Sraffa and the reconstruction of economic theory* (Aggregate demand, policy analysis and growth) (Vol. II, pp. 242–264). Basingstoke: Palgrave Macmillan.

Cesaratto, S. (2017). Initial and final finance in the monetary circuit and the theory of effective demand. *Metroeconomica, 68*(2), 228–258.

Cesaratto, S., & Di Bucchianico, S. (2020). Endogenous money and the theory of longperiod effective demand. *Bulletin of Political Economy, 14*(1).

Ciccone, R. (2012). Pierangelo Garegnani: rifondare la teoria economica. *Moneta e Credito, 65*(259), 243–267.

Deutsche Bundesbank. (2017). The role of banks, non-banks and the central bank in the money creation process. *Monthly Report.*

Dvoskin, A. (2016). An unpleasant dilemma for contemporary general equilibrium theory. *The European Journal of the History of Economic Thought, 23*(2), 198–225.

Dvoskin, A., & Petri, F. (2017). Again on the relevance of reverse capital deepening and reswitching. *Metroeconomica, 68*(4), 625–659.

Frank, R. H., & Cartwright, E. (2016). *Microeconomics and behaviour* (2nd European ed.). London: McGraw-Hill Education.

Garegnani, P. (1960). *Il capitale nelle teorie della distribuzione*. Milano: Giuffré.

Ginzburg, A., & Vianello, F. (1973, August 3). Il fascino discreto della teoria economica. *Rinascita*, 31. Retrieved February 20, 2020, from http://www.fernando-vianello.unimore.it/site/home/una-selezione-di-scritti.html

Giorgio Lunghini (a cura di). (1981). *Scelte politiche e teorie economiche in Italia (1945-1978)*. Torino: Einaudi.

Graziani, A. (1990). The theory of the monetary circuit. *Économies et Sociétés, 24*(6), 7–36.

Keynes, J. M. (1936). *The general theory of employment, interest, and money*. London: Macmillan.

Kurz, H. (Ed.). (2013). *The theory of value and distribution in economics: Discussions between Pierangelo Garegnani and Paul Samuelson*. London: Routledge.

Lazzarini, A. (2011). *Revisiting the Cambridge capital theory controversies*. Pavia: Pavia University Press.

Pasinetti, L. L. (2000). A critique of the neoclassical theory of growth and income distribution. *PSL Quarterly Review, 53*(215), 385–431.

Steedman, I. (1979). *Trade amongst growing economies*. New York: Cambridge University Press.

Trezzini, A. (2016). Early contributions to the economics of consumption as a social phenomenon. *The European Journal of the History of Economic Thought, 23*(2), 272–296.

4

The Incomplete Revolution

Abstract This chapter deals with Keynes's critique of marginalist theory. Keynes questioned the idea that market flexibility leads to full employment. He regarded aggregate demand as the main determinant of production and employment levels. For Keynes, as for Marx, increasing inequality in income distribution depresses aggregate demand. He believed that monetary policy could have real effects on the economy, but was hampered by distrust of the financial markets, and regarded fiscal policy as a necessary tool for full employment.

Keynes also believed that saving was not the driver of economic growth, but rather a factor that depresses aggregate demand. In his theory, investment depends on entrepreneurs' expectations of future aggregate demand. Keynes's main theoretical contribution lies in the idea that investment determines saving, and not vice versa as in mainstream economics. This theoretical innovation has important implications for the role of banks. According to Keynesian theory, banks do not intermediate saving, but create money out of nothing to fund investment. This view is called endogenous money theory. Finally, we examine the limits of Keynesian criticism of marginalism and how, by integrating Sraffa's criticism with that of Keynes, a complete alternative to marginalism can be developed.

© Springer Nature Switzerland AG 2020
S. Cesaratto, *Heterodox Challenges in Economics*,
https://doi.org/10.1007/978-3-030-54448-5_4

4.1   Keynes: Two for the Price of One

The year 2021 marks the 85th anniversary of John Maynard Keynes's *General Theory of Employment, Interest and Money*, his most revolutionary work.[1] The importance of Keynes last century is not second to that of Einstein or Freud, scholars who gave us a different view of the world. Before illustrating the central analytical points of the Keynesian revolution, let me recall the role of the English economist at the end of the two world wars. In 1919, after World War I, he represented the British Treasury at the peace talks in Versailles before resigning in disgust at what was happening, namely the humiliation of Germany, destined to have terrible consequences. The book he wrote about this experience, *The Economic Consequences of the Peace*, became an international bestseller. At the end of World War II, Keynes was head of the United Kingdom delegation to the Bretton Woods negotiations that redesigned the international monetary system. Also, in this case, his long-sightedness went beyond what was politically acceptable to the Americans.

The debate on "what Keynes really meant" is never ending. One story goes that if you put five economists, including Keynes, around a table, there will be six different opinions, two of which are held by the famous economist. This, in combination with his failure to break completely with the mainstream marginal theory, helped to fuel the many interpretations of his ideas. The research of Sraffa, personally invited to Cambridge by Keynes in 1926 and a member of his very limited *circus* of close younger colleagues, was probably still in too early a stage to have any influence on him. And perhaps the liberal views of Keynes made him unsympathetic to the socialist perspective of Sraffa. Indeed, the two only wrote one article together and this sprang from their common love of books. In a brilliant feat of literary detective work, they demonstrated that Adam Smith was not the anonymous reviewer of David Hume's *Treatise of Human Nature*, as generally thought, but that Hume wrote it himself because the reviewers had ignored the book.

The theories of Keynes have been very influential and it is not incorrect to define the first two or three decades after World War II as the "Keynesian epoch". Everyone knows that government spending to sustain the economy is the core of Keynesian policies. Politicians have always known this. Since the first emergence of a surplus, the political class has been aware that if the people agitate for lack of food or work it is well to spend some of the surplus to build pyramids and aqueducts. However, economists cannot see something

---

[1] Keynes (1936).

working in practice without asking if it can work in theory. And indeed, a sound idea has more force if it has scientific trappings. Keynes, who as a good liberal believed strongly in the force of ideas, fully appreciated this. As good followers of Gramsci, however, nor do we underestimate the battle of ideas. Of course, the ultimate struggle is elsewhere, namely in the concrete balance of power between the social classes.

4.2   Keynes the Copernican

The Copernican revolution triggered by Keynes's *General Theory* revolves around a proposition: investment determines saving and not vice versa. To understand the reach of this innovation, we return to Say's Law, which Keynes strongly criticised. As we saw in Chap. 2, in Ricardo's simple and straightforward understanding of the law, capitalists save to invest: if they abstain from buying caviar, they do so to purchase capital goods and the income–expenditure circle is complete. As we saw in Chap. 3, the marginalists have a more elaborate version of Say's Law based on a natural rate of interest. When the economy is at full employment, there is a certain supply of saving from households. However, there will be a "natural" rate of interest at which all saving is absorbed by firms for investment. Again, households' reluctance to spend is compensated by the investment spending of firms, and the circle is complete. Unfortunately, Keynes puts both versions of Say's Law in a melting pot he calls classical theory. He did not realize that in so doing, he created confusion. Although Ricardo accepted Say's Law, we find no analytical support in his writings for the idea that laissez-faire necessarily leads to full employment—Ricardo speaks, for example, of technological unemployment and believes that unemployment can only be absorbed through faster capital accumulation or a population decline—whereas marginalists accept Say's Law and at the same time presume to demonstrate that wage flexibility leads to full employment (Fig. 4.1).

While Keynes criticised Ricardo's version of Say's Law, he lacked the tools to contest it in the marginalist version: for that, we have to wait until the late 1950s, when Sraffa completed his criticism of the marginalist notion of capital. Keynes made do with claiming, contrary to Say-Ricardo, that saving decisions are made by households, typically the more well-to-do households, whereas investment decisions are made by firms, and there is no reason why Jones & Co. down the road would invest as much as lawyer Smith's family has decided to save, as we saw in Chap. 3. This argument works for Ricardo, but it is less effective for the marginalists. Indeed, the latter replied to Keynes that they agreed perfectly with him. Saving and investment decisions are made by

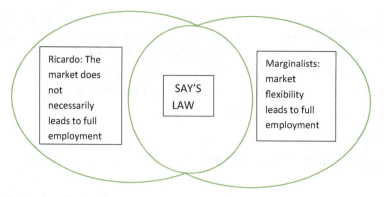

Fig. 4.1 Accepting Say's Law does not imply accepting that laissez-faire leads to full employment

different economic actors. This is why they pinpoint the rate of interest as the variable that can make firms want to invest exactly what households want to save.

Keynes has nothing to say, no arguments to demolish the marginalist reasoning. What he does is to replace one theory with another. In other words, he states that saving and investment are not brought into equilibrium by the rate of interest, but rather by income (we shall see how shortly), and that the rate of interest is consequently not determined as in Fig. 3.3. Keynes's weakness lies in the fact that in order to criticise theory A, it is not enough to propose theory B: it is also necessary to explain why A is wrong. Otherwise, theory A might simply assimilate theory B, which is what the marginalists later do, seeking to demonstrate that the theory proposed by Keynes (theory B) is interesting, but can be considered a special case of marginal theory (theory A).

Keynes's intention was to shake up the "formidable power" of the dominant theory by striking its fortified theoretical "citadel", a well-established doctrine that was never impressed by the external common-sense criticism of heretical economists—whom Keynes calls cranks. "I range myself with the heretics," Keynes wrote in 1934, but "I was brought up in the citadel and I recognize its power and might".[2] He realized that it was within the citadel that its weak point had to be found. Keynes's intentions were therefore radical—although he did not believe that the whole citadel should be demolished. His scalpel, however, did not go deep enough. Sraffa's criticism was still in gestation, and who knows if Keynes would have followed him in a more radical demolition. The fact remains that although it was later slowly reabsorbed, the blow to mainstream theory came from its most eminent exponent, and was therefore very effective.

----

[2] Quotations from Keynes (1934 [1987], pp. 488–489).

Keynes will need Sraffa, as we shall soon see. But let us not get ahead of ourselves. Let us look at Keynes's plan B and at how he sees the relation between saving and investment. Then let us consider how the marginalists' plan A tries to absorb Keynes, to whom Sraffa launches a lifebuoy.

4.3   Explain It Again, Gardner

Gardner Ackley (1915–1998) wrote one of the best and most carefully argued textbook of macroeconomics, before vulgarity took over with texts like Oliver Blanchard and Gregory Mankiw. Ackley was American ambassador to Rome in 1968–1969. Around the end of the 1950s, he was active at the Roman headquarters of the Association for Industrial Development of Southern Italy (SVIMEZ), a hotbed of Keynesian ideas not far from the *dolce vita* of Via Veneto. He was also an advisor to President John F. Kennedy. Somewhere I read that in this guise he explained the Keynesian multiplier to the US President. The multiplier is the mechanism by which investment generates saving (Copernicus) and not vice versa (Ptolemy); Kennedy was impressed. Sometime later, before a meeting, Kennedy, uncertain of the argument, asked Ackley: "Gardner, would you explain that story of Keynes to me again?"

Keynes's idea is that the level of production decided by firms depends on expected demand. If firms are optimistic about the demand for goods and services, they produce more; if they are pessimistic, they produce less. But so far this is only psychology. The expectations of firms will plausibly be based on the effective trend of aggregate demand, the total amount of demand for goods and services. (Clearly, each entrepreneur will also consider the specific demand for his product: if the product is innovative he will expect that demand will grow faster than average; if it is obsolete he will expect below-average demand; but we are only considering the average trend of aggregate demand.) We therefore ask ourselves what the average trend of aggregate demand depends on. Aggregate demand has various components. In defining them, Keynes also gave a big impulse to national accounting.

The question Keynes poses is whether aggregate demand generated by the free market is high enough to sustain aggregate production at full employment.

4.4 The Hen or the Egg

In order to spend, economic subjects (households and firms, let us say) first have to have an income; but to produce and distribute an income, firms at least have to wait for someone to spend. So if there is no income there is no expenditure, but without expenditure there is no income.

Another vicious circle, Prof? This is a vice of yours! True, but perhaps there is a way out. Actually, part of expenditure is not financed by income, but by banks. As we mentioned and as we shall see again in Chap. 5, banks create money in the form of credit in the deposit accounts of customers: credit that customers can use to pay by means of drafts, cheques or credit cards. To credit an account, the bank does not need to have first received new savings.

Let us identify two types of expenditure:

- induced consumption, requiring an income in order to happen; for example, the employee awaiting her pay cheque before going shopping;
- autonomous expenditure financed by banks; this includes investment by firms and also autonomous consumption financed by consumer credit. When we buy a car or an appliance on instalments, a bank has effectively paid on our behalf, crediting the seller's current account with newly created money that we will pay back in instalments with interest. Purchase of a newly built house by means of a home loan is also a form of autonomous consumption, although it is deceptively classified in national accounts as expenditure for investment; indeed, it is the most powerful form of autonomous consumption, as demonstrated by the American, Spanish and Irish construction bubbles that preceded and then triggered the financial crisis of 2008 (Chap. 5).

Then if we consider an economy in which there is the State, public expenditure, namely what the State spends to provide its services, is also autonomous expenditure. As we shall see in Chap. 5, and also according to the theses of Modern Money Theory, the State can spend even without having first collected taxes or without first financing itself through government bonds. We shall argue that the State can finance its spending by selling bonds to commercial banks that create credit in its favour as they do for private operators.

Then if we also consider foreign exchange, exports will be another item of autonomous expenditure. In fact, the expenditure of foreigners does not depend on our income. Sometimes domestic banks create credit for foreigners so that they can buy our goods, a mercantilist policy known as vendor finance.

Summing up, aggregate demand can be defined:

Aggregate demand = Induced consumption + Autonomous expenditure

where autonomous expenditure is in turn defined as:

Autonomous expenditure = Investment + Autonomous consumption
+ Public expenditure + Exports

If exports are demand for our products, imports are our demand for foreign products and must therefore be subtracted from internal demand. Thus, the level of national production will depend on aggregate demand, excluding the part of demand that concerns foreign products, namely:

National production = Aggregate demand − Imports

In a causal sense, from the Keynesian viewpoint, the relation should actually be read from right to left (←), i.e. aggregate demand generates aggregate supply. This is an inversion of Say's Law, according to which the relation goes from left to right (supply creates its own demand).

Armed with these definitions, let us return to the hen and the egg, that is to the problem of whether expenditure generates income or income generates expenditure. We now know that part of expenditure, the autonomous part, is independent of income. We can, therefore, suppose that autonomous expenditure, financed by bank-created purchasing power, is where it all starts (*you* can decide whether it is the hen or the egg). In other words, autonomous expenditure generates overall aggregate demand and this generates income.

4.5 Keynes Multiplied

To explain how autonomous expenditure can be the prime mover of aggregate demand and income, let us assume (Ricardian vice) that aggregate demand consists only of private induced consumption and autonomous investment, and that there is no foreign trade (economists say that we are in a closed economy without public administration):

Aggregate demand = Induced consumption + Autonomous investment

In a certain period, firms decide to make a certain amount of investment and they go to the bank for a loan. The banks evaluate the projects and provide the loans. The firms spend and set production of investment goods in motion. The factories produce the equipment required and distribute incomes in the form of wages to their workers and profits to their shareholders. Those receiving incomes spend part of them on consumer goods and save the other part. Expenditure for consumer goods sets production of consumer goods in motion. These factories produce and distribute further incomes which are partly spent on consumer goods and partly saved. Expenditure for consumer goods generates additional production and incomes, and therefore new consumption and saving, and so forth. *The process by which an amount of investment X generates a proportionally larger amount of income Y is called the income multiplier.*

This process is not simultaneous, but occurs gradually in the course of the year. If, for example, total investment last year was X, it is plausible that it was made approximately 1/12 per month, and every month we could observe a multiplication process and the consequent increase in consumption and saving. Annual income, consumption and saving are the sum of the monthly results.

The first point to understand is that the multiplier process becomes less and less powerful and tends to run out, because as it proceeds, part of the income is saved, and if it is not spent it does not generate further production. At the end of the process, an amount of investment X will have generated an amount of consumption C and therefore a final income $Y = X + C$.

The second point is that as we have said, most consumption is an induced component of income: it is generated by the process described; it does not set it in motion but helps to propagate it (albeit in a manner that tends to taper off, as we just said, since not all income is consumed). The investment decided by firms is the prime mover.

The third and fundamental point is that saving is the result of the process set in motion by investment, in other words investment is what generates saving, not vice versa as maintained by marginal theory! This is the heart of the Copernican revolution of Keynes. (With simple mathematical expressions that you can find in Wikipedia, it is easy to show that if entrepreneurs decide to invest an amount X, an amount S of saving will be generated exactly equal to X; we show it in a simple numerical example in the Appendix to this chapter.) In a certain sense, we can say that at the end of the game (ex post as economists say), but only at the end of the game, the banks have financed so much investment and hold the same amount in saving as bank deposits.

The fourth point concerns "morals". Keynes had a negative view of saving, whereas parsimony is a leitmotiv of moralists. In fact, since there is no reason why bigger investment follows if people decide to save more, an increase in saving damages aggregate demand and depresses the economy. A World Savings Day was established in 1924 during an international banking congress in Milan: it should be replaced with Spendthrift Day!

Fifth point: There is no reason to think that the level of investment decided by entrepreneurs will generate a sufficient level of production (income) to ensure full employment of labour and plant. Indeed Keynes held that in an advanced capitalist society, in which there has already been much investment, the level of investment is generally insufficient to generate full employment. According to Keynes, unemployment is therefore largely involuntary. Even if workers accepted lower wages, this would not increase employment; on the contrary, the fall in worker consumption would depress aggregate demand and destroy investor confidence in the economic situation. We now have a theory with which to oppose the marginalist thesis that the cause of unemployment is wage rigidity. Fathers are not competing with sons: if father or mother accepted a wage-cut, the only effect would be greater profits, while the family as a whole would certainly not be better off.

But Prof, Keynes again has nothing to say about the marginalists' labour demand curve, just as he had nothing to say about the investment demand curve. He just replaces theory A (if wages fall, employment rises) with theory B (if wages fall, aggregate demand and income fall). True. As we said in Sect. 3.10, we have to wait for Sraffa for a criticism of the marginalist demand functions for the factors of production. But we do not want to pit Sraffa against Keynes: the two are complementary.

Finally, Keynes held that a more equal distribution of income alleviates problems. Indeed, we expect wealthier classes to save a higher share of their income compared to the working class. So if income were redistributed to the working classes by increasing wages, the same amount of investment would generate a higher income, and therefore higher employment. The income multiplier would in fact be stronger. As we said, the propulsive effect of investment is damped because at every round of expenditure, a part of the income generated is saved. If the amount saved at every round is less, the propulsive effect is prolonged and final production is greater. This result is perfectly coherent with what we concluded about the theory of surplus in Chap. 2: the greater the inequality, the lower the aggregate demand and the more difficult it is to convert a physical surplus of commodities into money, what Marx would have called the "realization problem" (Sect. 2.17). Not by chance the great Polish economist, Michal Kalecki, obtained results identical to those of

Keynes in the early 1930s, starting from Marx. At that time, however, he wrote in Polish. In the 1940s he was at Oxford and later, as a renowned economist, he returned to socialist Poland where he tried with little political success to contribute to better planning.

4.6   Six of One, Half a Dozen of the Other

Economists are somewhat obsessed with the saving–investment relation. The economy produces consumer goods (food, clothing, etc.) and investment goods (equipment, etc.). At the end of the year, when the balance sheet is drawn up, the part of income (i.e. product) that has not been consumed by definition matches both saving and investment. In other words, saving and investment are both "non-consumption" in the form of unconsumed income and unconsumed product, respectively.

Suppose that the annual product (never mind whether gross or net) was 100 and therefore the income distributed to households (workers and firm owners) was also 100. If households spent 80, they saved 20. If households, therefore, consumed 80 of the annual product, the rest, 20, went on investment goods. (In economics, goods are classified as either consumer or investment goods).

Very well, Prof, but if households consumed 80, who is to say that the 20 saved were effectively absorbed by firms and used to purchase investment goods? I would not want to be examined by you, when you become a university professor! Unsold consumer or investment goods are classified as "(unintended) investment in inventories"—a situation that clearly cannot continue for long, but that allows us for now to balance the books. So 20 saved by households can for example be 15 invested in equipment and 5 invested in warehouse stock (they are probably accumulated involuntarily by firms that would have preferred to sell them).

As you can see, ex post, saving is identical to investment. The part of income that was not consumed was equal to saving and to investment, like two sides of the same coin. Please observe that we are talking about final results in national accounting. The final equality of *actual* saving and investment does not, however, imply that during the year *decisions* to save are identical to *decisions* to invest. In other words, it is necessary to explain how a balance is achieved between the two. In Keynes, saving adjusts to investment through the income multiplier…

But Prof, you just said that if decisions to save exceed decisions to invest, investment somehow adapts to saving by accounting unsold product as unintended inventory investment... True. Let me express myself more clearly. According to Keynes, investment determines aggregate demand and production, but effectively in many cases production has already been carried out by firms on the basis of *expectations* of demand. And firms can err, produce too much or too little. When they overproduce (they were over-optimistic about demand), there is an unintended accumulation of inventories. When production is adjusted to aggregate demand, i.e. production is equal to the level of aggregate demand justified by entrepreneurs' (voluntary) investment decisions, there is no involuntary build-up of inventories, and we can genuinely say that the level of saving is determined by those investment decisions.

According to traditional marginalism, as we saw in Chap. 3, the variable that balances saving and investment decisions is not income, but the natural rate of interest (Fig. 3.3). The economy is at full employment. The saving (or capital) demand curve expresses the demand for saving of entrepreneurs wanting to invest according to the rate of interest. The saving supply curve expresses the desire of households to save. If the central bank is clever, it adjusts the interest rate so that entrepreneurs invest exactly as much as households have decided to save out of the full-employment income. We can, therefore, say that the following relation holds for marginalists at the equilibrium (or natural) rate of interest:

$$Saving \rightarrow Investment$$

For Keynes, the relation between saving and investment is Copernicanly different from that of marginalists, and the process whereby saving and investment are ultimately identical is triggered by investment and takes place via "the income multiplier":

$$Investment \rightarrow Multiplier \rightarrow Saving$$

In the Appendix to this chapter, we explain more fully how the multiplier works.

Very well Prof, but if saving does not finance investment, who finances it? We touched on that in Chap. 3: the banks create credit "with a stroke of the pen". In Table 4.1 in Appendix to this chapter, we assume this very thing that investment is financed by bank credit created out of thin air. However, in the end, that credit is transformed via investment into saving, and ex post (but only ex post) the banks can say that they lent saving. It is not theory but a fact that banks create credit. At central banks they know this, even at Bundesbank, and even some marginalists know it! However, many marginalist economists consider it to be a bold theory, too bold to be taught at university. So the textbooks continue to plague you with the view of banks as intermediators of saving, or with the multiplier of bank deposits! We'll talk about the deposit multiplier in the next chapter.

The short, the long and the expected. *The General Theory* of Keynes examines how aggregate demand determines the degree of utilization of a given stock of production plant, on which the level of employment depends. Economists call this a short-period analysis, since the stock of plant (also known as productive capacity) is given. In this analysis investment is a component of autonomous expenditure. Heterodox economists in the Keynesian tradition hold that aggregate demand not only determines the *degree of utilization* of productive capacity in the short term, but also the *growth* of productive capacity in the long period; in other words it determines the accumulation of capital. The vigour of capital accumulation depends in turn on that of investment, which is precisely an increase in productive capacity (new equipment, plant, etc.). The heart of the theory of accumulation—or of growth, as a mainstream economist would say—is therefore the explanation of the circumstances that invigorate or weaken investment. A good theory is one that explains investment on the basis of expected demand: if entrepreneurs expect robust and persistent growth of aggregate demand they will invest a lot; and vice versa: they will invest little if they expect stagnant demand. So while investment is an autonomous component of aggregate demand in the short period, in the long period it is an induced component of aggregate demand. But then, what does the trend of aggregate demand depend on in the long period?

Prof, you confuse us with another hen/egg dilemma: in the short period aggregate demand depends among other things on investment, whereas in the long period investment depends on aggregate demand? I am sorry: the world is complicated. To explain the trend of aggregate demand in the long period, and therefore investment and accumulation, we must rely on the other autonomous components of demand (Sect. 4.4). It can be argued that the long-term trends of autonomous consumption (the part financed by consumer credit), public expenditure and exports ultimately drive aggregate demand and investment. And since these items of demand are backed by credit creation by banks, excessive financing of autonomous expenditure may give rise to debt crises, as we shall see in the coming chapters. A promising heterodox theory in this direction is that of the supermultiplier, an extension to the long period of the short-term Keynesian multiplier (see the Further Reading for more details).

Developing Keynes. The *General Theory* of Keynes was mainly concerned with developed economies in which the stock of industrial plants is generally sufficient, if fully utilized, to employ the whole labour force. Any involuntary unemployment could, therefore, be absorbed by a higher degree of utilization of the existing equipment. However, in catching-up countries, the industrial stock is unlikely to be able to employ the whole workforce, even when fully used. In these countries, unemployment is largely structural, which means that it cannot be absorbed by the modern sector of the economy. Thus these countries need industrial policies to develop this sector. Support for aggregate demand is still nevertheless important for this purpose, ensuring full use of existing plant and offering market opportunities for investment.

4.7   Implications for Economic Policy

The logic of the multiplier is also applied to public expenditure. In this case, too, Keynes suggests a Copernican revolution with respect to previous conventional wisdom, according to which the State spends by collecting money from the pockets of citizens. Indeed it is commonly held that public expenditure is financed by taxes or government bonds that gather citizens' savings. But that is not so. Actually, just as investment generates, via the income multiplier, the saving that finances it ex post, thus public spending generates, via the income multiplier, both tax revenue and the saving of those who buy government bonds that finance deficits.

Public expenditure → Income → Tax revenues + Saving

The state, therefore, does not steal anything: it provides public services and social transfers (education, pensions and so forth) and its spending generates income that goes into people's pockets, enabling them to consume more. Certainly, citizens pay for the services with taxes, but the State is Robin Hood, and by progressive taxation makes those who are better off pay proportionately more. If the government wishes to strengthen the multiplier, leaving more money in citizens' pockets, spending will be financed by issuing public debt, and in this case citizens will "pay" for public services by lending money to the state, and they will even receive interest. (Paying interest, provided it is sufficiently low, is not a problem for the state, as we shall see.) When the state spends, it therefore generates income which in turn gives rise to tax revenue and saving that citizens invest in public debt securities. By spending, the state generates the resources that finance it!

Very clear, Prof, But if the state spends before the taxes are paid and before issuing securities (that will finance deficit spending), how can it spend? Is there an analogy with the way firms finance their spending with money created by banks? Yes, from the Keynesian viewpoint it can only be thus. We already touched on this and we return to it in Chap. 5.

Public debt and deficit—an example. To explain the difference between public deficit and debt, I use the example of the student living away from home, who for several months spends more than she gets from home (or from a grant) by borrowing from her friends. During those months her balance is negative or in deficit. The sum of the deficits is her debt. Even a child knows that to get out of debt it is necessary to begin to have some positive balances. Our student will not pay interest, but if a "friend" who studies economics expects her to pay interest on the debt—empirical investigation suggests that the study of economics induces behaviour of this type—our poor student will have to include interest payments in her expenditure. When we draw the monthly balance of receipts (money from home) and expenses excluding interest payments, we obtain the primary balance. For the public sector (and also for the student), the primary balance is an important indicator. For example, the Italian State has had positive primary balances since the beginning of the 1990s: the balance of the public sector has been negative overall (deficit), but excluding expenditure for interest, the primary balance has been positive (surplus). What put the total balance in the red was spending for interest, while the positive primary balance indicates that Italian citizens paid more tax than what they received in public services, pensions, etc. This is why it is fundamental that the central bank intervene to keep interest rates on government bonds very low.

Expecting too much from expectations. Once Pierangelo Garegnani confided to me that Keynes had been a disaster for economic theory. Surprised, I asked him why. "Because he introduced the concept of expectations into economic analysis," he replied. Indeed, we have already seen that Sraffa and Garegnani were strongly against giving a central role to subjective elements in economic analysis. Not that expectations do not exist, but they do not have a life of their own; they are based on the objective circumstances that generated them and the circumstances are what must be investigated. It can be said that expectations crept into economic analysis from all sides.

On the conservative side, there has been much talk in recent years about *expansive austerity*, proposed by the late Harvard economist Alberto Alesina, well known to Italian readers for his articles with Bocconi economist Francesco Giavazzi in *Corriere della Sera*. The idea is that "healing public finances" (an unfortunate expression coined in the 1970s by the Italian Communist Party), increases entrepreneur confidence (subjective element) through expectations of future lower interest rates and lower taxation. Thus the recovery of investment more than compensates the fall in demand due to austerity policy. This theory had an amazing influence on European policy at the beginning of the last decade, and perhaps continues to do so. Heterodox economists maintained from the beginning that the collapse of demand could not fail to worsen expectations, as indeed happened. Many readers also know that the expected initial collapse, captured by the value of the "Keynesian multipliers", was underestimated. As we know, the multipliers translate a change in autonomous components of demand into changes in income. In 2010–2011, official circles continued to hold that a decrease of say €10 in public spending would lead roughly to a €5 decrease in GDP. The spate of subsequent studies showed that the decrease would be between €15 and €25, with a negative effect on expectations and investment. But this was not sufficient to induce Europe to change its austerity policies!

On the heterodox side, I think that the influence of critical economists was considerably weakened by abuse of notions like animal spirits and uncertainty. Animal spirits is a concept introduced by Keynes and refers to entrepreneurial investment impetus, sometimes optimistic and at other time pessimistic. This is an unconvincing explanation of investment decisions. Although subject to forecasting errors, these decisions largely depend on the trend of aggregate demand: if an entrepreneur expects expanding markets he invests; if he expects a contraction he makes no move. We should, therefore, investigate the historical-political circumstances explaining the trend of aggregate demand and the economic policies that affect them, and not remain on the surface, talking generically of optimistic and pessimistic expectations. Uncertainty is a fact in an unplanned economy. Many heterodox economists also speak of uncertainty squared, fundamental uncertainty, when entrepreneurs are not even able to estimate a probability for certain events. There is uncertainty about the weather tomorrow, but the forecasts can assign a probability of rain (e.g. 90% or 10%). However, there is fundamental uncertainty about the weather a month ahead, where only a windbag could assign a probability to the likelihood of rain. Thus entrepreneurs certainly do not know the trend of demand over very long periods—it is in fact the task of economic policy to stabilize these trends. Apart from this, attributing the problems of capitalism to fundamental uncertainty is incorrect. In any historical period, it is necessary to seek the objective circumstances, especially prevalent economic policy, that induce certain long-period trends of demand and the consequent investment choices.

The theorem of Podemos. In May 2015, I had a conversation in Madrid with Nacho Alvarez, then responsible for the economic programme of Podemos, the Spanish left-wing political party. Currently, Nacho is a member of Pedro Sánchez's government, supported by the Socialists and Podemos. The programme sprang from consideration of the low level of public expenditure and taxation in relation to the Spanish GDP: low compared to other European countries—about 35% in Spain against 45% in Italy. The idea was therefore to increase both expenditure and taxation to reach a percentage with respect to GDP, similar to the European average. In that way Spain could stimulate demand while maintaining a balanced budget to keep Brussels happy. I observed that they were applying the famous Keynesian theorem of the balanced budget (or Haavelmo theorem after the Norwegian Nobel laureate who "discovered" it in 1945, indeed simultaneously with economists in other countries). This helped the economists of Podemos to clarify what they were proposing. What then is the theorem of the balanced budget? It states, for example, that if public spending and taxation are increased by €10 (thus maintaining a balanced budget), income too will increase by €10. Why? The idea, on one hand, is that spending €10 (e.g. €10 more per week for the poorest pensioners) has an expansive effect on the economy. On the other hand, it is true that a tax of €10 (e.g. €10 extra tax on the highest incomes) has depressive effects, but that €10 taken by taxation would not all have been spent but partly saved. This would mean that demand would decrease by, say, €7. Hence spending makes demand increase by €10, the tax makes it fall by €7, so the net increase in demand is €3. Via the Keynesian multiplier, this net increase generates an extra €10 in income (the demonstration is banal, see Wikipedia).

A final consideration regards the nature of public expenditure to achieve full employment. Public spending fills the gap left by private investment. Keynes held that "'wasteful' loan expenditure [government deficit spending] may nevertheless enrich the community on balance," especially if "the education of our statesmen on the principles of the classical economics [by which Keynes meant marginalism] stands in the way of anything better". "It would, indeed, be more sensible to build houses or the like", Keynes bitterly concludes, "but if there are political and practical difficulties in the way of this", wasteful spending is "better than nothing".[3] In other words, a hospital or an environmental project are better than a jet fighter (without underestimating the topic of national defence). However, we should be wary of playing into the hands of moralisers, whose ultimate interest is to impede or dismantle public intervention (this is often called "spending review").

Prof, talking of Keynes, what is the final word on the question of public debt? Is it a problem or not? "It depends" economic logic holds here too. The size of public debt is usually expressed in relation to GDP which somehow gives the capacity of an economy to repay it over time. But there is no magic number: the fateful 60% of the European parameters, the present 130% of Italy [before the coronavirus crisis], the 230% of Japan. Whether or not we should be worried depends on two factors. The first is the amount of that debt held by foreigners: the more public debt involves net indebtedness of the country to other countries, the more we should in theory be worried. The reason is that a confidence crisis towards public debt securities is less likely to come from national holders of that debt, and it is easier for the government to act towards domestic holders with measures like freezing the debt or capital controls. From this point of view Italy is in a better position than Spain, which has a slightly lower public debt/GDP ratio but a net debt to other countries almost as large as its GDP. Two other elements count as well: the average rate of interest that the state pays on its debt and the rate of growth of GDP (both rates can be taken as real, i.e. adjusted for inflation, or nominal).

Let us assume, for the sake of the argument, a state with zero primary balance, i.e. that covers all its spending except interest payments through taxation. The only reason it would incur further debt is to pay interest on its existing debt. It follows that, if the average interest rate that the state pays on its debt is equal to the rate of growth of GDP, the public debt/GDP ratio does not change. Assuming a public debt of 2200 billion euro and a GDP of 2000 billion euro, the public debt/GDP ratio is 2200/2000 = 110%. If we assume

---

[3] Quotations from Keynes (1936, pp. 128–129).

that the average rate of interest i and rate of growth g are both 5%, i.e. $i = g$, the following year the ratio will again be 110% = 2310/2100 (both the numerator and the denominator rise by 5%). If, however, the mean rate of interest were only 2.5% (so that $g > i$), you can calculate that the ratio becomes 2255/2100, about 107%, i.e. it decreases. In this case, instead of lowering this ratio the government could decide to use the lower expenditure for interest for extra government spending. Thus the primary balance of the state, initially balanced, becomes a primary deficit. The effect on the economy is probably expansive, so that the rate of growth will increase and g will exceed i even more, and this will lead to a decrease in the public debt/GDP ratio! Just what Italy needs: very low interest rates on its debt, as low as those of Germany say, so as to relaunch public spending and support internal demand in a way that is compatible with a stable public debt/GDP ratio. High interest payments lead a government into a trap. Either it may be forced to achieve a primary surplus, i.e. to allocate part of taxation revenue for interest payments instead of sustaining demand, further depressing growth. The result can be an increase in the public debt/GDP ratio—conned and clobbered—more debt and less growth. Or the government may maintain an expansionary fiscal stance, which however may worry the markets, leading to a further increase in government bond spreads. Only low interest rates can open a fiscal space, that is provide room for expansive fiscal policy. We return to this topic in Chap. 6.

4.8   Keynes in the Long Run

It is well known that Keynes was exasperated with the mainstream belief that in the long run the economy would inevitably return to a state of satisfactory equilibrium. In the long run, we are all dead, he remarked in 1923.[4] This statement should not, however, lead us to underestimate the persistence and the continuous action of the long-period forces identified by marginal theory. Due to the very fact that they are long-period forces, their action is tenacious and such as to overwhelm the short-period forces that tend to cancel each other out. The scholastic example is the leaf that falls in autumn: the force of gravity (long-period force) may be hindered in the short period by other contingencies, such as wind, but is just as likely to be seconded by other transient events, such as violent rain that accelerates the fall of leaves.

Unfortunately, Keynes does not have enough tools to criticise the long-run forces at the core of marginal theory. In many respects, he considers the

---

[4] Keynes (1923, p. 80).

theory well-constructed, especially the demand curve for production factors illustrated in Chap. 3. He also advances the suspicion that the propulsive impetus of private investment has been damped in modern capitalism where there has already been much capital accumulation, and thus he seems to favour more equal distribution in order to revive aggregate demand, just as he favours a greater public role in investment. However, these remain relatively marginal reflections in the *General Theory*. On analytical grounds, Keynes is in great difficulty. More specifically, in accepting the marginalist factor demand curves, he accepts the conventional idea that investment is influenced by the interest rate. In other words, however depressed investment is, there will always be an interest rate sufficiently low to revive it and lead the economy towards full employment, validating Say's Law. In truth, Keynes strives to criticise the theory of the natural interest rate, arguing that the interest rate is not determined by the supply and demand functions of saving (or capital as in Fig. 3.3), but is instead the result of interaction between monetary policy and people's choices on how to hold their savings (in liquid form or as financial assets). But again, it is not enough to have a new theory, it is also necessary to explain why the old theory is wrong.

4.9   Keynes in the Trap

So Prof, Keynes proposed a revolutionary explanation of the relation between saving and investment, according to which the latter determines the former (via the multiplier), but at the same time he accepts the idea that investment decisions depend on the interest rate, and from this point of view he is in line with traditional theory. Exactly. As mentioned above, Keynes feels the need to criticise marginal theory, according to which investment lines up with (full employment) saving decisions via the natural interest rate (Fig. 3.3). However, he has no substantial criticism to offer (for that we have to wait for Sraffa). So he shuffles the cards and claims that the interest rate is not the price that makes investment adjust to full employment saving, so as to validate Say's Law, but the price of liquidity. Let me explain.

Keynes considers the interest rate to be the price of money. He argues that it is the price that each of us must be paid in order to give up liquidity. Try thinking of a situation you have experienced. Let us assume (Ricardian vice) you have €1000 of saving. Your alternatives are to keep it in your current account, in liquid form, or to buy public or private bonds. The current account pays no interest, but if you keep your money there, €1000 today will be €1000 a year from now (assuming zero inflation); bonds pay interest but they can lose value in the financial market (so that you can make a loss if you are forced to sell the bond). It is therefore your confidence in the trend of the financial market that determines the interest rate that you will ask in order to part with your liquidity. If you mistrust the market and expect a fall during the term of the bonds, you will ask a higher interest rate to cover the risk of holding bonds; vice versa, you are happy with a lower interest rate if you expect stability or an upturn in the financial market. Here a rule emerges:

Bullish bond market → The cost of parting with liquidity is low

Bearish bond market → The cost of parting with liquidity is high

With a bullish financial market, it is easier for firms to finance themselves by issuing bonds even if the interest rate they offer to savers is low. And according to the traditional theory that Keynes accepts, this stimulates investment.

The central bank, Keynes continues, has a large influence in determining the interest rate, and it does so by buying bonds on the market and therefore sustaining their price if it wants to lower prevailing interest rates, or selling bonds and depressing their value if it wants to raise them. The aim of the central bank is therefore to make the interest rate at which private investment balances full employment saving prevail on the market.

But Prof, this interest rate is the natural rate of interest! Keynes is therefore not far from the conclusions of traditional theory! Absolutely! Keynes realizes this and pulls another rabbit out of his hat, namely the liquidity trap. This can be explained as a situation in which the central bank is unable to lower interest rates as much as needed, especially long-term interest rates important for investment—long-term rates necessary to revive investment can even be negative, if entrepreneurs' expectations are particularly depressed (see the box "Negative interest rates" in Chap. 7).

Trap? How does the liquidity trap work? It is generally believed that the central bank can lower interest rates in the market by buying bonds and therefore increasing available liquidity. As we said, the interest rate is the price of money, the interest we ask for giving up our liquidity. If liquidity is more abundant, its price goes down.

> *Prof, but you are describing quantitative easing!* As we shall see in Chap. 7, quantitative easing (QE) is an evident form of this policy, although in normal times the ECB uses other instruments to regulate interest rates.
>
> With QE, the central bank withdraws bonds from the market in exchange for liquidity. However, if the market is avid for liquidity because confidence is low and it wants to get rid of bonds, the supply of liquidity may not become abundant in relation to demand and the interest rates may not fall: this is the liquidity trap. In other words, the liquidity created by the central bank is abundant, but the desire to hold financial wealth in a liquid form is also strong, so that the central bank's demand for bonds is met with strong sales and interest rates do not fall. Concretely, if market operators (e.g. savings managers or simply speculators) fear that the central bank could soon change its policy and reduce liquidity, and therefore in future the price of bonds may fall, they will tend to get rid of bonds (perhaps with the idea of buying them back again when the price is much lower), and therefore the central bank fails to obtain a rise in their value. The greater liquidity available will therefore not transmute into more favourable conditions for issuing of bonds with low yields (i.e. at lower interest rates), and investment will not pick up.
>
> Actually, recent experience indicates that determined action by central banks succeeds in lowering interest rates to zero and below, not only in the short term. The Federal Reserve (Fed) and the ECB in fact accompanied QE and other liquidity-easing measures with so-called forward guidance: the promise to keep monetary policy accommodating for an indefinite period of time—e.g. in the case of the ECB, until inflation returns to the target of "below but close to 2%" (see Chap. 7).

So experience indicates that central banks have powerful means for reducing interest rates in the short and long term. The liquidity trap, therefore, does not seem to be an effective defence of Keynes's main proposition, namely that investment is what determines saving. Once Keynes accepted that investment was sensitive to the interest rate, he (not the central banks) was trapped. Empirical experience suggests that investment is indeed insensitive to interest rates. To confirm the primacy of theory, it is, however, fundamental to demonstrate that what does not work in practice, does not work in theory either.

4.10   Keynes Assimilated

The liquidity trap is not an effective defence of Keynesian theory either in theory or in practice: in fact, recent events confirm the capacity of central banks to reduce interest rates. In effect, the assimilation of Keynes into traditional theory took place quickly: the so-called "neoclassical synthesis", the synthesis of Keynes and marginalism, is based precisely on the weakness of the liquidity trap. Nobel laureate Franco Modigliani provided the arguments in 1944. The synthesis claimed that Keynes was valid in the short period, when some price (e.g. nominal wages or the interest rate) proved to be rigid, or real or financial expectations particularly negative, while in the long period marginalist theory was true, possibly with support from economic policy, for example monetary policy aimed at fighting the liquidity trap or fiscal policy. Economics is a hypocritical science: the economists "of the synthesis" know that in practice interest rates do not influence investment (the "dirty little secret" as Krugman called it in his blog), and therefore they know that Keynes is right even without the liquidity trap: if investment is depressed this does not depend on the liquidity trap but on something else, for instance on inequality and low aggregate demand.

Well Prof, what I understand is that economists of the "neoclassical synthesis" know that Keynes is right in practice, but they want to prove he is wrong in theory. Yes, they want to show that in (marginal) theory, we are all alive in the long run, even if in practice it is not true and Keynes is right. This stresses the primacy of theory and it is why I consider Sraffa, Garegnani and Pasinetti's criticism of the foundations of neoclassical theory so essential. From them we know that Keynes's criticism of Say's Law is valid in theory and practice, and both in the short and long period. In fact from what we said in Chap. 3, investment decisions (the demand for capital) of firms do not depend on the interest rate. In theory. What happens in practice confirms the irrelevance of the interest rate in investment decisions, demonstrated by many empirical studies; those decisions depend fundamentally on expected demand, which in turn depends fundamentally on economic policy.

Secular stagnation. In 2013, Larry Summers, eminent Harvard economist and ex-secretary of the US Treasury, warned that capitalism was inclined to stagnation. This dire prophecy unleashed many comments in the international blogosphere and was promptly subscribed to by Paul Krugman in his popular column and blog in the *New York Times*. Briefly, Summers argued that capitalism can avoid secular stagnation only if it can reproduce stock market or housing bubbles similar to those that sustained it in the recent past, but which however gave rise to the financial crisis. As on other occasions during the crisis, mainstream economists realize late what critical economists have long been denouncing.

That such renowned economists indicate a deficiency of aggregate demand as the cause of a stagnating trend of capitalism is, however, remarkable. That one of the problems of capitalism is the lack of aggregate demand has always been daily bread for critical economists, the more solid of whom lean towards the theory of income distribution of classical economists and Marx. According to these economists, greater inequality of distribution worsens the deficiency of aggregate demand. In fact, capitalists and their retinue only spend part of the surplus they appropriate on luxury goods and investment. Financial and construction bubbles push the middle class to spend more, since saving invested in securities and houses increase in value, making further saving superfluous. Pressuring households to borrow in order to consume acts as a further stimulus to consume. It comes as no surprise to critical economists that capitalism ends up having to be driven by speculative bubbles, household debt and the indebtedness of whole nations—in the latter case at the service of the mercantilist interests of the élite of countries like Germany. That is capitalism, baby.

Summers and companions have therefore touched a nerve of capitalism: its need to rely on perverse mechanisms to support aggregate demand. This confirms that capitalism is a dysfunctional system, fundamentally because it is based on inequality that depresses aggregate demand, producing poverty when well-being is possible. (Naturally, there are also ethical reasons why capitalism is undesirable, such as obsessive consumption, competition between persons instead of cooperation, ecological reasons, etc.; here we consider but one.) In 2019, Larry Summers wrote in a post on his blog that he is more in tune with heterodox than with mainstream economists.[5]

Appendix

Of Bread and Fishes

Let us try to understand the logic of the Keynesian multiplier also in relation to the creation of credit by banks. We assume (Ricardian vice) an initial investment of €100 (or a million or a billion, whatever you like) made by entrepreneurs on the basis of purchasing power created by banks (see Table 4.1). The bank finances the firms by opening a deposit (first item column 5). The production of investment goods gives rise to a production and a corresponding income to households of €100 (first item in column 2). In period 2, this income is partly spent on consumption and partly saved. Assuming that

---

[5] http://larrysummers.com/2019/03/20/37441/

Table 4.1 The Keynesian multiplier in action

The multiplier carousel				
Periods	Change in investment (1)	Change in income (2)	Change in consumption (3)	Change in saving (4)	Change in bank deposits (5)
1	100	100			100 (initial loan)
2	(initial investment)	80	80	20.0	100
3		64	64	16.0	100
4		51,2	51,2	12.8	100
5		40,9	40,9	10.2	100
...		...	...	...	...
Final		500	400	100	100

households spend 80% for consumption (and save 20%), their spending gives rise to a production of consumer goods and the corresponding income of €80. Households employed in the consumer goods sector, therefore, receive €80 of income, of which they spend 64 (80%) on consumer goods and save the other 16 (20%). The production of consumer goods increases by 64. The households receive another 64 of income which they partly consume and partly save, giving rise to another round in the Keynesian merry-go-round. This shows that for subsequent rounds, from an initial expenditure for investment of 100, a product or final income of 500 is generated, which was partly spent on consumer goods (400) and partly saved (100). The saving generated is exactly equal to the initial investment. The banks initially generated credit out of nothing by creating a deposit of 100 in favour of the investor, i.e. lending without having first received saving as deposits (Keynes named this "initial finance"). At the end of the multiplication process, this deposit (which changed hands gradually as payments were made) consists of 100 in saving (named by Keynes "final finance"). In the end, we can say that the saving deposited matches the initial loan, but only ex post. As the multiplier process unfolded, the deposit always remained at 100, partly consisting of incomes and a gradually increasing part of saving. For example, in period 2, the 100 of income earned in period 1 is partly spent for consumer goods, so that 80 of the deposit changes hands, and 20 is saved; overall, however, the deposit remains at 100. The process stops exactly when the whole deposit consists of saving.

From the example we deduce that ex post, what we asserted for national accounting is confirmed, i.e. that investment is equal to the saving made during the year. While it is therefore right to say that investment is financed by the creation of bank credit out of nothing, it is also correct to say that ex post the investment and saving taking place in the economy are equal. Thus analysis of a monetary economy seems to confirm and strengthen the saving–investment relation that can be deduced from the Keynesian multiplier, namely that the latter generates the former.

In the example, we presume that production decisions follow the manifestation of demand, as when we go for a haircut or the restaurant prepares us a meal. However, in many sectors, such as manufacturing, firms undertake production on the basis of expected demand, so that we find the products already on the shelf when we want them. But if demand is less than expected, firms are forced to accumulate stock, which is a form of involuntary investment, as we saw. It is evidently a temporary situation. In the next period, if the lack of demand is expected to persist, they will reduce production, adjusting it to the demand ultimately determined by entrepreneurs' investment decisions, via the Keynesian multiplier.

Further Reading

The most complete biography of Keynes is by Robert Skidelsky (2004). In recent years Skidelsky has been a companion in disputing European policies. Keynes and Sraffa's essay on Hume and Smith can be found in Hume (1938). The story narrated in the booklet probably also intrigued and inspired Ludwig Wittgenstein, who at the time was engaged in an intense exchange of ideas with Sraffa in Cambridge, and was also a passionate reader of Agatha Christie, see Lucia Morra (2019).

Keynes's first biographer was Roy Harrod (1900–1978) (Harrod 1951). At the end of the 1930s, Harrod was also the initiator of modern growth theory. His was an attempt to extend Keynes to the long run. Keynes had in fact stated that in the short period, when productive capacity is given, the degree to which it is used depends on aggregate demand. In the long run, however, productive capacity (or capital stock) increases. The question is therefore what determines this increase. In the late 1930s, Harrod came up with a model as simple as it was intriguing, which was neither Keynesian nor marginalist. So much so that both the orthodox and the unorthodox growth theories departed from it. A good introduction to the theories of growth, albeit a little dated, is Hywel Jones (1976). A harsh judgment on recent marginalist theories of growth can be found in Cesaratto (1999). Robert Solow, founder of the modern neoclassical theory of growth (and "Nobel Prize" winner), appreciated this criticism of mine.

The state of the art in the unorthodox field is in Cesaratto (2015). Also as a result of this paper, the "supermultiplier" initially proposed by the Swiss

(Sraffian) economist Heinrich Bortis, a former professor at the University of Fribourg (Switzerland), and Franklin Serrano of the Federal University of Rio, is slowly but surely gaining ground among heterodox growth theories. An introductory text on the "supermultiplier", which also deals with "technological unemployment", is in Cesaratto et al. (2003). The supermultiplier takes up the idea, implicit in mercantilism, of foreign markets as an outlet for the surplus examined in the first chapter. This idea, developed by Rosa Luxemburg (1871–1919), who called them "external markets", was taken up by Michal Kalecki, who included state spending as an absorber of surplus. The supermultiplier includes autonomous consumption in the category "external markets". In a beautiful essay, Kalecki (1971) compares the solutions of Rosa Luxemburg and the Russian economist Mihail Tugan-Baranowsky (1865–1919) to the problem of surplus realization, i.e. its actual sale on the market. We have just mentioned Rosa Luxemburg's work. Tugan-Baranowsky argued that in theory, capitalism would not suffer from lack of demand as long as capitalists systematically invested all their savings (Kalecki assumes that workers' saving is negligible).

Invested in what, Prof? In industrial machinery, says Tugan. *But machines to do what?* To produce other machines. Kalecki comments that this implies economic planning, which of course capitalists don't want. In a famous aphorism, the Polish economist writes that "capitalists do many things as a class, but they don't invest as a class." Kalecki concludes, however, that although the hypothesis of production of machines by machines is only valid in theory, it indicates a bitter truth about capitalism: that its ultimate goal is not the production of consumer goods and the material well-being of the community. In principle, producing machines to produce other machines is just as good.

When a student applied to Garegnani to supervise his undergraduate thesis on a Keynesian topic, Garegnani suggested he study Alvin Hansen (1953). An old but unparalleled Keynesian macroeconomics manual, with a comparison between marginalist macroeconomic theory and Keynes's theory, is Ackley (1961). Ackley also published Keynesian studies on the Italian economy. One report has striking similarities with a contemporary study by Garegnani, both conducted for the same institute in Rome. I write about it in Cesaratto (2020), in a *Festschrift* dedicated to Marc Lavoie and Mario Seccareccia, two distinguished heterodox economists.

A useful critical review of recent mainstream macroeconomics can be found in Antonella Stirati (2016). The complementarity of Keynes's and Sraffa's critique of marginalism was initially identified by Garegnani (1978–1979). In a post on his blog in the *New York Times*, Krugman (2014) reveals the "dirty little secret of monetary policy", namely that "it normally acts through the housing sector, with little direct impact on productive investment". The important thing is not to say it in textbooks, right Paul?

But why don't they want to say it, Prof? Because they are very keen to say that saving and therefore thrift determine investment. Besides acclaiming sacrifice (parsimony is a bourgeois virtue), this provides a justification for the unequal distribution of income.

The fact that public debt is not a problem when the interest rate is less than the growth rate was recently "rediscovered" by Oliver Blanchard (2019). Take a look at the first pages, the rest is "vulgar economics" based on the concept of marginal capital product and natural interest rate. Luigi Pasinetti (1998) had already written about this at the end of the nineties.

The example in the Appendix to this chapter is inspired by Dalziel (1996). Two important economists, Claudio Borio and Piti Dysiatat (2011)—chief economists at the Bank for International Settlements, Basel and the Central Bank of Thailand, respectively—clearly support the narrative of the Appendix when they write (evoking similar passages from Keynes): "The true constraint on expenditures is not saving, but financing. … And it is only once expenditures take place that income, investment and hence saving, are generated" (ibid., p. 7). Borio and Dysiatat are exemplary marginalists, so for them the essential thing is that financing takes place at the natural interest rate. We of course disagree with them on this aspect.

But then, Prof, endogenous money and the Keynesian multiplier can be incorporated into marginalist macroeconomics. Yes, of course. In fact, dissent with the marginalists has shifted to the existence of a natural interest rate or a full-employment equilibrium wage and so on, as suggested by Sraffa.

Finally, Augusto Graziani (1990) suggested that the creation of bank credit is to finance production decisions, not investment. Cesaratto (2017) tries to reconcile the two points of view.

References

Ackley, G. (1961). *Macroeconomic theory.* New York: The Macmillan Company (2nd edition: *Macroeconomics: Theory and policy*, Macmillan, 1978).

Blanchard, O. (2019. *Public debt and low interest rates.* PIIE, Working Paper, No. 19-4.

Borio, C., & Dysiatat, P. (2011). *Global imbalances and the financial crisis: Link or no link?* BIS Working Papers, No. 346.

Cesaratto, S. (1999). Savings and economic growth in neoclassical theory: A critical survey. *Cambridge Journal of Economics, 23*(6), 771–793.

Cesaratto, S. (2015). Neo-Kaleckian and Sraffian controversies on the theory of accumulation. *Review of Political Economy, 27*(2), 154–182.

Cesaratto, S. (2017). Initial and final finance in the monetary circuit and the theory of effective demand. *Metroeconomica, 68*(2), 228–258.

Cesaratto, S. (2020). Garegnani, Ackley and the years of high theory at Svimez. In H. Bougrine & L.-P. Rochon (eds.). *Economic growth and macroeconomic stabilization policies in post-keynesian economics* (Essays in honor of M. Lavoie and M. Seccareccia) (pp. 121–136). Cheltenham: Edward Elgar (working paper version: WP Centro Sraffa N. 26. Retrieved February 28, 2020, from http://www.centrosraffa.org/).

Cesaratto, S., Serrano, F., & Stirati, A. (2003). Technical change, effective demand and employment. *Review of Political Economy, 15*(1), 33–52.

Dalziel, P. C. (1996). The Keynesian multiplier, liquidity preference, and endogenous money. *Journal of Post Keynesian Economics, 18*(3), 311–331.

Garegnani, P. (1978–1979). Notes on consumption, investment and effective demand, parts I and II. *Cambridge Journal of Economics, 2*(4), 335–353 and *3*(1), 63–82 (original Italian edition 1964-65).

Graziani, A. (1990). The theory of the monetary circuit. *Économies et Sociétés, 24*(6), 7–36.

Hansen, A. (1953). *A guide to Keynes.* New York: McGraw-Hill.

Harrod, R. (1951). *The life of John Maynard Keynes.* London: Macmillan.

Hume, D. (1938). *An abstract of a treatise of human nature 1740. A pamphlet hitherto unknown by David Hume.* Reprinted with an introduction by J. M. Keynes and P. Sraffa. Cambridge: Cambridge University Press.

Jones, H. G. (1976). *An introduction to modern theories of economic growth.* New York: McGraw-Hill.

Kalecki, M. (1971). The problem of actual demand in Tugan-Baranowskij and Rosa Luxemburg. In M. Kalecki (Ed.), *Selected essays on the dynamics of the capitalist economy 1933–1970.* Cambridge: Cambridge University Press.

Keynes, J. M. (1923). *A tract on monetary reform.* London: Macmillan.

Keynes, J. M. (1934 [1987]). Poverty in plenty: Is the economic system self-adjusting? *The Listener,* 21 November 1934, repr. in D. Moggridge (ed.), *The General Theory and after, Part I—Preparation* (vol. XIII of the Collected writings of J. M. Keynes). London: Macmillan.

Keynes, J. M. (1936). *The general theory of employment, interest, and money.* London: Macmillan.

Krugman, P. (2014). *Notes on easy money and inequality.* Retrieved February 20, 2020, from https://krugman.blogs.nytimes.com/2014/10/25/notes-on-easy-money-and-inequality/

Morra, L. (2019). Sraffa, Hume, and Wittgenstein's lectures on belief. *Nordic Wittgenstein Review, 8*(1–2), 151–174.

Pasinetti, L. L. (1998). The myth (or folly) of the 3% deficit-GDP Maastricht 'parameter'. *Cambridge Journal of Economics, 22*(1), 103–116.

Skidelsky, R. (2004). *John Maynard Keynes 1883–1946: Economist, philosopher, states-man*. London: Penguin.

Stirati, A. (2016). Real wages in the business cycle and the theory of income distribution: An unresolved conflict between theory and facts in mainstream macroeconomics. *Cambridge Journal of Economics, 40*(2), 639–661.

5

Money and the External Constraint

Abstract The focus of this chapter is twofold. First, we return to the theory of endogenous money, providing further details on how banks create money in the form of loans to businesses and households. Secondly, we open our economy to foreign trade and introduce another workhorse of heterodox economics, the "balance of payments constraint". We explain what the balance of payments is: far from being a boring accounting document in which foreign trade and financial transactions are recorded, it is a key to many important questions. In particular, it tells us how countries that want to grow faster in order to catch up with more developed nations often find themselves stuck in unsustainable foreign debt and financial crises. This is because when a country grows faster, it ends up importing more goods from abroad. These must be paid for in international currencies (e.g. in dollars), that can be obtained through exports or through borrowing from foreign banks. Debt in foreign currency is risky because the country may fail to increase its exports and therefore to repay its foreign debt. The final part of the chapter discusses the Modern Money Theory thesis that the balance of payments constraint is overestimated.

5.1 That Obscure Object of Desire

Although I have bored you since Chap. 1 with the importance of theory, with regard to money I will be very practical, because I have always found treatises on the "nature of money" somewhat metaphysical. So let us be practical: what is money for you? Something useful for receiving or making payments, you

© Springer Nature Switzerland AG 2020
S. Cesaratto, *Heterodox Challenges in Economics*,
https://doi.org/10.1007/978-3-030-54448-5_5

will say. Good. And how do you make them? Probably you will say: small payments with banknotes and large ones by cheque, bank draft or credit card; and we arrange with the bank to pay the electricity and gas bill and to credit our wages to our accounts. In the unlikely hypothesis that among my readers there are people who conduct illegal activities, you would probably have replied that you use mostly cash, for the obvious reason that it cannot be traced. It is certainly clear to you that payment by cheque, draft, card and money transfers implies a debit or a credit to your account. On the basis of daily experience, we therefore deduce that there are two ways of making payments: by cash or by transfers between bank deposits from one current account to another (from that of the employer to yours when you are paid, from yours to that of the electricity company when you pay the electricity bill, etc.). We can say that all of us, let us call ourselves the public, use two types of money: cash and bank deposits—the latter also known as bank money because it is a "product" of commercial banks, whereas banknotes are "issued" by the central bank. Let us see how this happens.

We see that the two types of money we (the public) use for payments, cash and bank deposits, are issued and therefore guaranteed by "higher" institutions, trusted by the two parties involved in a transaction: the central bank for banknotes and commercial banks for deposits. For example, all restaurants accept payment in cash or by credit card and are less enthusiastic about personal cheques because they have no way of checking that you have money in your account. In theory, we could even pay the restaurant with a promise to pay (an IOU: "I owe you"), a piece of paper on which we write: "I promise to pay the bearer of this note x euros in y months' time". The restaurateur is unlikely to accept this type of payment (unless you are the Godfather). And if he did, his suppliers would be unlikely to accept the note as a means of payment. Between firms where there is a relation of trust built by years of collaboration, or between the corner shop and the little old lady with her old-age pension, promises to pay of this type do exist, but they are relatively limited cases.

So in general, our counterparts do not accept payment with our promissory notes (IOUs), but want to be paid with means of payment issued by third parties, the central bank or commercial banks. (Defining money an IOU takes us back to the mythical epoch when the central bank promised to "pay the bearer" gold or silver in exchange for the banknote. If this was ever true, it is not true now, and everyone accepts banknotes only because everyone else accepts them. According to chartalist theory, shared by Keynes and many heterodox economists, including the proponents of Modern Monetary

Theory, money is accepted for payments as long as the state guarantees that taxes can be paid with it.)

Let us now ask: how do banks make payments with other banks? In other words, what happens when we get our bank to pay €100 to a bed and breakfast in another town that has its account with another bank? One possibility is that an armoured car leaves our bank in the evening and takes the banknotes to the other bank. However, this is dangerous. Armoured cars still exist, as we discover from the newspapers, but are mostly used to collect banknotes from supermarkets and take them to safety. Between banks there is another payment system. Just as we have current accounts with commercial banks, they have current accounts with the central bank, which in this sense acts as the banks' bank.

The money held by commercial banks in their accounts at the central bank is known as bank reserves. The latter are issued by the central bank (we'll see how). Bank reserves can be promptly converted into banknotes by the central bank, and the fact that commercial banks are obliged to hold a reserve, like for example in the European Economic and Monetary Union (EMU), reassures account holders that the bank can give us our deposit in cash at any moment. More importantly, reserves have the purpose of enabling payments between banks. In other words, when we ask our bank to pay €100 to the B&B in another town, our bank debits our account with the amount and instructs the central bank to take that amount out of its reserves and transfer it to the reserve accounts of the bank in the other town. Finally, the latter credits €100 to the account of the B&B. In summary, our payment orders through the banking system take place through the transfer of reserves between the reserve accounts that banks have at the central bank. These accounts are appropriately defined in Italy as "'reserve and settlement accounts'", meaning settlement of payments.

The compulsory reserve ratio, namely the amount of reserves that banks have to hold in relation to current account deposits is currently 1%, i.e. one euro for every 100 euro deposited with that bank. If you think this is low, in some systems compulsory reserves do not exist, for example in the United Kingdom. But banks hold reserves in any case in order to meet payments, reassure their customers, and pay cash on demand.

Summing up, our money transfer to a third person involves our bank cancelling the amount from our account, ordering the central bank to transfer the amount from our bank's reserve account to the reserve account of the bank of the third person, who finally sees the amount credited to his personal account. As you can see, there is a hierarchy of monies: in transactions between members of the public, bank money (transfer of deposits) or banknotes are used, both being means of payment issued by "higher" institutions (banks and central bank, respectively); the banks make payments between each other with money (reserves) issued by the institution above them, the central bank. Reserves are therefore a third type of money, but are used exclusively by commercial banks for payments among themselves: the interbank payment system is based on transfer of reserves. Reserves and banknotes issued by the central bank are often defined as base money, or monetary base. We will often refer to base money as central bank liquidity.

> **The books balance.** Since some of you know some accounting by virtue of work or study, you will follow me if I say that in the balance sheet of our bank, the deposit in our current account is a liability (money it owes), whereas the liquidity it holds in its reserve account at the central bank is an asset (liquidity that the central bank owes it). When we transfer money, our bank cancels €100 from our account and therefore has €100 less liabilities, but at the same time it loses €100 from its reserve account and therefore also has €100 less assets. The bank of the B&B to which we wish to make a payment acquires €100 of assets in its reserve account, and records €100 of liabilities when it credits €100 to the account of the B&B.

Repetita iuvant, we have identified three types of money: banknotes issued by the central bank and used by the public (by us); bank reserves issued by the central bank and used by commercial banks; bank deposits issued by commercial banks and used by the public.

Prof, how do central banks make payments between themselves?

Quod non mortalia pectora coges, auri sacra fames.[1] Payments can be made in gold, or more likely in the top currencies in the international hierarchy of currencies, especially dollars and euros (once in pounds sterling).

Also among the central banks of the Eurozone, Prof? To make transfers, the central banks of the Eurosystem, which is the network of all central banks of EMU countries and the ECB, use an IT platform known as Target2. Hardly any economists knew about Target2 until 2011, when the leading German economist Hans-Werner Sinn raised a storm by contesting the role it was playing in the European crisis. We will consider this intricate affair in Chap. 7.

Prof, please get round to explaining what it means that money is "issued" by the central bank or by commercial banks. How does money come into circulation? Lately there is talk of helicopter money: is that it? No, not exactly, although it is a possibility. As usual, we have to put the pieces of the puzzle together and

---

[1] What do you *not* force mortal hearts (to do), accursed hunger for gold (Virgil and Seneca).

some patience is needed. To begin with let us see how the creation of deposits and reserves is linked.

5.2   In the Beginning There Was a Bank

We just said that the compulsory reserve is 1% of deposits in the Eurozone. But what does the amount of deposits depend on? Here there is a fundamental step: the amount of deposits depends on the amount of credit created by commercial banks.

One minute, Prof! How can a bank lend if money has not previously been deposited? Let's return for a moment to real life. Which of these two situations is more true?

Laura a brilliant graduate with a good stable job goes to the bank to ask for a loan of €100,000 to buy a house from signor Neri. Even before asking for her credentials, the bank employee calls the teller on the ground floor and asks whether that morning at least €100,000 has been deposited. The teller says no, new deposits have been below that figure. The bank employee expresses his regrets to Laura and asks her to come back tomorrow. Puzzled, Laura crosses the street and asks the other bank for the loan. The bank employee phones upstairs and asks: "If I open a new current account with €100,000 of credit for a new customer, do we have €1000 of compulsory reserves available to cover the new deposit?" The answer is no, and this bank employee, too, expresses his apologies to our friend, asking her to phone the next day. Laura goes away puzzled. Are you puzzled too?

Let us turn to the second version of the story.

Laura goes to the first bank for a housing loan. A courteous employee asks about her job situation and once he has ascertained that she has a steady income, he grants her the loan, opening a current account in her name with a credit of €100,000. Obviously, the procedures are not quite so simple, but basically the only credential the bank cares about is her pay (and the mortgage on the house). If she has a steady income, the bank simultaneously creates a credit and a deposit. The deposit is how the bank grants credit. Naturally, Laura will use the credit to pay the seller of the house.

For my accountant friends, the credit granted is an asset on the bank's balance sheet, money that it will in time get back (while earning interest in the meantime), whereas the deposit is a liability, money that the bank owes its customer: the bank's balance sheet is balanced. The bank did not have to await a deposit in order to lend, it created the deposit. Repeat after me: banks do not lend deposits, they create them.

That's clear, Prof, but how does the bank stand for reserves? There is no hurry for the bank to collect the reserves. In the meantime, remember that the €100,000 will not remain in Laura's account. As soon as she receives it, she will go to the notary to sign the contract for the house and transfer money to signor Neri, who probably banks with a different bank from Laura's. As a result of this step, reserves move between the reserve accounts of the two banks, as we now know. Signor Neri in turn makes other payments, and so the €100,000 continues to go from bank to bank, becoming scattered among many credit institutes. The important fact is that by considering the banking system as a whole (think of it as a single bank), there is an extra €100,000 of deposits that give rise to the need for €1000 more in reserves.

The reserves requirement is however very elastic and depends on the average amount of deposits held in the previous "banking month" (more precisely, over the previous "maintenance period", the 6 weeks between one board meeting of the ECB and another). It is not observed day by day: if one day a bank has fewer reserves than it should have, it will make up for it in the following days by holding more than it should have. For example, if the bank held a billion (=1000 million) in deposits in the previous "maintenance period", in the current period it has to hold an average of 10 million euro in reserves (1% of a billion), and if one day it only holds 5 million, the important thing is that another day it should hold 15 million. The ECB is a tolerant bank! In addition, the Eurosystem has weekly auctions in which it offers reserves to the banks in exchange for bonds (generally government bonds). The ECB creates reserves for commercial banks through an accounting entry on the computer (it does not have to hold gold or anything else in order to issue reserves). So at the next auction, the banks with which Laura's deposit is scattered will ask the ECB for €1000 of reserves—technically they ask their own central bank, e.g. the Bank of Italy, that acts as a branch of the Eurosystem—receiving in exchange for a deposit of €1000 in bonds (commonly called "collateral"), a corresponding credit in its reserve account.

Technically the operation by which the Eurosystem creates reserves for a commercial bank is a repurchase agreement, namely the central bank creates reserves for the bank in exchange for bonds and the bank promises to repurchase the bonds after a certain period of time. In "normal times" the most common operations are the "Main Refinancing Operations" that occur weekly and last one week (at the end the bank has to repay the liquidity and repurchase the bonds, repeating the operation if necessary). During the crisis, the ECB increasingly implemented the "Longer-term Refinancing Operations" (LTRO), normally with a duration of 3 months, but progressively extended up to 4 years. (As we shall see in Chap. 7, in addition to regular refinancing operations, banks also have emergency desks at the central bank, where they can obtain liquidity.)

For my accountant friends, the central bank enters the reserves created in its balance sheet as a liability (liquidity that it owes) and the bonds deposited as an asset. The commercial bank enters the reserves acquired as an asset, but at the same time has to cancel from its assets the corresponding bonds temporarily relinquished to the central bank.

In the long run, of course, a bank must try to balance the deposits created with credit operations, which may be followed by loss of reserves when the money created is used for payments, attracting deposits from other banks, so that new reserves flow in.

But Prof, why do banks need deposits when they can create them? As we said above, banks create bank money in the form of deposits for the public—they do so through credit operations. When we use these deposits to make payments, our bank loses reserves. It is cheaper for the bank to recover reserves by attracting deposits than by borrowing them on the interbank market—the market in which banks exchange reserves—or at the central bank.

We can therefore conclude that loans create deposits and deposits create reserves:

$$Credit \rightarrow Deposits \rightarrow Reserves$$

Note that if the central bank did not promptly create the reserves necessary for banks to meet their reserve obligations, the banks would have to get them on the interbank market, where banks lend and borrow reserves, making the interest rate on this market increase. Since the central bank generally wants to avoid variations in this interest rate—unless they are the result of its own monetary policy decisions—it meets the banks' demand for reserves.

But Prof, if banks can create money, how can they go bankrupt? Attention, banks create money in our favour in exchange for an asset, our promise to repay the debt. A bank cannot do this favour for itself. It can create money for us, but not for itself.

Everything is created and everything is destroyed. We have seen that through the creation of credit, banks create deposits, i.e. bank money. But then every time a debtor pays a mortgage instalment, we perform an act of destruction of bank money. In fact, the repayment of debts implies a decrease in the bank deposits of the debtors. Correspondingly, our banks will need fewer reserves. Only when the creation of new credits exceeds the repayment of old ones is there a net creation of money.

Prof, when in the example of Laura the bank loses €100,000 to the other bank, you taught us that it loses €100,000 of reserves, of which it has to hold a flexible but compulsory amount. What happens if at that particular moment it does not have enough reserves to make the transfer? No worry. The central bank takes care of that. In the Eurosystem, this is the task of the central bank of each country (jurisdiction as the ECB says). Even if Laura's bank did not have enough reserves, the central bank concerned (e.g. Banca d'Italia) would make an intraday loan (daylight credit) to Laura's bank and credit the equivalent amount of reserves to signor Neri's bank.

So signor Neri is sure to receive payment? Yes. Of course, the first bank has to pay back the loan received from Banca d'Italia before nightfall, but in the meantime its reserves have probably been topped up by payments received from other banks.

And if by nightfall the bank is still unable to return the loan? Well, it borrows on the interbank market, and so it can pay back the central bank. The second bank could, for example, have excess reserves and lend some to the first bank—and it is worth its while to do so because while the ECB pays interest on compulsory reserves, it pays nothing on excess reserves (presently the interest rate on excess reserves is even negative, as we will see later). If the second bank lends to the first bank it receives interbank interest which is usually positive.

Normally the central bank ensures that the reserve requirements of all banks are met—if they have 100 billion in deposits, the central bank will meet the reserve requirement of one billion. However, this billion of reserves could be poorly distributed: some banks have excess reserves, others are in deficit. The interbank market serves precisely to exchange reserves from banks in excess to those in deficit, as with communicating vessels (if this metaphor helps you). The interbank market plays a fundamental role in the monetary policy through which the central bank influences interest rates.

But Prof, why do banks need deposits when they can create them? As we said above, banks create bank money in the form of deposits for the public—they do so through credit operations—but they cannot lend to themselves. When we use these deposits to make payments, our bank loses reserves. It is cheaper for the bank to recover reserves by attracting deposits than by borrowing them on the interbank market or at the central bank. However, it is normal for a bank on a particular day to need to resort to the interbank market.

And if the banks do not trust each other, as happened in the crisis of 2007–2008? No problem. The central bank transforms the daylight loan into an overnight loan. These loans are issued by what the Eurosystem calls the "marginal lending facility" (the US Federal Reserve's "discount window") and are always available to banks. However, the rate of interest on marginal lending is higher than that on the Main Refinancing Operations. Moreover, having to resort to emergency lending does not put the bank in a good light, since it means that interbank finance has been refused because other banks do not trust its financial solidity. Indeed, from the first presages of the crisis in mid-2007, when banks began to lack mutual confidence, the ECB progressively opened its coffers, making unlimited liquidity available to banks through the normal refinancing channels, the Main and Longer-term Refinancing Operations (so that only limited use was made of the discount window, see Appendix 1 in Chap. 7).

The central bank never leaves the commercial banks in the lurch! Certainly not, at least for as long as the banks are solvent, i.e. whenever they may be short of liquidity, but they have sufficient capital to withstand losses on credits (creditors who do not pay, the famous non-performing loans). In so doing, the central bank not only prevents banks from collapsing like dominoes, but also prevents short-term interest rates, that measure the price of liquidity on the interbank market, from rocketing as a result of a shortage of liquidity. Explain that to the social forum economists who are always condemning state support to the banks!

These principles of the central bank as lender of last resort were established by Walter Bagehot (1826–1877), the famous first director of *The Economist*.

Prof, a friend of mine who is studying economics says that in a lecture it was explained that the amount of deposits (thus credit) in the economy depends on the reserves created by the central bank. Get your friend, or rather his lecturer, to buy this book. Universities are still teaching that money is exogenous, namely that the central bank decides the quantity of reserves and thus the quantity of deposits that the banking system can create:

$$Reserves \rightarrow Deposits \rightarrow Credit$$

In other words, credit made available to Laura (that implies creation of a deposit) is said to depend on the availability of unused reserves to the bank. Hard to believe? This story that the central bank creates a billion in reserves for the banks, and if the compulsory reserve is 1%, then banks will create 100 billion in credit/deposits is known as the monetary multiplier (or bank deposit multiplier). It even goes so far as to say that the banks lend excess reserves, which is nonsense because reserves only circulate between banks' current accounts at central banks and never ever end up in the current accounts of we poor mortals. The idea that reserves are a prerequisite for the creation of deposits/credit is not only false in theory and in practice, but demonstrates how little the mechanisms of monetary policy continue to be understood among mainstream economists. More about this in Chap. 7.

5.3   Keynes the Endogenous

Prof, when you told us about Keynes, you said that investment determines saving, and now you say that banks do not lend saving but create money. We sense a relation between Keynesian theory and endogenous money, but could you please explain better? This is a good question that allows some interesting considerations. We can effectively say that investment is initially financed by credit creation by banks. When the entrepreneur spends the deposit created for him by the bank, this expenditure generates a more than proportional increase in income via the Keynesian multiplier. As we saw in Chap. 4, at each round, part of the deposit is spent and part is saved. The multiplication of the loaves and fishes stops when the initial deposit has all been converted into saving. So we see ex post (at the end of the game), but only ex post, that the initial deposit (initially an accounting entry) has been transformed into saving. But at the start, the deposit was money created out of thin air.

The foreign merchant and parallel money. Kalecki told of a colleague in the 1930s who was summoned by a colonel in the junta that governed Poland. The colonel wanted to know how the economy worked: "In a very poor town," the colleague recounted, "where the people could hardly get by, one day a rich foreign merchant came to the local inn and paid in advance for a room. He also left a hundred dollar banknote in custody with the inn-keeper, but left unexpectedly at dawn the next day, leaving the banknote behind. The inn-keeper waited a few days and then concluded that the merchant was not going to return. He decided to use the money to fill the pantry of the inn, buying supplies from the local emporium. The owner of the emporium gave the banknote to his wife to mind. She, however, seized the opportunity to order a new coat from the dressmaker, who in turn was able to pay the rent. Her landlord used it to pay the favours of the local Rosamunde, who offered her services at the inn where she rented a room. Thus the banknote returned to the inn-keeper. All the townspeople were happy. Then the rich merchant returned and the inn-keeper, with a sigh of relief, gave him back the hundred dollar bill. The merchant took it and to the inn-keeper's consternation, used it to light a cigar". "It was counterfeit", explained Kalecki's colleague. The colonel, sweating from the effort to understand, was satisfied and announced the moral of the story: "He could tell at once that there was something suspicious about that foreigner!" Unfortunately, people tend to reason like the colonel, concluded Kalecki (sadly not only from the point of view of monetary theory, we can bitterly add). Clearly, the true moral is that the creation of means of payment gives rise to production and income. And these means of payment can be any piece of paper, provided everyone accepts them. An example is the Portuguese fraudster Artur Virgílio Alves dos Reis, who at the end of World War 1 reacted to the deflationary policies of the government by getting counterfeit escudos printed in England. With the money, Reis opened his own development bank in Angola, through which he was able to generate an economic boom in Portugal. When the fraud was discovered and Reis was arrested, there were popular protests. When Reis's game ended, Portugal went back into recession.

The tale can also give credit to the idea, which has crept into Italian political debate of a currency parallel to the euro that the government could issue, distributing it with certain criteria among households and firms. By reviving demand, such a currency would lift the economy. Everyone would accept it because the government would also accept it to pay taxes. It is a masked form of Keynesian deficit spending, financed by the issue of currency, not by the central bank, which is prohibited from doing so by the European treaties, but by the Treasury. As in the inn-keeper story, the money would eventually return to the government as taxes, so the government budget would balance in the end. No problem, but perhaps Berlin and Brussels would not agree: we are not stupid, they would say, this is deficit spending with surreptitious issuance of a national currency, which is not allowed. Moreover, I fear that this simplistic ploy to solve the euro problems will distract us from the need for more radical changes.

With regard to the financing of state spending, the story is similar to that of investment financing with credit created ex nihilo. In year zero, how does the state spend if there is no income to tax or saving to soak up with bonds? Like private entrepreneurs, the state becomes indebted to the banking system by selling it bonds, in exchange for which the banks create a deposit in the state's name out of thin air. Public expenditure generates a subsequent multiplication of income, and so the state begins to receive taxation revenue that it uses to pay its debt with the banks, thus absorbing part of the bonds initially issued. The multiplier process also leads to the generation of saving that people use to buy the remaining bonds from the banks—or, in any case, leave deposited with banks, which may say ex post that the government bonds were purchased with the savings deposited with them. While in the beginning public spending was financed by creation ex novo of bank money, it is therefore possible to say ex post that public spending gives rise to taxation revenues and saving, with the latter financing the part of the expenditure in deficit. Many here will have recognised elements of Modern Money Theory.

But then the government can spend without limits, Prof? In some ways yes. It has the power to do so, but attention! It only makes sense to do so until all domestic resources are fully employed, making up for the incapacity of the market to lead us to full employment. Beyond full employment, indeed, unlimited spending may cause inflation. More importantly, full employment policies may generate an external trade deficit before the objective has been reached, as we will discuss later in this chapter. The exponents of MMT are only partially aware of this, and the rather Messianic way they broadcast their message probably made many believe that there is an easy and miraculous answer to social problems.

The capitalism of instalment purchasing. This box is about "autonomous consumption" and gives another very topical example of how Keynesian logic chimes well with the theory of endogenous money. Autonomous consumption is defined as the expenditures that consumers make even when they have insufficient disposable income. This may be the case for households in difficulty living on subsidies; but we are referring here to the generally superfluous mass consumption, which, alas, characterises our economies, financed by consumer credit. In short, autonomous consumption is that financed not by income (e.g. wages) but by consumer credit. Simplifying a little, there are two types of households: those that spend more than their income, and those who spend less than their income and save. According to traditional marginal theory, one plus one, the first borrow from the second through the banks. Simply put, the profligate behaviour of some households compensates for the thriftiness of other households, so that the effects on aggregate demand are clearly zero. Experience gained in recent years suggests, however, that consumer credit, far from having no effect on the economy, drove aggregate demand in countries like the United States and Spain, especially through facilitation of housing purchases. So it is better to tell the story differently. Before the great financial crisis of 2007–2008, the commercial banks of Spain and the United States, favoured by the expansive monetary policy of their central banks (the ECB and the Fed) and by taxation laws that favoured housing purchases, increased the supply of housing loans, creating deposits for those who applied for them. Expansion of the construction sector, which is a formidable driver of the economy, had a multiplier effect on income. As a result, other households saved more. We are familiar with the mechanism: the initial deposit to the home buyers, after passing through the hands of the builders (workers and entrepreneurs), was partly spent by the latter and partly saved. The spending generated further incomes, partly spent and partly saved. The multiplication of loaves and fishes stopped when the whole deposit had become saving. Read my lips: the deposit has become saving, at the beginning it was just bank money. The "autonomous" spending of certain households generated income and saving for other households. Ex post, and only ex post, we can say that the saving of some households is equal to the dissaving of other households—so in a way, we can say that ex post the former finance the latter (what Keynes called "final finance"). But be careful not to get confused, this is an ex-post accounting result, while in fact, it was an ex ante creation of bank credit that financed autonomous consumption (what Keynes termed "initial finance"). In the same way, we noted that ex post the saving of households also matches private investment and deficit spending of the government (final finance), but initially it is a creation of purchasing power ex nihilo by the banks that finances businesses and states (initial finance).

Excuse me, Prof, but didn't you just say that saving is equal to investment? Now saving has to do with autonomous consumption. Could you please explain? You are right. Effectively, on one hand, it is true that autonomous consumption by certain households, financed by consumer credit created by banks, gives rise to new income and new savings for other households. The net result, however, is that the net saving of households generated by autonomous spending is zero, since the saving of households that spend less than their income exactly compensates the negative saving ("dissaving" for the English) of households that spend more than their income. Similarly, the households' saving that finances public deficits is offset by a dissaving of the state. This does not happen for investment-expenditure, in which case the saving of households generated by this expenditure turns out to be equal to the investment made by firms.

This is true in an economy closed to exchange with other countries. We can extend the reasoning to an open economy. Before the eurozone crisis, the autonomous expenditure of Spanish households, directed above all at home purchases, also generated income and saving for German households, for example, through greater imports of German products by Spain. In this case, the saving of German households matched ex post the dissaving of Spanish households. Again, using Keynes's terminology, we can say that the initial finance to support autonomous spending in Spain was created ex nihilo by banks, and that ex post this generated corresponding saving of German households or final finance. Spain as a whole has a saving deficit and Germany has a saving surplus. We can guess that the deficit of saving in Spain goes with a trade deficit, since the country consumed more than it produced. On the other hand, the German surplus of saving goes with a trade surplus, since Germany consumed less than it produced.

So Prof, German households lent their saving to Spanish households? Ex post yes. As we said, Spanish household's home loans were financed "out of thin air" (initial finance) by Spanish banks or by branches of foreign banks, it doesn't matter. In turn, the construction boom generated imports from Germany and higher German income and saving. As we know, through payments to Germany, Spanish banks were losing reserves. Symmetrically German banks accumulated reserves while at the same time German savers' deposits increased (my accounting friends know that for banks, reserves are an asset and deposits a liability). Finally, German banks lent the excess reserves to Spanish banks via the interbank market. This loan is the concrete manifestation of the fact that at the end of the sequence, or ex post as economists say, German households were lending their savings to Spain (final finance). We shall come back on this in Sect. 5.10.

5.4   Let Us Open Our Minds and Draw a Balance

When I was in kindergarten, some relatives from Paris came to visit us in Rome. I proudly showed them the single Roman underground train line and had them listen to Adriano Celentano (an Italian pop singer) singing on the radio (we did not have a television set). It was a shock to learn that the Paris metro had many lines and had been built years before, and that in France they had never heard of Celentano. My little world was shattered. In those days, parents did not take you on low-cost flights to see the great cities of Europe. It was a small pain. Opening the mind is sometimes painful and can be expensive if you do it with the help of a shrink.

To put the cards on the table for those, often influenced by Modern Money Theory, who think monetary sovereignty is the cure for all ills, let me say that not all national currencies are on the same plane. There are currencies which by virtue of the economic and political strength and financial reliability of the issuing country (that for example does not have a history of financial failures) are commonly accepted in international payments. Principally the American dollar, since the euro has not yet achieved a full status of international currency (which is not surprising, considering its problems). Countries that issue currencies accepted in international payments are in a special position because they "print" the money with which they can make their own payments—it is as if we could print money to go shopping or play poker! Other countries, such as Italy when it had the lira, have to obtain international currency in order to finance imports. Italy could perhaps pay in lira if it guaranteed its convertibility to international currency. This convertibility depends on having abundant currency reserves (international currencies are in fact also called reserve currencies). For the dollar it is different. Until 1971, the United States in theory guaranteed convertibility of the dollar to gold, making the dollar as good as gold. Since 1971, one dollar is as good as a dollar. The guarantee is American economic and military power.

Prof, but now with the euro is it not easier for us than in the days of the lira? We are almost Americans. Indeed, behave like Americans is what Europe ought to do, but unfortunately does not. Much more about this later. For the moment let us return to the case of the Italian lira, the case of a country that has to procure international currency, presumably dollars, in order to buy goods abroad.

A first channel for procuring international liquidity is through exports. If others ask us to pay in dollars, we can do the same. Liquidity is then lost in the first place, paying for imports. The difference between exports and imports is the trade balance.

$$Exports - Imports = Trade\ balance$$

Let us consider this point. If a country has a negative trade balance, it spends more dollars on imports than it acquires for its exports. Unless it is the United States, which prints dollars (as Minister of Finance under De Gaulle, Giscard D'Estaing called this the *exorbitant privilege*), the country has two ways of procuring the dollars it lacks. The first is to take them out of the drawer in which it keeps its official reserves. This is the little treasure that the country has accumulated in the fortunate years when it had a positive trade balance. But, alas, if negative trade balances persist, that treasure will soon be used up. The second way is to borrow dollars. Naturally this is possible, but if deficits persist, i.e. last many years, the country accumulates foreign debt on which it has to pay interest. Moreover, if foreigners see our debt increase, they will begin to worry, even more if the credit has not been spent well (as experience teaches). They may continue to lend us money, but at higher interest rates. If we do not restore our trade balance, we will continue to accumulate debt. The trade balance needs to become a trade surplus in order to pay the interest on previous debt. If this is not done, foreigners will stop giving us credit and will probably want their dollars back at the expiry of the loan, without extensions. Default is inevitable. We declare bankruptcy because we can neither pay the interest nor return the dollars. We take our books to court, which used to be the International Monetary Fund. This was considered extortionist and hated in the global South, but in recent years some European countries have had to do with Wolfgang Schäuble, who has in some ways been worse. Later we shall see how these debt courts function.

5.5   The External Constraint

Together with the concept of social surplus (Chap. 2), the external constraint is the key concept of this book. We draw a fundamental rule from what we have recounted so far, namely that in the long period, a "normal" country cannot afford to have a persistently negative trade balance, because it will end up in the debt trap.

Prof, but then in order to avoid the trap, a country has to be run like a regular family that lives within its own means. Yes, in a certain sense. The point is that even well-to-do households may borrow to buy their children a house or to send them to university. Firms, too, borrow in order to grow. Ideally, countries that want to rise up the scale of economic development need to import products that incorporate technology (e.g. innovative plant and the corresponding know-how). If they do not have primary materials or energy resources, expansion of internal demand will also require more imports, while as per capita income increases, households will want to consume more imported products. What these "catch-up" countries should do is to use foreign borrowing to strengthen their production apparatus and gradually become net exporters. At that point they will sell more abroad than they import and have more dollars coming in than going out, thus enabling them to pay back their foreign debt.

Does it work this way? Almost never, really. History shows that long periods of foreign indebtedness lead a country to default since the country is unable to become a net exporter and to pay its debt back. We shall see more about this when we look at the case of Europe.

Prof, but how come many countries, especially Asian countries, succeeded in developing, driven by export? "Singapore… vado a Singapore, benedette care signore!" went another (rather funny) Italian song. Before I answer: two premises. Economists do not know the mysteries of development. Those who pretend to know them, like many conventional economists, are only bluff-ing. Certainly, many important circumstances are known. Jared Diamond gave us an excellent example of objective facts that help to explain the emergence of the surplus in prehistory. Certainly that method must also be applied in the case of more recent economic take-off. Secondly, I am not an encyclopaedia. On the economic development of Asian countries, I can list some circumstances that may have been favourable. Japan and the first generation of countries that developed in its wake, the so-called Asian tigers (Taiwan, Hong Kong, Singapore and South Korea), shared borders with communist countries. Their governments, therefore, received much American aid, also through military spending. This helped them overcome the external constraint: dollars came directly from Uncle Sam. The United States also opened its markets to these countries. Finally, they equipped themselves with industrial policies guided far-sightedly by the state so as to rely not so much on import substitution strategy, as in Latin America, but rather on developing advanced technology with promising foreign markets, especially the enormous market that the United States offered them. So, rather than solve the problem of the external constraint by decreasing imports, they tackled it by increasing exports. Other factors are evoked, such as Confucianism (the Asian equivalent of the protestant spirit mentioned by Max Weber) and the importance given to education.

5.6   Socialists Are Autarkists

The external constraint not only concerns emerging countries but also industrialised ones. Any industrialised country wanting to relaunch its economy by supporting internal demand through appropriate monetary, fiscal and distributive policy, i.e. sustaining public spending, wages and autonomous consumption, in a context in which the countries with which it trades do not do the same, soon finds itself with a persistent trade deficit and increasing debt. Imports are in fact linked to growth: the more the GDP of a country increases, the more it imports, whereas exports might be nailed to their initial level by the stagnation policies of its trade partners, who are obviously taking advantage of the Keynesian policies of the expansionary country. The latter could devalue its currency. This generally has the effect of promoting exports and decreasing imports. By devaluing, we make our goods cheaper abroad and foreign goods more expensive at home. However, devaluation also has drawbacks (economists always have two hands, as explained in the next box): we actually give more of our products in exchange for fewer foreign goods. Moreover, we cannot do without certain imports, such as petroleum, and now we pay more for them. So devaluation brings relief, but in the long run we cannot rely on it alone.

> While it may seem rigorous, economic reasoning often does not give univocal answers. Sometimes because the results of certain actions are not well understood, other times because a measure has both positive and negative effects, or may favour one interest and penalise another, so the ball is in the politicians' court rather than in that of the economists. If you ask an economist about the effect of a certain economic measure (say a new tax), he will often reply that on one hand it is this and on the other it is that. American President Harry Truman, tired of the ambivalence of his economic advisors, is famous for saying: "Give me a one-handed economist!"

Applied to the European economic situation, this means that even if by some magic we could abolish the euro and re-establish reasonably flexible exchange rates, German mercantilist reliance on exports rather than on internal demand would still be a problem, as it was before the euro and continues to be also for economies outside the euro. The German élite opportunistically exploit other countries' Keynesian policies.

> **Keynesianism in a single country.** Not only socialism but also Keynesianism in a single country is difficult to achieve, and for very similar reasons. This is the central problem of any left-wing government. Autarchy is an option to consider when unemployment is high, although obviously international Keynesianism, i.e. adoption of expansive policies coordinated between countries, would certainly be better as it would avoid damage to international trade.
>
> The classic case of the failure of Keynesianism in a single country is François Mitterrand's France in the early 1980s. A fine essay in *Jacobin*, an excellent magazine of the American left, compares the capitulation of Tsipras in July 2015 and that of Mitterrand in 1981–1982, both not incidentally due to Germany.[2] Though France was not small and wretched like Greece, the parallel is striking. Mitterrand went to power on a very advanced programme of nationalisations, redistribution of income and support for aggregate demand—a Keynesian programme with socialist ambitions. The lack of economic cooperation from its German partner, which pursued rigorous fiscal policies, put an end to the experiment. The German government effectively had a brief Keynesian season in 1978–1979 on the insistence of America: the argument was the famous locomotive theory according to which world aggregate demand had to be drawn by all large economies (at the time the United States, Japan and Germany) and not only by the US economy. In 1979, there was a second oil shock, inflation increased in Germany and the German élite swore that it would never adopt Keynesian policies again (and it kept its word).

---

[2] Birch (2015).

The reason why France capitulated to the German government's refusal to implement concerted expansive policies is well known: any trade deficit country that decides to grow more by supporting internal demand, for example by increasing wages and social spending, soon encounters trade balance problems. Trade balance problems, therefore, emerged punctually in France. Only if all partners adopt similar policies—so-called international Keynesianism—do the economies develop harmonically: all buy more from the others, which means that all also sell more to the others. With one of the many about-turns that distinguished his long political career, the French President converted to *rigeur*, deciding to maintain France's participation in the European Monetary System (the precursor of the Euro system) and since then France has become the dame of honour of Fräulein Deutschland. If the courage to go one's way was lacking in the case of the proud and advanced France, things were certainly much more difficult for poor Greece.

In the years immediately preceding the Mitterrand experience, the left of the English Labour Party faced the same problem and proposed an Alternative Economic Strategy (AES). The left was represented in Harold Wilson's Labour government by its top exponent, Tony Benn, as Minister for Industry in the period 1974–1976. The Labour right posed many obstacles to his radical programme of industrial policy, aimed at actively promoting the manufacturing sector to decrease dependence on imports (and for greater industrial democracy). Faced with balance of payments problems and the possible collapse of the pound, in autumn 1976 the government rejected the protectionist measures proposed by Benn and contemplated by the AES, opting for restrictive fiscal measures and a loan from the International Monetary Fund (IMF).

In fact, the AES consisted of limitations to speculative movements of capital (with which even the IMF now condescends to agree), but also and above all controls on imports. The authors of the AES presumably held that foreign exchange rate flexibility would not be enough to ensure the equilibrium of the balance of payments when faced with expansive domestic policies, and moreover that depreciation of the exchange rate would have negative effects on wages, depressing internal consumption and popular consensus for the left-wing government. Over the years, even Nicholas Kaldor (1908–1986), the most influential and prestigious economist of the Labour left, became more sceptical about the positive effects of devaluing the pound. The idea of controlling imports is simple and is first addressed to economic partners: dear partner, our country intends to use monetary, fiscal and distributive policies to sustain internal demand and employment. We are aware that if you do not do the same, our country will find itself with a balance of payments deficit. Since we do not want to damage you, we promise to continue buying what we already buy from you. However, it would not be fair of you to take advantage of our expansive policy to sell us more products without at the same time buying more from us. So we intend to block imports from your country at their present level (so as not to damage you), so that our citizens, who elected us on the promise of full employment, will use the increased income resulting from our expansive policies to buy our products and not yours. Naturally, this is not the best solution. If you too adopt the same policies of full employment, we will both benefit from increased employment. In that case, no major control of imports will be adopted. And even if we are forced to limit imports *below* current levels to correct the grave deficit in our balance of payments, it would be the same to you if this happened by internal deflation. In either case, we buy less from you, but the latter option is much more painful for us in terms of employment.

Bob Rowthorn (University of Cambridge), an influential heterodox economist and member of the English Communist Party, explained and defended the AES, extolling its national character on the basis of the common-sense argument that justice, work and well-being in a country cannot await the chimera of left-wing governments coming to power in other countries. Underlining that the AES envisaged exit of the United Kingdom from what was then known as the European Common Market, because belonging was an obstacle to public intervention in industry, he concluded with a revealing story about the current situation of the pro-Europe left:

> The crisis which is affecting millions of British people is upon us now. If the left is to exploit the present situation, it must have a programme which offers these people some hope, and it must think in terms of something more practical than a European or world revolution. Those who attack a national strategy for socialism in Britain as doomed to failure, and call for a European or world revolution, may sound very revolutionary. But in fact theirs is a doctrine of despair, and however much their views may inspire a small vanguard of sympathisers, they can only breed demoralisation amongst the mass of workers to whom they offer nothing.[3]

Mitterrand himself had occasion to say: "In economics, there are two solutions. Either you are a Leninist. Or you won't change anything".

National strategies for full employment are possibly more difficult than several decades ago, also due to the disappearance of the socialist countries, possible alternative trade partners. The pursuit of national solutions is also said to run up against the growth of interdependence between countries with so-called global value chains and the interests of national and international capitalism, while it requires broad support from the people. US President Donald Trump's threats of tariff retaliation, particularly against German products, in the absence of trade rebalancing policies have shown, however, that import control is not an economic concept of the past. Moreover, the growing vulnerability to which countries have felt exposed as a result of the health and economic consequences of the COVID-19 outbreak has also highlighted the need to protect many national productions. Greater national independence does not necessarily mean hostile closure within national borders, but greater mutual security.

5.7   Adding Up the Bill

After these long and I hope interesting digressions, let us now complete our description of the balance of payments, which is essential to master.

Simplifying somewhat, we said that a country like Italy in the days of the Italian lira paid for its imports in dollars, procuring them through exports. The difference between imports and exports is the trade balance. We also

---

[3] Rowthorn (1980).

discovered that payment of interest and dividends on debt (including foreign investment) is another sink of dollars. Every country has both foreign debts and credits. On debts it pays interest, on credits it receives interest and dividends. In general, if a country has more debts than credits, it pays more interest than it receives. The balance of revenues paid and received—payments made to foreign lender and investors minus earnings on our loans and foreign investment abroad—is the "net capital income" from abroad.

Prof, why did you say "in general"? I said so because the rates of interest for debtors and creditors are not necessarily the same. For example, the United States receive high interest on what they lend and pay low interest on what they borrow because, for instance, US government bonds are considered a safe investment for foreign capital.

Another net income from abroad is net labour incomes from abroad (actually a minor item). When an Italian engineer, say, resident in Milan, does a consultancy in Switzerland, his pay is income from abroad (incoming); vice versa if a Swiss engineer resident in Lugano does a consultancy in Milan, she too receives income from abroad (outgoing). And here too we can make a balance between the two flows. Bear with me! If we sum the balances of net capital income and net labour income, we have the balance of net incomes from aboard. (Lamentably sometimes this is also called "net factors income from abroad" referring to the marginalist expression "factors of production". "Whoever talks bad, thinks bad," as film director Nanni Moretti once said).

Prof, but where do migrants' remittances sent home go? They are not included in "labour income from abroad", because immigrants are considered residents (the consultant from Lugano was not resident in Italy). Remittances go under another current account entry known as net foreign transfers. Let us linger on this question a moment.

Money sent home by migrants is a major source (for the receiving country) or sink (for the sending country) of international currency. In the case of Italy, a net positive influx of remittances in strong currencies from Italian emigrants was fundamental in loosening the external constraint in two key phases of its growth: the early 1900s and in the period leading up to the economic boom in the late 1950s. Italy had indeed little else but physical labour to sell abroad. The other fundamental source of revenue was tourism. Reasoning as cynical economists, emigrants not only got out of the way and were less of a burden on the meagre peasant income, but sent money home, raising the economic situation of their households and above all allowing the home country to spend that foreign currency to import technological goods. As you can imagine, in the last 30 years, the sign of migrant transfers in the Italian case has reversed: now immigrants send much more money to their countries of origin than our emigrants send back to Italy. Oh well, Italy, along with other southern European countries, has again become a labour exporting country, this time an exporter of young, often intellectual labour. Another source/sink of currency concerns official transfers, that is, transfers of funds between countries, such as aid to developing countries, or funds that European countries transfer to the European Union, which in turn allocates them to support the most depressed regions (Italy being a net giver).

Finally, if we sum the trade balance with the balance of incomes from abroad and the balance of foreign transfers, we obtain the famous current account balance (I say famous so that if you did not know it you will feel guilty and make an effort to understand this important concept). This is a key concept because it tells us whether the country has had a net influx or efflux of dollars. The current account balance sums up the first part of the balance of payments, which as we shall now see, contains two other components.

Prof, would you please give us a summary? Certainly. To start with:

$$Trade\ balance = Exports - Imports$$

$$Trade\ balance + Balance\ of\ net\ income\ from\ abroad * + \\ Balance\ of\ foreign\ transfers ** = Current\ account\ balance$$

* Includes the balance of interest received (capital income) and paid and the balance of labour incomes.
** Includes the balance of remittances and the balance of official transfers.

The balance of the current account is the first component of the balance of payments. If the country has a negative current account balance, i.e. at the end of the year more dollars left the country for imports, interest on foreign debt and remittance outflow, than incoming dollars from exports, interest on foreign credits and remittance inflow, this means that it has contracted new foreign debt (foreigners lent the missing dollars) or has spent dollar reserves (dollars accumulated when the current account was positive). In short, if the country spends more dollars than it collects, either it borrows the difference, or takes them out of the drawer (if not empty). The dollars respectively borrowed and lent abroad are accounted for in the balance of capital movements (also known as financial account), the second component of the balance of payments. The dollars taken out of the drawer are accounted for as a change in official reserves. The variation in official reserves is the third component of the balance of payments.

Panic? Let us see an example.

Let us assume that a country has a negative current account balance of 20 billion dollars, in other words, considering the trade balance, the balance of interest on debt and credit, the balance of remittances and that of official transfers, the country spent 20 billion dollars more than it received. This means that the country has received net foreign loans of $20 billion (net in the sense that the country has given and received loans, but the latter exceed the former). In this case we see that:

Current account balance = Capital movements balance

or in numbers:

$$\$20M = \$20M$$

or

Current account balance – Capital movements balance = Zero

$$\$20M - \$20M = 0$$

If you are still not sure that you understand, for my students I sum it up thus: if you are living away from home and in a month you spent more than your monthly cheque from home, a friend has lent you some money. It is as simple as that.

The above equation is not yet quite complete as a description of the balance of payments, however. There is another possibility: you put some money aside. For a country, official reserves are the money set aside. To understand let us change the example. Assuming that net foreign loans were 15 billion dollars, not 20. Evidently, the country covered the gap by drawing 5 billion in official reserves. Thus we have:

Current account balance – Capital movements balance ≡
Variation in Official reserves

$$\$20M - \$15M = \$5M$$

Prof, but why that strange equal sign, with three lines, in the penultimate expression? It is a sign of "identity", that is, a relationship that is always true. But if this complicates your life and you are not a student of economics, you can ignore it.

If we consider the symmetrical case of a country with a positive current account balance, that net inflow of dollars could be used to grant net foreign credits (yes, German vendor finance) or put under the mattress in the form of official reserves.

When we talk of external constraint, we therefore refer to the current account balance and not to the trade balance, although if the latter is negative it can be an initial cause of deterioration of the current account. Remember: negative trade balances lead to greater debt and greater interest payments which in turn help worsen the current account (hence there are two items that can typically worsen the current account, trade balance and expenditure for interest on debt). Briefly:

Worsening trade balance → worsening current account balance → new foreign debt → greater expenditure for interest → further worsening of current account balance → further foreign debt, etc., in a downward spiral into increasing debt (like a business that is preyed on by loan sharks).

We tied one to zero. Take the above expression:

$$Current\ account\ balance - Capital\ movements\ balance \equiv Variation\ in\ Official\ reserves$$

$$\$20M - \$15M = \$5M$$

and rewrite it (get your daughter to help you):

$$Current\ account\ balance - Capital\ movements\ balance - Variation\ in\ official\ reserves \equiv Zero$$

$$\$20M - \$15M - \$5M = 0$$

On the basis of this, it is said that the balance of payments has a balance always equal to zero.

But Prof, before you said that the balance of payments and the current account balance are the same thing, now you say that the balance of payments balance is always zero. We do not understand. You are perfectly right, they are two contradictory expressions. The first, more substantial, indicates that the root of balance of payments imbalances lies in the current accounts—in the everyday language it is equivalent to say, for example, negative current account balance or negative balance of payments balance. The second expression, more of an accounting nature, suggests that in the end a positive or negative current account balance must be completely offset by the capital movements balance or by a variation in reserves—the current account may have a positive or negative balance, but the balance of payments is always zero in accounting terms.

A great Calabria. One of the commonest misunderstandings regarding the European Monetary Union is that a balance of payments crisis cannot happen within its bounds. Whoever heard of a balance of payments crisis of Calabria in the days of the lira, or of Corsica in the days of the franc, or in Saxony in the days of the Deutsche mark? So why should we talk about a balance of payments crisis in Europe under the euro?

Actually, Calabria does have a balance of payments, although it would perhaps be complicated extracting it from the regional data of ISTAT (the Italian Institute of Statistics). We would probably discover that Calabria has a negative trade balance with the rest of Italy (especially towards the northern regions) and has had it ever since Italian unification. However, we have never heard talk about a debt crisis in Calabria. This is because fiscal transfers between north and south (via Rome) have enabled this region to live beyond its means, as is logical in a united country that seeks to equalise the standards of living of its regions. The external constraint restricts the growth of Calabria, but is loosened by inter-regional transfers.

5.8   Opera Buffa

In Rome, the word for debts is "buffi"—it may come from the French "faire pouf" (scrounge money). The mythical German Swabian housewife, accustomed to using the same word, Schuld, for debt and sin, will at this point raise her eyebrows. Just as some households from year to year spend more than they earn, and from month to month borrow from friends, relatives and banks, accumulating debt, so do countries. Current account deficits are a *flow* that increases the *stock* of debt. More precisely, a country generally has both foreign credits and foreign debts. The difference between them is the Net foreign position:

Foreign credit − Foreign debt = Net foreign position

(technically the Net foreign position is also called Net international investment position)

Obviously, if a country has more credit than debt, its position will be positive, i.e. it will be a net creditor to other countries; vice versa if it has a negative foreign position it will have a net debt towards other countries. The first position is clearly that of countries in persistent current account surplus, like Germany. This country typically pursues a trade surplus, uses the net revenues to lend to countries in deficit (so they can continue to buy German products) and pockets interest on the credit.

Foreign debt should not be confused with public debt. Public debt arises from public deficits, i.e. from the difference between public revenues (taxation) and expenditure. Net foreign debt arises from foreign deficits, i.e. from the difference between what the country spends abroad and what it receives from abroad. Is there a relation between the two debts? There are many combinations of the two, and with a third balance: that between credit and debt of households and firms, the so-called private sector balance.

They Call Me Trinity. In economics, three sectors are considered: private, public and foreign. Each has its current balance between outgoing and incoming flows of payments. If the payment outflow exceeds the payment inflow, each sector accumulates debt towards the other two sectors. If, conversely, the payment inflow exceeds the payment outflow, each sector accumulates credit towards the other two sectors. It is very important to note that the relations we are going to talk about are derived from national accounts, that is, they are ex-post relations. The current balance of the public sector is the difference between public expenditure and taxation revenue; the current balance of the private sector is the difference between the expenditures and incomes of households and firms; finally, the current balance of the foreign sector coincides with the current account balance. Current balances, and consequently the balance between debt and credit, can be combined in various ways. Here are three examples.

- If the public current balance is negative (i.e. the state spends more than its taxation revenue), but that of the private sector is sufficiently positive (households and firms spend less than they earn), national saving is enough to finance the public deficit; so there is no need to draw on foreign saving and thus the current balance of the foreign sector is zero. This is the case of Japan. The Land of the Rising Sun has enormous public debt (well over 200% of GDP) but has negative net foreign debt (the balance between total foreign debts and credits is zero), indicating that current surplus in the private sector covers public deficits. Public debt is all held by Japanese households and banks.
- If the public current balance is in deficit but the private current balance is positive but less than the public deficit (households and firms save, but not enough), national saving is insufficient to finance the public deficit and it is necessary to resort to foreign saving. In this case, the foreign current balance will be negative. In certain years this happened in Italy. Currently, however, Italy is more like Japan, with high public debt but insignificant net foreign debt. This means that in recent years, the saving of Italian households was enough to finance the government deficits.
- A third example concerns pre-crisis Spain (pre-2007), when private sector saving was lower than the sector's investment and booming autonomous expenditure (a result of the construction boom); the public sector was roughly balanced by the good tax flows from the construction boom; the foreign sector financed the deficit of the private sector (banks lending money to Spanish households indebted themselves in turn to foreign banks, as already explained). Overall, the country was living above its means and was indebted abroad, as we shall see better in the next chapter. Nowadays Spain no longer lives above its means, but its accumulated net foreign debt is still formidable (almost 100% of GDP).

A country's foreign debt can, therefore, consist of private foreign debt (e.g. of banks) and public foreign debt (i.e. state bonds held by foreigners). In the years before the crisis, for instance, Spanish foreign debt consisted largely of private debt, debt contracted by the Spanish banking system with foreign banks during the housing boom, as noted above. When the bubble burst, the Spanish government took on part of the bank debt. It did so by issuing bonds, most of which were bought by foreigners, and in 2012 also made use of an official European loan. "Private" foreign debt became "public" foreign debt. Spanish foreign debt has remained substantially the same, except that it changed form when the state took on the private foreign debt. This operation is generally justified because the shoulders of a state are broader than those of a private bank, however, big it is. Nonetheless, the breadth of public shoulders has limits, especially in the case of countries that incur foreign debt in a currency they do not issue, as we shall soon see.

And Germany, Prof? German perfectionism (which in other fields, from music to technology, is a great virtue) leads it to have all balances (private, public and foreign) positive (or at least balanced, like the ill-famed *schwarze null* balance of the public sector). So Germany is a country that lends massively to other countries, a manifestation of its mercantilist policies of living below its means.

5.9   Original, That Sin!

But why, Prof, are certain countries stupid enough to fall into the debt trap? It is a vicious circle. These countries need to finance current account deficits but have a history of financial unreliability (financial defaults). The only chance they have to attract foreign loans is to borrow in foreign currencies (or join a monetary union!). This trap has been called "original sin"; only countries like the United States that have the exorbitant privilege of printing a currency accepted by everyone for international settlements, or countries with solid foreign accounts, like Japan and Germany, and a handful of peripheral Commonwealth countries like Canada, Australia and New Zealand, who have a solid tradition of financial reliability and are rich in natural resources can escape it.

But Prof, some friends of mine who are MMT sympathizers say that if public debt is in the currency of the national central bank it is super-secure. The state can never go bankrupt because if investors, including foreigners, do not wish to renew the debt, the central bank can always print currency and buy the bonds itself. In other words, if the state has the mint it is always solvent. So in their opinion, it is always possible for a state to finance itself abroad, enjoying the trust of foreign investors. The problem is that the central bank can, yes, ensure solvency in national currency of debt issued by the state in the same currency, but cannot guarantee the value in terms of foreign currency, i.e. cover foreign investors against exchange risk, namely against depreciation of the value of the state bonds in terms of foreign currencies.

So? And so, since a country that resorts to foreign debt generally has fragile foreign accounts at risk of currency depreciation, foreign investors will ask very high interest rates to cover the risk of holding assets denominated in a weak currency.

If I understand rightly, peripheral countries therefore issue bonds in foreign currencies to reassure investors of the value of the bonds and pay a lower interest rate? Yes. However, even in this last case, interest rates tend to rise, perhaps not immediately, but when debt grows and the risk of default on payments increases.

In principle, foreign debt is not always a problem. As in the case of public debt, the sustainability of external debt—measured by the debt-to-GDP ratio—depends on the relationship between the average interest rate on debt and the GDP growth rate. With low interest rates and high growth, the country can continue to borrow without increasing that ratio. Unfortunately, experience has shown that countries that have more recourse to foreign debt end up paying interest rates that are higher than the growth rate.

> **Judicious Keynesianism**. *Incidentally Prof, MMT exponents often also say that debt is desired wealth. For example, households willingly lend to the state, accumulating financial wealth. Indeed, the state, by helping households desirous of saving through its deficit spending, ensures that such saving does not depress the economy. The same happens between states. Basically, even thrifty households of rich countries are happy to accumulate financial wealth by buying the bonds of peripheral countries.* This is very true and very Keynesian, and suggests that debt and deficits should not be demonised, quite the contrary. The question is whether the debt is transformed into investment and economic growth, and therefore into the ability to repay it with interest. Often foreign credit ends up encouraging public and private waste or superfluous imports. "Pedro, adelante con juicio", as in Alessandro Manzoni's *Promessi Sposi* the Spanish Grand Chancellor turns to the coachman as they pass through a crowd of Milanese angry with famine.

Let us now consider the case of European countries that issue state bonds in a currency they do not print, indeed a foreign currency (the euro is a foreign currency even for EMU member countries). Issuing bonds in a foreign currency is not necessarily a problem. It is not, for example, for Germany which has limited public debt in relation to GDP and which above all does not have a negative net foreign position (indeed it is a strong creditor). Countries where issuing state bonds in a foreign currency is a problem are those in which a large part of the debt is held by foreign investors following current account deficits. If they see a worsening negative net foreign position due to persistent current account imbalances, foreigners will worry about the future capacity of those countries to redeem their debt in a currency they do not print, and they will demand higher and higher interest rates, until they stop renewing the loans at maturity, which means default for those countries.

Let us take the case of two countries, Spain and Germany, with public debt to GDP ratios that were relatively similar in the first decade of the euro. In Spain, foreigners held a large portion of public bonds, whereas Germany did not have net foreign debt, so public bonds were fundamentally held by German investors (and in any case, if held by foreigners this was compensated by a much higher amount of foreign securities held by German savers). In both cases, the debt was in a foreign currency (euro). In the case of Spain, foreign investors who saw an increase in public and foreign debt began to suspect that the country could choose to convert its debt into a new national currency, which would devalue, so they would lose on bonds in the new currency (a €10 bond in "new pesetas" would initially be worth 10 pesetas but the euro–peseta exchange rate would rapidly go from 1:1 to say 0.7:1, making the bond worth only 7 euros; since you paid €10 to buy it you would lose 30%). In returning to a national currency, Spain would restore its own central bank, and its solvency would be ensured by control of the printing press. Foreign investors, therefore, asked higher interest rates to cover the risk of redenomination: and there we had the rocketing spread of 2011–2012, when panicking foreigners began to call home their capital invested in Spanish and Italian bonds. [Technically the spread is the difference between the yield of a 10-year state bond of any European country (e.g. the Italian BTP) and the same German bond (Bund). The comparison is with the Bund because it has the lowest yield, being considered safe]. In the case of Germany, as recognised by the IMF in 2016: "Irrespective of the state of its public finances, no country that had a current account surplus experienced a crisis".[4]

---

[4] International Monetary Fund (2016).

The profiteer. Incidentally, since 2010 everything that has afflicted eurozone countries in crisis has been benign for the German economy. With the creation of the euro, it is as if Germany enjoyed a Deutsche Mark that is undervalued with respect to the currencies of the other eurozone countries. The weakening of the euro against the dollar following quantitative easing (QE) sustained German exports outside Europe (a boost that Germany did not need), not only the exports of peripheral countries (a boost they needed). Capital flight from state bonds of peripheral countries meant strong demand for German public bonds that have even begun to show negative returns since the start of ECB policies like QE. In recent years, the German government has thus easily succeeded in bringing its public debt to GDP ratio back to within the famous 60% of the Maastricht Treaty and in pursuing a balanced budget policy: this is all very easy with negative interest rates on debt! Sadly, it can be said that the Germany economy systematically gained from the misfortune of others. More about this in the coming chapters.

In Chap. 7, we shall see that the ECB first put a patch on the looming fiscal crisis prompted by the high spreads on Italian and Spanish bonds by implementing the VLTRO operation, also exploiting the existence of Target2, and since 2012 it has adopted more radical measures such as OMT and QE—don't be scared, I use these mysterious abbreviations only to get you used to the European foolish acronymia; I shall explain them later. In fact, the two countries only came out of a fatal crisis of the euro when Draghi announced in his famous speech of 28th July 2012 that he would do whatever it takes to save it. Shortly after, the ECB declared that investors could rest assured that should they wish to get rid of peripheral government bonds it would buy them in unlimited amounts, exactly as the Bank of Japan does for the debt of the Japanese government (or any other central bank for that matter). The spread crisis had for the moment slackened (but not the European crisis).

Sovereign debt crises are therefore generally associated with foreign debt crises—the case of a "pure" sovereign debt crisis is almost a school-book case. Foreign debt crises—also said balance of payments crises—typically occurs in latecomer countries with fragile current accounts that therefore tend to incur foreign debt. To facilitate access to foreign loans, these countries often liberalise capital movements and adopt fixed-exchange regimes—like endorsing the gold standard, setting parity and convertibility of their currency in gold; or adopting a currency board, i.e. pegging parity and convertibility to the dollar; or joining a monetary union like the EMU. In the case of the euro, the debt of peripheral countries although partly unexpected, was initially considered not surprising: the more wealthy, capital-rich core countries lent to the capital-poor periphery, as prescribed by mainstream theory. Historically, the "original sin" (contracting foreign debt in foreign currency) has been the pre-condition for financial crises in developing countries. Nobody expected this to happen in developed Europe. We will deal with this fully in the two final chapters on the European crisis.

So Prof, if we understand rightly, foreign debt incurred in foreign currency is decisive for triggering a financial crisis; it can initially be incurred by private banks or the public sector. In the end, however, public bail outs of banks transform the financial crisis into a sovereign debt crisis that foreigners want to get out of, making it impossible for the state under attack to honour its principal and interest payments. And if we understand rightly, you say that that the country committed the original sin of borrowing in foreign currency, because otherwise it would not have been able to obtain international loans at convenient rates. These countries do so to finance external deficits due to faster growth. The problem is that such growth is often fictitious, the country is not able to expand the exporting sector, foreign deficits worsen (also due to payment of interest on the debt) and the situation collapses when the pushers, the international lenders, stop providing the drug.

You summed it up better than I could!

5.10   Can Countries with Monetary Sovereignty Avoid the External Constraint?

Still on the topic of foreign debt, the greatest point of division between Modern Money Theory and the positions of many other heterodox econo-mists concerns the importance or otherwise of the external constraint. Is it true that a country with its own currency can borrow freely abroad provided it does so in its own currency? I have expressed my position on the question clearly: no, nein, niet, 没有. An ordinary country that needs to borrow abroad generally has low financial reliability and is therefore forced to borrow in for-eign currency. This is not true in all cases, but certainly for most. The MMT authors are prolific and also generally coherent, though rather stubborn, in what they say. I therefore decided to examine two posts by an eminent MMT author, Bill Mitchell.[5]

The economic model that MMT criticises most is that of Kaldor-Thirlwall, named after the great heterodox economist Nicholas Kaldor and after Anthony Thirlwall, another distinguished unconventional economist. These two authors ascribe limits to the possibility for growth and therefore full

---

[5] Mitchell (2016a, b).

employment in a country subject to the external constraint. In practice, a country's level of exports determines how much it can import without incurring foreign debt, and it therefore constrains the GDP and employment levels and growth compatible with the equilibrium of the trade balance. For example, if a country imports 20% of its GDP and its exports are 50 billion, the GDP of that country cannot exceed 250 billion. In fact at this level of GDP, the country has 50 billion in imports, equal to exports. If by supporting internal demand, a progressive government pushes GDP to 300 billion, imports will rise to 60 billion causing a trade deficit and debt. Structural policies, e.g. industrial policies, which can increase exports or decrease dependence on imports, are therefore crucial. But they are not easy policies, especially today when gaining a share of international markets requires advanced technologies, and they take time to be implemented.

So we can ask two questions: (a) How much does exchange rate flexibility increase a country's competitiveness? (b) If this flexibility proves insufficient or even counterproductive, can the country sustain prolonged balance of payments deficits by incurring foreign debt in its own currency? On the first point I partly agree with Mitchell; on the second I disagree with him.

(a) A competitive exchange rate, i.e. slightly depreciated with respect to equilibrium value, can help—indeed it can be the only true prefabricated industrial policy. In other words, considering the uncertainty and in any case long-period effectiveness of industrial policies, exchange rate flexibility is the only chance a country has. But it may not be enough if exports do not react with sufficient vigour to this stimulus (by increasing), and if imports react with insufficient vigour (by decreasing). According to some heterodox economists, moreover, devaluation can depress real wages and demand for national products (presumably if imported consumer products, now more expensive, cannot be replaced with internal production). Bill Mitchell however seems to have faith in the miraculous function of completely flexible exchange rates, which in his opinion should dissolve the problem of the external constraint. As often happens in economics, there is endless literature on the effects of exchange rate flexibility for adjusting foreign accounts, but no univocal conclusions. Personally I am inclined to think that a competitive exchange rate can help, but I do not trust magical recipes.

(b) Regarding the second argument for asserting the irrelevance of the external constraint in countries with their own currency, the MMT exponent argues that many countries, including his native Australia, have had balances of payments constantly in the red without incurring financial crises. WASP Commonwealth countries do seem to enjoy this privilege, associated with that of being able to avoid the original sin of having to incur debt in foreign currencies (paradoxically old mother Britain seems to have partly lost this privilege). The economic, social and institutional stability of these countries has probably favoured this privilege, as has their immense natural wealth. Moreover, being in constant debt with other countries counts for little if the economy develops and the debt/GDP ratio is stable.

Unfortunately, like Latin American countries and extremely poor countries for which Mitchell acknowledges the external constraint—even invoking import control just as English left-wing economists did for their country—also many European countries, including Italy, do not seem to have enjoyed this privilege.

If Italy were allowed to return to the lira, this could certainly loosen the external constraint, as far as exchange rate flexibility can have positive effects on the trade balance, but it would definitely not allow the country to incur foreign debt in lira ad libitum. On the basis of empirical results, my anti-euro colleague Alberto Bagnai (currently a Senator of the Italian Republic) concludes that in the case of Italy, the main advantage of adopting a new national currency "would be to allow some fiscal space. Without a new currency, any expansive fiscal policy would upset external equilibrium."[6] This is a reasonable conclusion. The problem is that Italexit is not a simple affair.

National egg or foreign hen? In the mainstream view, capital movements between the core and peripheral countries of Europe are justified in so far as the former lend their excess saving to the latter, thus allowing them to invest and export more, grow faster, fall into line with the former and pay their debt. This is the usual story of saving determining investment, seen and criticised in Chaps. 3 and 4. Apart from the fact that experience suggests that capital movements do not finance productive investment but rather housing and financial bubbles, something basic is wrong. The sequence is not triggered by saving of core countries, but by endogenous money; saving, like General De Gaulle's *intendance*, suivra! Let us look in more detail at an example typical of the eurozone before the crisis.

As we shall see in Chap. 6, in the period 1999–2007, the context of liberalisation of capital movements, unified currency and low interest rates of the ECB prompted Spanish banks to expand credit in an alluring way for households. We can imagine the following sequence of events. A Spanish bank grants a home

---

[6] Bagnai et al. (2017).

loan to Pedro. As we know it does so with a stroke of the pen. Pedro buys a house, and the builder pays the workers, himself and the suppliers. In this way, as we saw, Pedro's deposit ends up in a thousand hands, and at every round, part is spent and part saved. We also know that the income generated is a multiple of Pedro's initial purchase. By now, we should also be aware that part of this income is generated abroad, for example in Germany, since part of the purchases consists of imports. At the end of the story, the Spanish trade balance (part of the current account) deteriorates and the German trade balance improves in equal measure. The trade surplus corresponds to a German foreign saving, i.e. Germany produced more goods than it consumed, so it saved. Instead, Spain consumed more goods than it produced, so it shows negative foreign saving (we discussed these relations also in boxes in Sects. 5.3 and 5.8, if you remember). In other words, the trade balance—or more precisely the current account balance that is the larger aggregate—equals the foreign saving of the country: positive if there is a surplus (Germany) or negative if there is a deficit (Spain). Positive (negative) current account balances match positive (negative) "foreign saving". But as we see, the saving that Germany lends to Spain was originally credit created out of nothing by the Spanish bank. As argued by an eminent economist of the International Bank of Settlements, Claudio Borio, "by definition a current account deficit on one side must be compensated by a surplus somewhere else. However, countries with a current account surplus do not finance those with a current account deficit. The underlying expenditure for consumption and investment that generates those positions can be financed in a myriad of ways, either domestically or externally".[7]

The "myriad of ways" refers to the fact that finance "out of thin air" granted to Pedro can be created by a Spanish or a German or even French bank (which in turn incurs a debt with the German bank). The ways of international finance are infinite.

But in practice, Prof? If your brain is not overheating, there is also a financial (and practical) equivalent of what we have seen—we already touched it in Sect. 5.3.

When part of the demand generated by Pedro's initial purchase of a new house concerns German products, the Spanish bank system loses reserves to the German banks (remember? Payments between banks happen by reserve transfer). The Spanish banks will be short of reserves and the German banks will have a surplus. Normally, when banks trust each other, as they did until 2007, banks with surplus reserves lend them to banks in deficit. That German saving in favour of Spain manifests in this loan of reserves from German to Spanish banks. This is also coherent with the logic of the balance of payments: the Spanish current account deficit (due to more imports) is balanced by a loan from the country with a current account surplus. As said, Keynes called the initial credit creation "initial finance", and the eventual lending of saving "final finance".

And if the initial loan was issued by French banks? They would play an intermediation role, lending to Spain and incurring debt with Germany. France does not have a record of current account surpluses and could therefore not be the ultimate lender.

---

[7] Borio (2014).

Liquefaction. *Prof, what you say is pretty clear, however there is much talk of "global savings in search of lucrative yields". Can you explain that?* Anyone who expresses himself like that "talks bad and thinks bad". Saving does not have a life independent of the investment (real capital) in which it is incorporated. It is like your soul, if you believe in souls: it is attached to your body and doesn't wander around on its own (at least for as long as you live).

But then Prof, what is it that goes round the world "in search lucrative yields", maybe causing financial bubbles? It can only be liquidity. Let us take QE as an example: it will be the topic of Chap. 7, but you probably already know about it. When the central bank buys bonds, it creates liquidity in exchange for private financial wealth. If, for example, the central bank buys obligations from pension and investment funds, the savings immobilised therein are transferred from the private sector to the central bank. The private sector is left with liquidity, which often goes round the world in search of higher yields. But it is only liquidity, nothing more than liquidity. It was Ben Bernanke, former president of the Fed, who caused misunderstanding with the idea that housing and financial bubbles (including the American bubble that degenerated into the crisis) were caused by "an excess of saving", especially Chinese, that wanders around in the world.

We come back to this in the box on "negative interest rates" in Chap. 7.

Further Reading

On endogenous money I suggest reading two papers available from the Bank of England website: McLeay et al. (2014a, b). The fact that official authorities not only at the Bank of England, but also at the ECB, the Fed, the orthodox Bank for International Settlements in Basel and even at Buba (cited in the Chap. 3), embrace the theory of endogenous money suggests that this theory can also be accepted by conventional economists. Indeed, the greatest marginalist economist ever, Knut Wicksell (1851–1926), supported it. However, it remains a fact that this theory has a role, so to speak, ancillary to the orthodox theory, which is basically the same with exogenous or endogenous money, while it has an essential role in the heterodox economics. The fundamental heterodox text for endogenous money is Moore (1988), in which you also find criticism of the multiplier of bank deposits. Importantly, Moore mentions Garegnani and the controversy on capital theory, arguing that this is essential to criticise the concept of natural interest rate. What a pity that many unorthodox people, although followers of Moore, do not understand this point. From the more practical point of view of banking, the endogenousness of money has been analysed by Richard Werner (2016). The fact that banks cannot lend out reserves, as stated in the monetary multiplier theory, is ironically denounced by the chief economist at Standard and Poor's Paul Sheard (2013). Standard and Poor's gives conventional economists a low rating! Kalecki's story is adapted from Jan Toporowski (2015).

Among the recommended books on the Modern Money Theory I suggest Randall Wray (1998, 2015). A very balanced paper on MMT is by Marc Lavoie (2013). One objection sometimes made to the central proposition in the MMT (that the State spends through the central bank that credits citizens' current accounts) is that with the independence of central banks, the State cannot at present finance its expenditure through issuance of money by the central bank. This is expressly prohibited. The result would be that the State can only spend after collecting taxes or collecting saving by issuing bonds. However, this conflicts with the Keynesian principle that taxes and saving are a consequence of public spending and cannot precede it. In support of the MMT case, Cesaratto (2016) and Cesaratto and Di Bucchianico (2020) put forward a number of arguments that take the objection into account, but further research is needed.

The import substitution strategy is linked to the name of the Argentinian economist Raúl Prebisch (1901–1986), development theorist, arguably among the most outstanding heterodox economists of the twentieth century. On the Alternative Economic Strategy see also Rowthorn (1981). Keynes (1933) expressed himself in favour of national self-sufficiency, contrary to mainstream opinion, identifying the germ of international conflict in the obsession to conquer foreign markets and the germ of financial instability in free capital movements. In the mid-seventies, a heated debate on import control took place in the pages of *Rinascita*—the excellent political–cultural weekly of the Italian Communist Party. In support of import control, Giancarlo De Vivo and Massimo Pivetti, against Luigi Spaventa. In a sarcastic article Fernando Vianello (1977) commented on "not properly respectful [expressions] used by Spaventa to reprimand the younger and less illustrious companions [De Vivo e Pivetti]". They refused to accept that inflation was "a priority for the workers' movement" and that deflation was its "greatest victory" snatched from "those big spenders, the Christian Democrats". Besides, Vianello adds ironically, it seems that as students De Vivo and Pivetti "visited a certain Garegnani, who often hung out in Campo de' Fiori [a beautiful square in the centre of Rome, once a freak meeting place, where Garegnani lived]. An edifying environment! Then they come home and campaign for import control" to "loosen, they say, the balance of payments constraint and increase employment. Not this employment story again! What about the European Common Market? [the prior name of the European Union]…they don't care about the Common Market." It is curious, observes Vianello, that only 3 years earlier Spaventa supported that very thesis

---

[8] Amato and Ranci (1974).

in a major volume (that we mention at the beginning of next chapter).[8] "But fortunately Spaventa has come to his senses. And we gladly forgive him the sins of his youth. We don't know how he came to repent. It would be nice if he told us himself, like Moll Flanders, to show sinners the way to salvation, illustrating the dangers of vice and the consolation of virtue. Without omitting, of course, the story of previous sins, which is always the best part of any edifying narrative". An implacable pen that of Vianello. Of course, the question of import control is complicated, but high unemployment levels may evoke extraordinary measures!

The main objection to MMT is that its exponents seem to ignore the foreign constraint. In 2012, I discussed this with Randall Wray, the main academic exponent of MMT, in a series of exchanges that you can find on my blog (http://politicaeconomiablog.blogspot.com/). MMT is accused of being America-centric, namely to express propositions that are probably only valid for the United States, due to its "exorbitant privilege" of issuing the international currency par excellence (the United States does not have to incur foreign debt to finance balance of payments deficits).

References

Amato, G., & Ranci, P. (Eds.). (1974). *La Congiuntura più lunga: materiali per una analisi della politica economica italiana, 1972-1974*. Bologna: Il mulino.

Bagnai, A., Granville, B., & Mongeau Ospina, C. A. (2017). Withdrawal of Italy from the euro area: Stochastic simulations of a structural macroeconometric model. *Economic Modelling, 64*, 524–538.

Birch, J. (2015). *The many lives of François Mitterrand*. Retrieved February 20, 2020, from https://www.jacobinmag.com/2015/08/francois-mitterrand-socialist-party-common-program-communist-pcf-1981-elections-austerity/

Borio, C. (2014). *The international monetary and financial system: Its Achilles heel and what to do about it*. BIS Working Papers, No. 456.

Cesaratto, S. (2016). The state spends first. *Journal of Post Keynesian Economics, 39*(1), 44–71.

Cesaratto, S., & Di Bucchianico, S. (2020). Endogenous money and the theory of longperiod effective demand. *Bulletin of Political Economy, 14*(1).

International Monetary Fund. (2016, July). *The IMF and the crises in Greece, Ireland, and Portugal: An evaluation by the independent evaluation office*. Washington, DC.

Keynes, J. M. (1933). National self-sufficiency. *The Yale Review, 22*(4), 755–769.

Lavoie, M. (2013). The monetary and fiscal nexus of neo-chartalism: A friendly critical look. *Journal of Economic Issues, 42*(1), 1–31.

McLeay, M., Amar, R., & Ryland, T. (2014a). Money in the modern economy: An introduction. *Bank of England Quarterly Bulletin*, No. 1.

McLeay, M., Amar, R., & Ryland, T. (2014b). Money creation in the modern economy. *Quarterly Bulletin*, No. 1.

Mitchell, B. (2016a, February 10). *Balance of payments constraint*. Retrieved February 20, 2020, from http://bilbo.economicoutlook.net/blog/?p=32931

Mitchell, B. (2016b, February 11). *Ultimately, real resources availability constrains prosperity*. Retrieved February 20, 2020, from http://bilbo.economicoutlook.net/blog/?p=32938

Moore, B. J. (1988). *Horizontalists and verticalists. The macroeconomics of credit money*. Cambridge: Cambridge University Press.

Rowthorn, B. (1980). The alternative economic strategy. *International Socialism, 2*(8), 85–94.

Rowthorn, B. (1981, January). The politics of the alternative economic strategy. *Marxism Today*, 4–10.

Sheard, P. (2013, August). *Repeat after me: Banks cannot and do not 'lend out' reserves*. S&P Economic Research.

Toporowski, J. (2015). *A Kaleckian fable on debt and the monetary transmission mechanism*. LSE Financial Market Group Paper Series, Special Paper, No. 239.

Vianello, F. (1977). Il castigamatti [The Chastiser], *Sinistra '77*. Retrieved February 20, 2020, from http://politicaeconomiablog.blogspot.com/2016/11/il-casti-gamatti.html

Werner, R. A. (2016). A lost century in Economics: Three theories of banking and the conclusive evidence. *International Review of Financial Analysis, 46*, 361–379.

Wray, R. (1998). *Understanding modern money: The key to full employment and price stability*. Aldershot: Edward Elgar.

Wray, R. (2015). *Modern money theory: A primer on macroeconomics for sovereign monetary systems* (2nd rev. ed.). London: Palgrave Macmillan.

6

Dying of Europe?

Abstract This chapter deals with current economic problems, particularly those in Europe, the world's developed region most in difficulty. It starts with Italy, the weakest link in the European Economic and Monetary Union (EMU), examining its path from the economic miracle of the 1950s and 1960s to recent decades of stagnation and even decline.

The European crisis of the past decade resembles foreign debt crises that have involved many emerging countries in the past. Europe is divided into "core" and "peripheral" countries. Peripheral countries borrowed from core countries, which happily granted loans to expand their exports to the periphery. Subsequent austerity measures were designed to bring the resulting imbalances under control. However, coordinated use of monetary and fiscal policy could have avoided much unnecessary suffering.

The chapter finally examines two obstacles to change in Europe. The first concerns German "monetary mercantilism", a problem for the EMU and the global economy. Secondly, history teaches that a monetary union is only viable if supported by political solidarity between the units that compose it, as in the case of the United States. Americans feel part of a nation. In Europe, mistrust and a divisive doctrine, ordoliberalism, prevail.

6.1 From Miracle to Decline

The first economic crisis that I remember (1963–1965) was termed "congiuntura" (conjuncture). *La congiuntura* was also a film directed by Ettore Scola starring Vittorio Gassman (it came out in English with the title *Hard Time for*

© Springer Nature Switzerland AG 2020
S. Cesaratto, *Heterodox Challenges in Economics*,
https://doi.org/10.1007/978-3-030-54448-5_6

Princes). The term "congiuntura" evoked a difficult but temporary transitional situation in the midst of the Italian economic boom that began in the 1950s. Sadly, a few years later a book titled *La congiuntura più lunga*[1] (The longest conjuncture) indicated that the difficulties were not that temporary. *La congiuntura* initially arose from the Italian bourgeoisie's response to the first cycle of workers' struggles (1962–1963) in northwest Italy, where the "economic miracle" had led to full employment. Higher wages and vigorous aggregate demand brought the balance of payments to a deficit, which could not be addressed by currency devaluation due to the system of fixed exchange rates of Bretton Woods. The situation was solved by severe measures by the Bank of Italy (governed by Guido Carli), aimed at deterring investment and quickly generating unemployment. By 1965, the Italian economy was already back on the path of growth, with the foreign balance back in order, but the economic miracle and the previous *Chinese* growth rates were over. This is when the economic troubles of Italy began, due to failure to meet social claims in a country that had grown, albeit with too many imbalances, for example between north and south; pitiful living conditions in city outskirts; technological lags with respect to advanced economies; poor social services and unequal educational opportunities. Moreover, the upturn was not guided by internal consumption or by investment, even though the current account surpluses would have allowed this. The most active component of demand was indeed exports. Rather than modernising their industrial plants, entrepreneurs increased labour exploitation, and this was met with a second season of worker insubordination and social unrest known as the "hot autumn" that begun in 1969 and lasted until the mid-1970s.

Nonetheless, in those decisive years there was no lack of awareness that after the miracle the country had the resources to tackle its imbalances. This is reflected in the "Additional note to the Budget" presented to the Italian Parliament by the Sicilian politician Ugo La Malfa in May 1962.[2] This awareness led to an entente of the Christian Democrats with the Socialist Party, until then an ally of the Communist Party. Political historians will judge whether it was a genuine opening to the left or rather a political move to divide the Italian left. The outcome was that the reforming zeal of the first centre-left coalition boiled down to only two reforms. The first was nationalisation of the electricity system, which brought electric power to vast areas of the country hitherto without (1963!), albeit with excessive compensations for the private power companies. The hope was that the

---

[1] Amato and Ranci (1974).
[2] La Malfa (1962).

compensation would be invested in other industrial sectors, fostering industrial modernisation. Unfortunately, most of it ended up in large financial and industrial operations in the chemical sector, which became a giant with feet of clay, built on obsolescent technologies (basic chemistry) and collapsing miserably within a decade or two. The second reform was a unified middle school, to avoid the streaming of workers' children and those of the bourgeoisie towards vocational schools and high schools, respectively, immediately after primary school. The prospect of two more reforms worried the Italian bourgeoisie: full identifiability of holders of financial securities for tax purposes and a bill for a new land planning law. The bill took the name of Minister Sullo of the Christian Democrat left. It envisaged effective expropriation of buildable land to avoid land price speculation in areas earmarked for urbanisation. Such expropriation had already been put into act in other countries. There was extreme opposition to this bill on the part of landowners (including the Vatican in Rome). "The rattle of sabres", namely the threat of a coup that loomed over Italian democracy for a long time, put an end to reformist ideas. Plans for a coup were drawn up in 1964 by General Giovanni De Lorenzo, commander of the Carabinieri (the Italian national gendarmerie), as later revealed by the magazine "L'Espresso". The centre-left government had to content itself with a largely disorderly model of economic growth. Economic planning, the idea of guiding development, was relegated to the book of dreams. The Christian Democrats and the Socialists vied to occupy the centres of power, particularly in the vast state-owned industrial and banking conglomerates, guided until then by long-sighted *commis de l'état*, which had been driving industrial modernisation. Italian technological independence suffered a mortal blow when the electronic sector of Olivetti and the independent nuclear programme were dismantled, choices that were probably influenced by foreign interests. Annoyed by his policy of energy independence and dialogue with Middle Eastern regimes, foreign oil companies were clearly behind the assassination of Enrico Mattei, founder of ENI (the Italian, State-controlled, multinational oil and gas company), in 1962. Workers' claims were met with increased exploitation of labour, fuelling the *hot autumn* revolt in 1969 that brandished the flag of working and social conditions in addition to wage claims.

Ever since I have known them, Italian economists have been full of regret for what might have been: "If only…" However, it is true that in the 1960s Italy missed the opportunity of a progressive social contract and full modernisation. The country was evidently unable to muster a political class up to the challenge.

Neoclassical communists. A booklet written by Leonardo Paggi and Massimo D'Angelillo in 1986 had a profound influence on me.[3] Inspired by the economic analysis of Sraffa and Garegnani, it shows that Scandinavian reformism sprang from acknowledging the conflicting interests of labour and capital, and solving it by a compromise beneficial to workers. As we saw in Chap. 2, one of the fathers of Scandinavian reformism, Gunnar Myrdal, was inspired by Ricardo's conflict view of income distribution, and (not incidentally) sponsored the award of an important prize to Sraffa in 1961. According to Paggi and D'Angelillo, the Italian Communist Party was obsessed with the existence of "general national interests", above the interest of the working class; this essentially rendered any serious workers' advancement subversive for the system, and hence at risk of triggering a violent reaction by capital. There is a clear marginalist imprint in this tradition, which was quite strong in the party leadership (Giorgio Napolitano, later President of the Republic and fervent Europeanist embodies this tradition). Curiously, this path chosen by the fathers made a greater impression on the progeny: we could reconstitute a central committee of the party with the names of children of the Italian communist leaders who later became mainstream economists! Not one is heterodox; if anything, some are of the most militant orthodoxy. A thought provoking coincidence.

So as to not place all the responsibility on the Italian Communists, Paggi and D'Angelillo accuse the Italian bourgeoisie of failing to elicit a reformist workers' force (in Myrdal's sense) in Italy, preferring to repress popular claims with the cannons of Bava Beccaris in 1898, the batons of Mussolini's fascists, the bombs detonated in the 1970s by fascists protected by part of the secret service ("strategia della tensione"), or by fomenting rifts between communists and socialists or in the trade union movement. A wonderful essay by Albert Hirschman shows how acceptance and democratic management of distributive conflict is the salt of democracy and of economic development in advanced economies.[4]

Mean annual growth rates of GDP were 5.5% in 1952–1956, 6.6% in the boom years 1957–1963, and still 6% in 1964–1970 (with a sudden dip to 3.8% in 1964) (Source: Bank of Italy, historical series).

6.2   Italy, Argentinian Style

The "hot autumn" was marked by worker spontaneity. In the universities and schools, bourgeois culture was criticised and democratic access to education was demanded. All this was part of a broader undercurrent throughout the

---

[3] Paggi and D'Angelillo (1986).
[4] Hirschman (1994).

industrialised world. *Progressive* emancipation of developing countries, which had already begun in the 1950s, saw the Vietnam War as the apex of resistance to American imperialism. The Chinese Cultural Revolution was depicted as an example of grassroots socialist democracy. It was necessary to "bombard the headquarters". Were I an easy pen, I would add that—alas!—many later took this slogan a bit too literally.

Much of this was wrong, but a lot was positive. Besides the dreaming of building a different society together, which lasted a couple of generations, the new winds of democracy encouraged the attempt to socialise medicine, psychiatry, the court system and science to some extent. The book opposing mental asylums by Franco Basaglia[5] was the work that influenced me most in those years, far more than those of Marx or Sraffa. Basaglia, whose work led to the abolition of mental hospitals in Italy, brought home to me the elementary truth that normality does not exist. In this and much else, we may have gone too far. Perhaps. But sometimes it is necessary.

In the first half of the 1970s, the confederated unions regained control of the worker movement and directed its claims towards "reforms": from pensions to health and public transport. The mythical FLM (the united federation of metalworkers) presented increasingly advanced contractual platforms, until 1975 when they demanded union control over industrial investment. In 1975, a friend and union leader of the catholic metalworkers union that was often more radical than the socialist–communist union, told me that they did not know what more to ask for. Of course, it was a swan song. However, much was obtained in those years and the condition of workers improved considerably. Public industry was used systematically to save jobs and technology.

Terrorism ("la strategia della tensione") was the right-wing reaction, and may have been tolerated by the upper echelons of the Christian Democrats, the powerful centre party. The other response was disorderly use of public spending to meet a wide range of demands, without any overall plan of income redistribution or adequate industrial policy for the new challenges facing the country. Taxes were not brought into line with the greater expenditure necessary for bringing social services up to European standards. However, recourse to public debt did not involve uncontrolled risk: the role of the Bank of Italy as purchaser of last resort of government bonds combined with high inflation enabled the Treasury to borrow at negative real interest rates. The words of Guido Carli, then governor of the Bank of Italy, justifying this policy (to do otherwise would be "seditious"), were read on the occasion of the presentation of the Bank of Italy's 1975 *Annual Report* and have gone down in history:

---

[5] Basaglia (1968).

We asked and we ask if the Bank of Italy could have refused or could refuse to finance the public sector deficit by abstaining from exercising its legal faculty to purchase Treasury bonds. Refusal would have made it impossible for the State to pay the wages of employees in the armed services, the courts, civil servants and people's pensions in general. It would appear as an act of monetary policy; in substance it would be seditious, leading to paralysis of public institutions. Continuity of the State must be ensured, even if it makes the economy stagnate, since the consequences of administrative chaos would be worse. We cannot prevent the fall with monetary policy alone but we can endeavour to make it less severe.

The front page of *Der Spiegel* showed a P38 pistol in a plate of spaghetti.

In a long interview before he died, Carli gave this reconstruction of the climate in those years and the reasons for the "accommodating" monetary policies. I was among the 14-year-olds he mentions!

Our analysis of monetary policy, designed to meet the change, cannot be divorced from the historical and political context that gives it meaning. How is it possible to explain the logic and the brief and intense credit squeeze that we created in 1963, without considering the nationalisation of electrical energy and the social tension that manifested violently in the industrial cities, in urban peripheries fresh with cement, gigantic dormitories that harbour people uprooted from their lands? How can we judge the policies of the early seventies, that some erroneously called "lax", unless we consider the demonstrations of 14-year-olds that I saw every morning from the window of my office in *Via Nazionale*? Public opinion was shaken by mysterious tension-strategy episodes. Should we have ignored it? The monetarist shrinks in horror when faced with such considerations. He maintains that the central banker should only have eyes for the graph of the money base and that all he has to do is to keep its growth gradual and constant. Nothing else exists. The Cartesian solipsistic ego of the monetarist lives in a historical and material vacuum, but at the same time requires that the central banker behave heroically. If his graph says that the growth of money should be stopped, he should stop it even if a million people lose their jobs, even if there are the Red Brigades, if sabotage prevails in the factories, if far-left "autonomous workers" are shooting in the streets. No, I have never been a monetarist. [6]

The possibility of defending external competitiveness by devaluing the lira (a possibility that was precluded in 1963–1964) allowed the country to

---

[6] Carli (1996, p. 261).

accommodate the high inflation caused by the conflict over income distribution, Hirschman's tug o' war. In 1973, the first oil shock made that conflict even more dramatic, since a third participant, the sheiks, began the tug o' war in a third direction. Agreement on the "scala mobile" (wage indexation), stipulated in 1975 by Luciano Lama, head of the CGIL (the largest union), and by Gianni Agnelli, head of *Confindustria* (the Italian employers' federation), marked those years: the industrialists preferred 100% alignment of the minimum contractual wage with inflation in order to avoid continual strikes about the cost of living.

The external constraint, that the Italian economy had long forgotten, re-emerged in the seventies. Through most of the sixties, sustained growth was accompanied by a current account surplus, to such an extent that policy makers were criticised for not sufficiently exploiting this opportunity to achieve full employment. Internal demand had not been stimulated enough to seize the possibilities of domestic expansion offered by the foreign surplus. This expansion would also have implied a much larger direct and indirect wage increase, via the pay packet and social services. It would of course have meant regulating distributive conflict to prevent unsustainable wage increases from reversing the sign of the current account (which in fact had happened in 1963). However, the Italian bourgeoisie was unable to regulate distributive conflict in a social-democratic manner. Malicious words—yes, Pivetti and De Vivo as usual—suggested that the export-driven model of growth pursued especially in the second half of the 1960s relied on illegal capital flight[7] (which at the time still occurred in the rustic manner of suitcases full of banknotes). In fact, trade surpluses put the lira under pressure to revalue; in the fixed exchange rate system of the time, this would have forced Italy to expand internal demand to balance the surplus. The flight from the Italian currency, taken abroad and exchanged for other currencies to invest in foreign assets, prevented revaluation of the lira. In other words, Italy was pursuing its own mercantilism.

The first blow to Italian external competitiveness came from the increase in the unit cost of labour (average cost of labour per unit output, a measure of labour cost competitiveness) after the *hot autumn*. It followed sharp increases in nominal wages, well beyond productivity gains. The oil shock was the second blow. Too much conflict, first due to the bourgeoisie's incapacity to accept social reforms (except as patronage), and second due to a lack of entrepreneurial ability to guide Italian industry in a further technological leap (after that of

---

[7] De Vivo and Pivetti (1980).

the boom years), weakened the manufacturing sector. This was later exposed to competition from the first "Asian tigers", which then paved the way for China and other Asian countries. The crisis of large Italian firms began in the 1970s, and was only partly offset by development of the network of small and medium firms grouped in the much studied industrial districts. Occupation of key posts by political appointees, followed by dismantling of public industry, contributed to the decline of high technology in Italy. Public industry had been the foundation of reconstruction and the economic boom.

6.3   The "Historical Compromise"

During the night of 1st January 1976, *Radio Citta' Futura*, a glorious free Roman radio station, announced that a coup was happening and that tanks were already in Piazza Venezia in the heart of Rome. One of us who always thought he knew best, and who also frequented the editorial board of the radical left newspaper *Il Manifesto*, invited us to "stay calm and call the national news agency" (a rather naïve idea because the agency would already have been in the hands of the coupists). Of course, it was a joke. However, this was still the climate in Italy years after the coup of 11th September 1973 in Chile. The Italian Communist Party was deeply disturbed by the events in Chile and believed that the social conflict of those years needed to be channelled into a programme of moderate reforms, the "historical compromise", negotiated with the more progressive part of the Christian Democratic Party. However, this caused a split in the popular movement, a part of which considered this strategy to be a betrayal. The more extreme elements of the radical left had already gone underground, probably when the trade union movement regained control of the workers' movement and sought to steer it in a more reformist direction. Let me be clear: this widespread extremism was the product of a backward society trapped between a regressive ruling class and frustrated social claims.

One may ask whether the response of the Communist Party could have been different. This is difficult to know without further study. Certainly, the dominant wing of the party considered worker struggles basically incompatible with western democracy. This analysis differed from that of Nordic reformism, which saw conflict as the salt of progressive democracy and considered a cooperative outcome, favourable to workers, to be possible (see above the box on Paggi and D'Angelillo). The fact is that the Italian Communist Party was never reformist (in a Scandinavian sense), as the Italian extreme left believed, led by the fatal misunderstanding that reformism means moderatism rather than social advancement and control of the government by workers' parties, albeit in the framework of Western democracy. One top leader of the party, Giorgio Amendola, saw the seeds of fascism in inflation, rather than conflict as the salt of democracy! Hence the control of inflation, and consequently nominal wages, became a priority of the Italian Communist Party and the unions. For my generation, the term "austerity" was associated with the party leader, Enrico Berlinguer. More sober and eco-sustainable lifestyles are to be hoped for, but not as an excuse for deflationary policies.

6.4   1977 Blues

Depressing years followed. The most committed youth ended up identifying with disparate autistic fringes. It was called *desencanto* in Spain and *riflusso* in Italy. For many of us, the end of hopes for a change, which had shone only two years earlier, was dramatic. It was a rude awakening that followed the results of the parliamentary elections of 1976: the Italian Communist Party gained votes and seats, but so did the Christian Democrats (in the 1975 local elections the communists had made great advances, winning all major cities). This was followed by coalition governments composed of communists and Christian Democrats, justified politically as a united front against the alleged threat of red terrorism and the difficult economic situation. The convergence of communists and Christian Democrats could only lead to further divisions, because the most radical public opinion saw the Christian Democrats as protectors of right-wing terrorists and corruption. The conflict of the radical youth movement with the Communist Party in 1977 was dramatic. In retrospect, it was absurd on both sides: desperation on one hand and stubborn defence of a government of national unity that was patently blocked in its social aspirations, on the other. In the government, the communists supported strategic industrial policies, measures doomed to early oblivion.

In spite of the political instability, the economic policy of the 1970s succeeded in safeguarding growth through expansive fiscal and monetary policy (with several stops and go's) and exchange rate flexibility, sacrificing price stability.

GDP rates of growth, which had averaged 6% in the period 1964–1970, fell to 3.9% in 1971–1979 (with a drop of −2% in 1975).

6.5   The New Regime

The Communist Party seemed to come to its senses when faced with Italy's ratification of the European Monetary System (EMS) in 1979, which led to a break with the Christian Democrats. The EMS was a system of fixed exchange rates between European currencies, a sort of grandfather of the euro. Alberto Bagnai amused us ("we laugh so as not to cry" says a song) with his report of Giorgio Napolitano's anti-EMS speech to the Camera di deputati, the lower chamber of Parliament. Bagnai appropriately writes "euro" instead of ECU, the EMS unit of account, a sort of virtual European currency, that preceded the euro. *Mutatis mutandis*, the speech of the communist leader rejecting the European fixed exchange rate system—because it would have favoured the German economy and penalised Italy—turns into a tirade against the euro. This shows Napolitano's about-face once he became President of the Republic (2006–2015) and started to support the European diktats. In 1979 the communists understood that fixed exchange rates regime were designed to stop the conflict over income distribution. In other words, trade unions could no longer expect higher inflation rates and consequent loss of competitiveness, caused by "irresponsible" labour wage claims, to be accommodated by devaluation of the Italian lira, as done during the seventies. Thus intolerable wage claims would be blamed for any future loss of Italian competitiveness. In retrospect, the strategy of joining the EMS consisted in *importing* the wage discipline that the country was unable to give itself through social-democratic regulation of social conflict.

In the following years, inflation decreased, but not enough to avoid loss of competitiveness, so that Italy had to ensure sufficient capital inflows to finance its balance of payments deficits. Attracting foreign capital involved paying high interest rates. This of course affected public accounts through greater expenditure for interest payments. In the meantime, international interest rates increased due to the deflationary policies brought in by Ronald Reagan's economic team in the United States.

> Bearing in mind what we said in Chap. 5, a country with a balance of payments deficit is a country that lives beyond its means. In the Italian situation, this meant that during the 1980s internal saving was not sufficient to finance public deficits, making it necessary to induce foreign capital to invest in Italian government bonds. This required paying high interest rates due to the simultaneous increase in international interest rates and due to the risk of devaluation of the lira, a real risk despite the fixed exchange rate regime. This risk implied the possibility of losses for foreign investors holding bonds denominated in lira, a risk that had to be remunerated with satisfactory yields.

The "new economic policy regime" initiated with the import of external discipline through EMS membership was sealed with the so-called "divorce" between the Bank of Italy and the Treasury in 1981. The former was no longer obliged to be lender of last resort to the Treasury at interest rates set by the latter.

This "divorce" was later defined as a "white coup", in that it was stipulated without parliamentary debate through an exchange of letters between Carlo Azeglio Ciampi (1920–2016), then Governor of the Bank of Italy (later Treasury Minister, Head of Government and President of the Republic), and Beniamino Andreatta (1928–2007), an influential Christian Democrat economist and politician from Bologna who inspired the new regime. Today, Ciampi and Andreatta (as well as Napolitano) are inviolable figures, and yet…

"Divorzio" and the EMS caused a chasm of expenditure for interest payments on debt, contributing to a swelling of public debt. The tax evasion of the years of *Milano da bere*, a prelude to the Berlusconi era, completed the picture. *Milano da bere* was the jingle for a well-known tonic liquor that ended up labelling the rampant yuppie era of socialist Bettino Craxi (1934–2000), when Italy emerged from an epoch of ideological violence and it was fashionable to go to Milan on the *Pendolino* (a high-speed tilting train of Italian design, later irresponsibly sold off to the French). The anti-union stance culminated in defeat of the trade unions at Fiat in autumn 1980, after a massive dismissal of thousands of militant workers. There was no longer any obstacle to mass dismissals and the road was paved for subsequent labour market reforms. The wind had changed and the union movement has never recovered (nor has it tried to reverse the trend, also by supporting research in alternative economic approaches).

The 1980s were defined by the eminent economist Marcello de Cecco as "a fool's paradise".[8] In this wonderland it seemed possible to reconcile the hard discipline of the fixed exchange rate, supported by the Christian Democrats, with an expansive fiscal policy, supported by the socialists. This combination led to significant external debt and the need for foreign loans at high interest rates, which pushed up the cost of public debt. The result was a disaster for both the external and public balances.

Prof, can you please further clarify why the combination of fixed exchange rates and expansive fiscal policies may be impossible? In a fixed exchange rate regime, member countries must have the same inflation rate. If a country, as was the case for Italy, has a higher rate of inflation, its products become more

---

[8] De Cecco (1994, p. 30).

expensive and this generates a trade deficit that cannot be solved by devaluation of the currency. Therefore, participation in the fixed exchange rate system implies restrictive fiscal and wage policies in order to align the inflation rate with that of competitors. The rate of inflation decelerated in Italy, but not enough to match that of the European partners. Inconsistently, in fact, fiscal policy continued to support domestic demand, worsening the trade deficit. As Joseph Stiglitz put it, countries losing external competitiveness may be forced to run fiscal deficits to maintain aggregate demand: "Without fiscal deficit, they will have high unemployment".[9]

To sum up, due to the combination of fixed exchange rates and the higher inflation rate than its competitors, Italy lost external competitiveness in the years of the EMS. In the period 1979–1986, the lira was devalued repeatedly, but never enough to regain competitiveness. Current account deficits were accompanied by growing foreign debt, which roughly matched the share of public debt incurred abroad. The loss of competitiveness affected public and foreign debt in three ways: (a) higher demand for foreign goods and lower growth of exports reduced national income and therefore taxation revenue (already penalised by not pursuing tax evasion), as well as domestic saving, which was insufficient to finance the deficit; thus an increasing proportion of public debt consisted of foreign debt; (b) the need to attract foreign financing of public debt increased interest rates, causing additional public debt; and (c) finally, fiscal policy in support of domestic demand also contributed to the fiscal and external imbalances.

During the "hard EMS" period (1987–1992), the lira never devalued and it was purported that the credibility of a stable lira would decrease interest rates on debt, helping restore the public and foreign balances. This strategy is based on subjective concepts, such as "credibility" that settles exchange rate "expectations", in a sort of autosuggestion game. Judgement day arrived in 1992 when the markets decided that Italian foreign debt was unsustainable and attacked the lira.

All in all, Italy still enjoyed reasonable growth rates in the 1980s; however, the expansive fiscal stance was not compatible with the rigidity of the exchange rate. The public and external balances were the victims of the "new regime": public debt grew in relation to GDP and the external account failed to balance.

Mean annual growth rates of the Italian economy fell from 3.9% in 1971–1979 to 2.3% in 1980–1992 (Source: Bank of Italy, historical series).

---

[9] Stiglitz (2010, p. 235).

6.6 The Trap

A detailed historical study of Italy's ratification of the single currency project has yet to be written. What is surprising is that Italy did not learn anything from its experience with the EMS. Despite various realignments, which were evidently insufficient to restore external competitiveness, Italy was caught with years of current account deficits and considerable foreign debt at the dawn of the speculative attack in September 1992. The attack forced the lira to abandon the EMS. Devaluation was useful to adjust foreign accounts and did not cause inflation due to the timely complete abolition of wage indexation. However, despite Italy's negative experience with the EMS, the country obstinately set out to ratify the single currency project, as if missing this appointment would brand it as a second rate European partner.

Some of us suspected that the fiscal parameters of the Maastricht Treaty signed in 1999—the famous limits of 3% of GDP for public deficits and 60% for the debt-to-GDP ratio—would have deflationary effects; we guessed that the fixed exchange rate with the Deutsche Mark would damage our competitiveness. However, in the collective imagination (possibly with few exceptions), the new European currency seemed to promise some kind of stability for the Italian economy after years of turbulence. We all became pro-Europeans. This was an even greater "fools' paradise", as became evident only 10 years later. I remember that after a post-Keynesian seminar that I held in Cambridge in 1996, I was invited to the High Table in Jesus College by Geoff Harcourt, a well-known heterodox economist. The dean of the College was advisor to the then Chancellor of the Exchequer, Kenneth Clark, a convinced Europeanist who favoured UK entry into the euro. I spent the evening (the food was not very interesting) trying to convince him that it would be a mistake. This shows that we had some doubts, but who of we elders did not celebrate with the children the novelty of the first new coins in circulation? In the following years, the idea increasingly emerged that the grip of Europe had become the biggest limit to the Italian economy. Thus in 2005, at an economic conference that I organised with a colleague, these were my words:

> The process of European unification has dealt a mortal blow to the Italian economy. European deflationary policies and loss of the weapon of devaluation (ugly as it is) have slowed Italian growth, exacerbating the difficulty of meeting increasingly stringent public finance targets. As far as Europe is concerned, the centre-left parties are incredibly consenting. It is not necessary to be an extremist to understand that European economic policy is a demented plan. Monetary policy is unified with the sole objective of fighting inflation (i.e. wage increases). Fiscal policy is off the agenda, except for constraints. Employment and growth objectives are delegated to national market flexibility policies (especially that of the

labour market), without forgetting to preclude any direct public industrial policy intervention because it is contrary to competition. To say that, with the EMU, Italy benefitted from lower interest rates that facilitated public finance targets has little meaning, since low interest rates can also be obtained by an independent monetary policy accompanied by controls over international capital flows, although to talk of such things today sounds like a heresy [...]. The creation of a European fiscal policy through creation of common public debt is a reasonable and elementary measure, upheld by European Commission documents until the end of the seventies (e.g. MacDougall Report) as a prerequisite for creation of the common currency, and underlined by many eminent economists [...]. If we want to create a united Europe, economic policy cannot be different from that of the United States. Is this impossible? Then perhaps we had better retrace our steps, or at least do everything to defend our national interests within Europe, even threatening to leave the EMU (a terrifying idea for other countries). This is not being anti-European. However, the pro-European rhetoric of the Italian left must cease (indeed, it is not so loud since the French referendum).[10]

I regret that I did not say these things 10 years earlier.

In 2009, my article in the first issue of an online journal (*Economia & Politica*) was entitled *The Sick Fräulein of Europe*. It accused the German government of acting irresponsibly in the face of the financial crisis. For several years after that I was treated by friends and colleagues as a madman blind to Italy's many sins and obsessed about Germany.

In the years of the euro (pre-crisis), Italian economic policy was more consistent: constant fiscal austerity (uninterrupted since the early 1990s), and the lower interest rates that followed the single currency, led to a decline in the ratio of public debt to GDP. The victim, however, was economic growth, and discussion about Italian economic decline began at that time.

The mean annual growth rate of the Italian economy fell from 2.3% in 1980–1992 to 1.4% in 1993–1998 and 1.5% in 1999–2007 (Source: Bank of Italy, historical series).

6.7   Short- and Long-term Troubles of an Authoritarian Currency

The crisis of the euro arrived in unexpected ways. This was quite similar to the many crises afflicting emerging countries in the recent and distant past, indicated by Bagnai as manifestations of the "Frenkel cycle" (after the Argentinian

---

[10] Cesaratto (2006, pp. 45–46).

economist Roberto Frenkel) and by Carmen Reinhart as "an unfortunate series of events" (from the novels of Lemony Snicket).[11] Both labels refer to the cycle of economic growth based on foreign debt, followed by a financial or balance of payments crisis, typical of developing countries participating in fixed exchange rate systems. Absolutely nobody had predicted this kind of event in the EMU. In truth, many forecast a deflationary trend in the EMU. This is certainly true in the long term, as many economists had already warned when discussions began at the end of the 1950s on the advisability of European monetary unification. I refer specifically to the debate on Optimal Currency Areas, the results of which were in fact rather negative in this regard. The "Frenkel cycle" overlapped with this underlying trend in the first decades of the euro, initially creating the illusion that the single currency worked well, at least for some countries. Around 2015, after the Frenkel cycle had terminated, the eurozone finally seemed to settle into its disappointing long-term low growth trend.

Only recently have we begun to understand that the plan to hand national sovereignty over to supranational institutions was a quasi-authoritarian project of expropriation of national democratic sovereignty, which was already crushed by the globalisation of capital. This led many of us to reject not only the monetary union, but also Europeanism, viewing it as an appealing ideology hiding a dangerous political agenda. But let's deal with the Frenkel cycle now.

6.8 The Frenkel Cycle at the Tour of Spain

The First Bike Ride

When we introduced endogenous money in the previous chapter, we said that when a bank grants a loan, it creates a deposit at the same time. So when a bank gives you a loan, it requires you to open a new bank account. In accounting terms, the loan is an asset for the bank (money you owe the bank) and the deposit it opens in your name is its liability (money the bank owes to you). However, the bank knows that when you use the account to make payments—for example to pay for the house you bought—the payments will probably go to people who have an account at another bank. We already said in Chap. 5 that when you draft €100 to Paolo at another bank, the central bank transfers €100 of reserves from the reserve account of your bank to the reserve account

---

[11] Frenkel (2014) and Reinhart (2011).

of Paolo's bank. Your bank loses €100 of reserves. Reserves move in all directions between banks, so your bank is likely to receive reserves from other banks. Of course, it can happen that a bank that is very active in giving loans will tend to lose more reserves (when the credit is used to make payments) than it attracts by collecting deposits. Let's take an extreme case of two banks, one specialised in loans and the other in collecting deposits: the former continuously loses reserves and accumulates a deficit of reserves, which the other acquires, accumulating a surplus of reserves. The interbank market (where banks loan to each other) ensures that if the two banks trust each other, the one in deficit borrows reserves from the one in surplus. We explain in the next chapter that the interest rate for overnight loans on the interbank market is normally close to the target interest rate decided by the central bank.

In the context of the monetary union, a large European interbank market developed when the exchange rate was fixed in 1999 and capital movements were liberalised. It was therefore the same for Deutsche Bank (DB) to lend to Santander or to Commerzbank on the interbank market, since the denomination of the loan was the same. Before the euro, a DB loan to Santander ran an exchange rate risk on both sides: if the loan was in pesetas and the peseta lost value, the lender (DB) was penalised; vice versa if the loan was in Deutsche mark (DM) and the peseta lost value, Santander was penalised.

Suppose that DB lends Santander DM100 when the exchange rate is 1:1, i.e. DM100 equals 100 pesetas. If the peseta devalues and the exchange rate becomes 1:1.1, Santander's debt becomes 110 pesetas if the loan is in DM (Santander has to pay back DM100 that now cost it 110 pesetas); or DB's credit becomes about DM90 if the loan is in pesetas (Santander pays back 100 pesetas that are now worth about DM90). One of the two parts is penalised. In a fixed exchange rate systems this "devaluation risk" disappears, which is why international loans are favoured by these regimes.

Another element that favoured credit expansion in European peripheral countries was the convergence of long-term interest rates on their government bonds with those of Germany. Indeed, while the European treaties denied European bail-out (e.g. by the ECB) of any public debt as a matter of principle, the markets and rating agencies assumed that there would in any case be a bail-out—i.e. no country would be allowed to go bankrupt—and therefore European government bonds were all considered equally safe. This meant that interest rates on all eurozone government bonds fell in line with that of the Bund, the 10-year bonds issued by the German government. Since long-term interest rates on government bonds are a benchmark for lending conditions for banks to the private sector, that alignment led to a reduction in the interest rates charged by banks all over the eurozone.

Finally, ECB monetary policy settled on relatively low short-term interest rates, aiming at sustaining aggregate demand in the leading country (Germany), which was growing very slowly, due to its mercantilist policy of compressing domestic demand. Normally a central bank uses short-term interest rates to drive long-term interest rates in the same direction (in Italy, for instance, the variable interest rate on mortgages is tied to a European short-term interest rate called Euribor, plus a spread, that here is the percentage added by the bank to ensure a profit).

The combination of these elements led to particularly favourable conditions for loans. Spain, for instance, was emerging from a situation that could be called financial repression. Credit for the economy had been strictly controlled so that the country would not incur foreign debt. With development of the European interbank market, obtaining reserves became simpler and interest rates were attractive, so it is not surprising that the Spanish banking system enormously expanded its supply of cheap home loans. As was explained to me in Spain in 2011 during a tour of one of the many ghost settlements composed of new, uninhabited houses, prior to the euro it was only possible to get 10-year mortgages at high interest rates. With the introduction of the euro, it became possible to obtain 25- to 30-year mortgages at very attractive interest rates. The ghost settlements were of course the result of the collapse of the housing bubble.

Prof, why didn't anyone notice anything? This is typical of the first phase of the Frenkel cycle: construction booms are strong engines of the economy. The economy seems to be going well, giving further impulse to the construction and purchase of new houses, until the mechanism jams. Similar situations occurred in Ireland and less dramatically in Portugal in the years immediately preceding the creation of the euro, when the escudo had a fixed exchange rate with the ECU. Greece also had its real estate bubble, but here the government contributed greatly to foreign debt by borrowing cheaply, for example in order to finance imports of weapons from conniving countries (France and Germany).

Breakaway and Final Sprint

The construction sector is an important driver of the economy: it is labour-intensive and impacts a formidable number of supply chain activities (e.g. construction materials, equipment and furnishings). The Spanish economy was growing fast and Zapatero announced that Spain was overtaking Italy in per capita income. A paper tiger, or a brick tiger, I told my students, winking

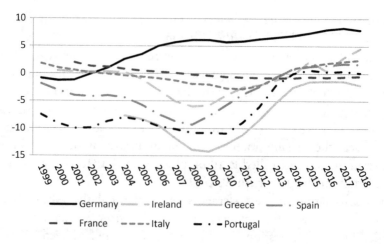

Fig. 6.1 Current account balances of some Eurozone countries as percentage of GDP (3-year average). Source: Eurostat, Macroeconomic Imbalance Procedure Scoreboard, June 2019. Note: The current account balance is the difference between the resources (goods and services, and labour and capital services) that a country sells and buys abroad, respectively. Here it is expressed in relation to GDP, i.e. to the size of each economy. According to European regulations approved in 2011 (Six-pack), the balance should not exceed 6% or −4%.

at the Spanish Erasmus students. Spanish current accounts fell deeply into the red (Fig. 6.1) as foreign debt rocketed (Fig. 6.2).

An Unlucky Fall

The price of houses began to fall and unemployment to grow in mid-2007. This was also driven by the winds of crisis arriving from the United States. Spanish (and Irish) banks were sitting on a mountain of loans to the construction sector and to households, both with repayment problems. Governments in these countries had to intervene to save the banks. The cost of doing so, in addition to the fall in taxation revenue resulting from the collapsing real estate sector and general economy, transformed a banking crisis into a sovereign debt crisis.

In 2010–2011, Greece, Ireland and Portugal were the first countries to have their bonds turned down by foreign investors. In 2011, the confidence crisis regarding sovereign debt infected Spain and Italy as shown by the increasing divergence of government bond spreads (the difference between the yields of 10-year Italian and Spanish government bonds and the yield of the corresponding German government bond).

In October 2010, as the fire was breaking out, a "romantic" event occurred: Nicolas Sarkozy and Angela Merkel promenaded along the beach at Deauville. The French president was of course a puppet, useful for Angela Merkel to

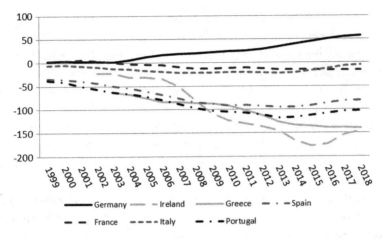

Fig. 6.2 Net foreign position of some Eurozone countries as percentage of GDP (3-year average). Source: Eurostat, Macroeconomic Imbalance Procedure Scoreboard, June 2019. Note: The net foreign position (or net international investment position) of a country measures the balance between the country's assets and liabilities with respect to other countries. Here it is expressed in relation to GDP, i.e. to the size of each economy. According to European regulations approved in 2011 (Six-pack), the balance should not exceed −35% of GDP (why not +35%? Another European asymmetry)

show that the great European decisions were shared by at least one other presumed European power. During the stroll, private sector involvement in any sovereign debt bail-outs was decided. In other words, if any sovereign state should fail, private banks holding its sovereign debt would have to pay from their own pockets. The French and German banks involved in the Greek crack had in any case been bailed-out in May 2010 with the money, among others, of Italian taxpayers. Indeed, the European plan to save Greece was designed to make sure that the credits held by transalpine banks were paid back. Private sector involvement fuelled the sovereign debt crisis, since it increased the risk associated with government bonds of peripheral countries, triggering the spread crisis.

We all became financial experts, checking the trend of the government bond spreads several times a day. When the small peripheral countries (Greece, Ireland and Portugal) began issuing government bonds at patently unsustainable rates, they had to resort to European loans to service the interest payments on their foreign debt.

For the Italian and Spanish governments as well, a too large increase in interest rates would have made it impossible to borrow on the market. Borrowing at excessively high interest rates would mean mortgaging future public finances with a mountain of interest payments, forcing the country to apply ferocious austerity measures and probably go bankrupt. This situation is like that of a business in the hands of usurers, who impose such high interest rates that the entrepreneur, unable to repay the accumulated debt, is forced to sell them the business. If he had been duly supported by the banks with low interest rates, he might have been able to restore the business. *Mutatis mutandis*, the ECB had to wait until Draghi took office to intervene decisively, but in the meantime, Italy and Spain were brought to their knees.

Under such conditions of evident social unsustainability, a country, unlike a shopkeeper, has one chance: to resume printing and redenominate its public debt in a currency of its own. The solvency of the country is thus ensured, as well as the end of the euro.

So Prof, if I understand correctly, the markets know about this possibility, which is why they demand such high interest rates. They are afraid that if you leave the euro, they will be left with bonds in a currency destined to lose value. Exactly. If the central bank does not do its job to help a country and leaves that country at the mercy of the markets, the markets will not only charge high rates, but the rates will continue to rise as expectations that the country will leave the monetary union increase. Draghi called it "redenomination risk": the risk of the country returning to its old currency and redenominating government bonds in the currency issued by its central bank. No country can fail on government bonds denominated in the currency it issues.

Prof, but as states without their own central bank can fail, Europe was right to impose the fiscal constraints decided in Maastricht! That is correct. It is very dangerous to leave fiscal policy to national governments that are not backed by a national central bank. In Italy, for example, the individual regions are required to respect the "internal stability pact", in short, a balanced budget, and I presume something similar happens for the German Länder and the states of the United States of America. In the United States, however, there is also a federal budget that redistributes federal tax revenues from richer to less fortunate states, and has the task of fighting recessions through fiscal policy. The federal government can do this because it is backed by the central bank (the Federal Reserve or Fed). None of this exists in Europe. The European monetary union was designed very badly on the basis of bad mainstream economic theories, while the political feasibility of a union with more comprehensive institutions continues to be very low.

6.9   Super Mario

In the absence of resolute ECB measures to settle the government bond spread crisis, in early November 2011 I wrote in the (left wing) newspaper *L'Unità*: "We can say that *this* Europe is making Italian debt explode, not vice versa.

Italians must be told the truth!" The next day Giuliano Ferrara, editor of another (right wing) newspaper, *Il Foglio*, created a prize for "the most important statement of the year". I won the first (and only) edition of the prize. That evening, Ferrara also spoke about it on the main television channel.

In July 2012, it seemed extremely doubtful that Italy and Spain would remain in the euro. Either the solvency of the two countries would be ensured by their returning to national currencies, or the ECB had to take control, acting like a normal central bank as it should have done from the beginning, i.e. as lender of last resort. National central banks were invented for this purpose. And so that is what Mario Draghi, who in the meantime had taken over from the inept Jean-Claude Trichet, did. In his famous speech of 26th July 2012, Draghi declared that the ECB would do whatever it took to save the euro: "Within our mandate, the ECB is ready to do whatever it takes to preserve the euro. And believe me, it will be enough". The ECB had, at last, produced its big bazooka, so-called Outright Monetary Transactions (OMTs), unlimited purchase of government bonds of countries in trouble.

> These transactions are called "outright" because the ECB purchases bonds without any promise of the seller to repurchase them as happens with the repurchase agreements used in the refinancing operations mentioned in Chap. 5. Quantitative Easing (QE) is also an OMT. More on this in Chap. 7.

Dear investors, Draghi was saying, are you afraid to hold Italian and Spanish bonds for fear that Italy and Spain leave the euro and redenominate their bonds in new currencies? Well, if markets panic, you can always sell your bonds to me. I will buy them in unlimited quantities at their current price. The markets calmed down and the spread crisis slowly settled. Mario Monti, Italian Prime Minister at the time (de facto nominated by the European institutions), boasted that he had saved the country, a pathetic claim that will not detain us here. The spread crisis was downscaled, but not the crisis itself.

Let us examine several points. In the first place, the spread crisis concerned the risk of redenomination. In other words, the difference between Italian and Spanish government bond interest rates and the corresponding German interest rate covered the risk that the former two countries might leave the EMU and redenominate their sovereign debt in new currencies, which would plausibly devalue with respect to the euro (or with respect to what would remain of the euro). So hypothetically, the foreign investor who bought a bond with a face value of €100 would find himself with a bond having face value of 100 new lira or 100 pesetas, worth, say, €70 if the new currency devalued from 1:1 to 0.7 euro to one new lira or new peseta.

In the second place, we learned that interest rates are determined by the central bank, and the market decides them only if allowed to do so by the central bank. Draghi did not have to buy a crumb of Italian or Spanish public debt: it was enough to threaten (or promise) to do so, without limit, in order to reduce the spread.

> Today people still ask what would have happened if Axel Weber, the iron governor of the Bundesbank, had succeeded Trichet as president of the ECB in 2011. Weber resigned as president of Buba (a position that included the right to sit on the Governing Council of the ECB) in April 2011, when he understood that his chances of being nominated had fallen in favour of Draghi. This resignation was followed in September 2011 by that of Jürgen Stark from the ECB Executive Board, which consists of six members, including the president. The Governing Council includes the Executive Board and the presidents of the central banks of Eurozone countries. Every 6 weeks it makes monetary policy decisions. Weber and Stark both sharply disagreed with the timid policy of sustaining government bonds of peripheral countries, the Security Market Programme (SMP), begun in 2010 for small peripheral countries and resumed in 2011 for Italy and Spain. The SMP was practically ineffective: only the promise of unlimited support, the big bazooka, convinced the markets.

What economists call a problem of moral hazard was associated with Outright Monetary Transactions as far as indebted governments were concerned. Moral hazard, which could also be called temptation to sin, refers for example to irresponsible behaviour of an adolescent who feels protected by his parents, or people who do not lock their houses because they have insured their belongings. Thus ECB support to troubled European countries was accompanied by conditions.

In particular, countries supported by the OMT have to sign a Memorandum of Understanding (MoU) with the European Stability Mechanism (ESM), a European "state-saving" fund created in 2012. This fund is endowed with a capital of 80 billion euros, paid in by the member countries of the monetary union, and can finance itself on the market (guaranteed by member states) up to 620 billion euro, with which it can bail out member states. The memorandum typically contains fiscal adjustment measures aimed at putting public accounts, but above all external debt, on a sustainable path. Leaving aside the precedent of the MoU traditionally imposed on developing countries by the International Monetary Fund, examples are the MoUs imposed on Greece in the three "bail-outs" that left that country socially and economically devastated.

In the meantime, between 2010 and 2013, European fiscal regulations became progressively stricter and more complex (and therefore incomprehensible even to the best-informed Europeans), immobilising countries in the grip of austerity. In April 2012, the Italian parliament approved the so-called Fiscal Compact, including the requirement of a balanced budget in the Constitution. The German government, which could have expanded its economy, sustaining the European economy, opted to do the opposite. Fiscal discipline was not a sacrifice for Germany after enormous savings on interest payments for public debt, estimated in 2015 at 100 billion euro by the Leibniz Institute for Economic Research in Halle: the fruits of the German Bund being considered a safe haven by the markets and of the ECB's policy of low interest rates.[12] According to more recent German news sources, the Bundesbank estimated these savings to be 436 billion euro in the period 2008–2019.[13] It is true that the ECB policy may have penalised German savers, as claimed by the German media, painting Mario Draghi as a vampire, but the German government could well have compensated them in other ways. The enormous German savings on interest on public debt are symmetrical to the sacrifices imposed on other European countries. As a matter of fact, the German economy never ceased to gain during the crisis: the weak euro strengthened its exports to extra-European countries and interest rates on its public debt were negative. For the European peripheral countries this added insult to injury. The German government's fiscal rigour is a major cause of weak European growth and a problem for the world economy.

Mean annual growth of the Italian economy fell from a meagre +1.5% in 1998–2007 to −1.4% in 2008–2015 (Source: Bank of Italy, historical series).

A negative sign for many years and the notion of deflation of prices was something that only a few years ago would have been considered a distant memory of nineteenth-century capitalism.

6.10   Monetary Mercantilism

The policies of the German élite are not only a problem for Europe, but also for the world economy. Since the end of World War 2, German governments have applied "monetary mercantilist" economic strategy, as defined by the major German economic historian Carl-Ludwig Holtfrerich. This strategy implies an international monetary regime of fixed exchange rates, like that of Bretton

---

[12] Leibniz-Institut für Wirtschaftsforschung (2015).

[13] https://www.n-tv.de/politik/Bund-sparte-mehr-als-400-Milliarden-Euro-article21521447.html

Woods (until 1971), the EMS (1978–1998) or the EMU (since 1999). As early as 1950, the powerful German Minister for the economy, Ludwig Erhard, observing the upturn in world demand after the Korean War, declared:

> A great opportunity for the future of German exports has arisen out of the current situation. If, namely, through internal discipline we are able to maintain the price level to a greater extent than other countries, our exports strength will increase in the long run and our currency will become stronger and more healthy, both internally and with respect to the dollar.[14]

Likewise, Wilhelm Vocke, President of the Bank Deutscher Länder (as the German central bank was then called), who inspired this policy, made a similar declaration in the same year:

> You will see, with satisfaction, that we have consistently remained below [the competitors' inflation rate]. And this is our chance, that is decisive, for our currency and especially for our exports. Raising exports is vital for us, and this in turn depends on maintaining a relative low price level and wage level ... As I have said, keeping the price level below that in other countries is the focal point of our efforts at the central bank, and it is a success of those efforts. That should be born in mind by those who say to us: your restrictive measures are too tight, are no longer necessary[15].

The recipe of monetary mercantilism is therefore clear: adopt domestic wage moderation and price stability; let the others adopt Keynesian policies and show a higher tolerance for inflation, so that they import more, also due to their loss of price competitiveness; buy a beer (German of course) and sit on the banks of the Rhine, watching the passage of the barges transporting national exports, without the partners being able to build dams by devaluing their exchange rate.

Returning to the present day, another German economist, Heiner Flassbeck, denounced violation of "implicit European agreements" by Germany: where the ECB set a common objective inflation of 2%, German governments pursued below-threshold inflation through a policy of wage dumping, maintaining the growth of German wages below that of productivity.

If you return to Sect. 2.3, you will recall that mercantilism enables capitalists to have their cake and eat it too: relatively low internal wages and

---

[14] Holtfrerich (2008, p. 45).

[15] Ibidem.

therefore high profits, offsetting the consequent compression of the internal market by exporting. Of course, there is much more than this to the German model: trade union cooperation; a central bank that has traditionally been a wage... (oops!) *inflation* watchdog; a very strong national system of research and training; a government that makes commercial penetration policy the axis of its foreign policy (in 2010, a German president resigned after candidly admitting that Germany had intervened in Afghanistan for economic reasons; the next president resigned in 2012 due to corruption); a national ideology that unites the country around the sacred cow of exports. The German state is therefore authentically mercantilist, showing an intimate bond between the public and private sectors, with the former at the service of the latter. A sense of community and pride in work well done, and other admirable qualities of the German people, such as thoroughness, do the rest (let us avoid facile comments; rather, there is a lesson here for Italians). I doff my hat to them.

Unhappy Italy. *Prof, all that is clear, but I have a doubt. Italy did not have a construction boom and its external imbalances were smaller than those of the rest of the Club Med. Italy has been closer to France from this point of view. So those who say that its problems are due to public debt are they right? And Italy's economic decline, which seems to date much further back, how did it arise? Why has its productivity been stagnant for so long? Is it really all due to the euro?*

There is no complete answer to these questions: a full history of the events of the Italian economy in the last 30 or 40 years has yet to be written. As Tolstoy reflected in his foreword to *Anna Karenina*, "All happy families are alike; whereas every unhappy family is unhappy in its own way". One thing I have learned from life is that an outcome has many causes. A mistake, a wrong decision or move, can certainly be harmful, but only in combination with one or more other concomitant circumstances can it lead to a truly alarming outcome. Regarding Italy, every analyst has a preferred list of causes, probably with the country's national defects, including cunning—cheating others, preferably the state—at the top. But this line of reasoning leads us too far afield. It is preferable to stay with more concrete hypotheses, even if at this stage they are little more than working hypotheses. A hypothesis alluded to in Sect. 6.5 is that Italy tried to put down social conflict, which manifested as relatively higher inflation than its competitors and badly managed public finance, through a self-imposed external constraint (the "new regime"). This happened first with the EMS, when adopting "monetarist policies" no longer seemed a "seditious act", and later with the euro. A more long-sighted answer to social conflict would have been possible. There is no sense in debating whose fault it was, whether an excessively maximalist left or a selfish bourgeoisie, but we should at least apply the lessons learnt to the present.

In the 1970s and 1980s, social conflict was tackled by trying to keep everyone happy, among other things by increasing public expenditure but not taxation. In the 1980s, the EMS and separation of the Treasury from the Bank of Italy detonated public debt. The loss of external competitiveness due to the fixed exchange rate regime meant less growth from exports, while for a given aggregate demand, a larger part of demand began to turn to foreign products. The same aggregate demand generated less domestic product and therefore, for a given level of public expenditure, less taxation revenue. Public accounts worsened further with the high interest rates aimed at attracting foreign capital, as we already said. This brings to light an important and relatively unexplored causal link that leads *from* the desire for external discipline *to* the growth of public debt (and not the other way round as in the mainstream narrative).

Alas, in mainstream fiction the causal link is inverted: instead of attributing increasing public and foreign debt to a self-imposed external constraint (in the form of fixed exchange rates), all responsibility was laid on public accounts. Thus the country entered the 1990s obsessed with stopping the deterioration of public finances. Fiscal adjustment measures and loss of external competitiveness harmed aggregate demand growth and the trend of productivity. While traditional economists see productivity as depending exclusively on supply factors—market flexibility and, more plausibly, state efficiency, research and training policies—heterodox economists see productivity as also having to do with aggregate demand. Do you remember the Smith-Keynes theorem in Sect. 2.5? Innovation depends on the size of the market. Only with a growing market can firms fully exploit industrial plants and build new ones. Of course industrial, technological and training policies are very important. It is in order to implement these policies that we need a proactive state, a state that is not concerned solely with cutting expenditure, privatising public enterprise and humiliating public hospitals, schools and universities, as in Italy. The effects of the self-imposed external constraint also ended up affecting the supply side as well as the demand side, through fiscal cuts to social and education spending. Every outcome has many interacting causes. Indeed, competitiveness was also affected by the appearance of new Asian competitors. Moreover, productivity was badly affected by the availability of cheap labour after labour market reform; this combined with the massive influx of migrant labour made the pursuit of competitiveness through innovative investment somewhat superfluous.

Finally, there was the advent of the euro. I don't know why in Germany they say that Italy plays dirty (violent) soccer, perhaps to excuse themselves for being repeatedly beaten (at least until the European tournament in June 2016). Certainly with the euro, the German government played dirty through stagnating real wages in the presence of growth in labour productivity. The French played clean, letting real wages and productivity increase at the same rhythm. The Italians saw stagnation of real wages as well as productivity. Here, however, lies the trick: Italian wages increased in nominal terms (albeit not in real terms), and with fixed exchange rates (the euro) this was enough to lose competitiveness. Austerity and the collapse of internal demand did the rest, devastating domestic production capacity and ruining public finances. How can firms survive, even with a good share of exports on output, if their main market, the home one, contracts? Again the country pays for the self-imposed external constraint, in the name of internal discipline that it was unable to achieve through a political compromise centring on social justice. We are very far from the reformist inspiration of the early sixties, La Malfa's "Additional note"!

Mean annual growth rates of the Italian economy fell from 1.4% in 1993–1998 and 1.5% in 1998–2007 to −1.4% in 2008–2013 (−0.3% in 2008–2019) (Source: Bank of Italy, historical series; Ameco).

6.11 Can Europe Change?

What is the back-up question? No, Europe cannot change. A frequent observation is that the error of Europe was to create monetary union before political union, and therefore a stateless currency for currency-less countries. A stateless currency means that when monetary unification causes imbalances, there is no federal body designated to restore balance through fiscal transfers. Moreover, in the absence of a federal fiscal policy, countercyclical measures implemented by monetary policy are less effective.

> Although monetary policy can stimulate private spending through low interest rates, in a depressed situation households and businesses are reluctant to spend ("you can lead a horse to water but you can't make him drink"). The only entity that can do this is therefore the State, by increasing deficit spending. The central bank supports fiscal policy by using low interest rates to prevent this expenditure from bringing about an increase in the ratio of public debt to GDP.

The existence of currency-less states implies that the weaker ones are likely to catch cold with the first draught once they have lost the sovereignty to adjust their exchange rate and the national central bank's guarantee of the nominal value of public debt. All this leads us to conclude that monetary unification implies political integration and a federal budget with redistributive and countercyclical tasks. But is it possible in Europe? The answer is no. A European federal state with a large redistributive budget would not enjoy public consensus in richer countries, although it would be well accepted by poorer countries. The stronger countries would even be willing to concede a few crumbs, but only in exchange for a definitive end to the fiscal sovereignty of peripheral countries (fiscal sovereignty is already lame since they gave up monetary sovereignty). The conservative economist Friedrich von Hayek[16] pointed this out as early as 1939: a federation of

---

[16] Von Hayek (1939).

unequal states can only exist with a minimum federal state, a state that sets rules and does little more: an "ordoliberal" state (see the next box). The monetary union we have, or the one we will have if the proposed Eurozone reforms are implemented, for worse not for better, is therefore the only one possible. The reform proposals in circulation are mostly aimed at strengthening the powers of control of the markets over the states, and not the other way round, as required by an authentic social Europe. In actual fact, the EMU has emptied national states of their monetary and fiscal powers, depriving the working classes of their natural battleground: their nation-state. Thus democracy is reduced to civil rights campaigns (the market does the rest). The incompatibility of the euro and supranational Europe, on one hand, and democracy on the other, is complete.

In this light, the euro reveals its true nature, sweeping pro-European rhetoric aside. It is an instrument that disciplines the working classes, especially in the undisciplined south, France included. It is untrue that the euro is a failure; it is a success. Tommaso Padoa-Schioppa (1940–2010), one of the influential technocrats who designed the monetary union, in 2003 warned that the euro would teach the hardship of living that recent generations of Europeans had forgotten under welfare state and full employment policies.[17] Padoa-Schioppa was Treasury Minister in the second centre-left Romano Prodi government (2006–2008). I heard him defined as a "saintly man" by an exponent of the Italian "radical" left. Pro-Europeanism arises from shame felt by the Italian left for its communist past, from which it emerged with surprising superficiality.

Unfortunately, it is difficult for the left to re-learn the idea that the national space is where the struggle for the redistribution of wealth, which is the core of democracy, takes place. Historically, the struggle for socialism and the struggle for national independence coincided. Of course, the untiring internationalist will say that faced with the globalisation of capital, labour must also become international and create supranational fronts. History, however, has no examples in this direction. "Between each individual and all humanity ... stands ... THE NATION" (capital letters in the original), wrote the great German economist Friedrich List (1789–1846).[18]

But Prof, what about the social classes? You are a Marxist... A non-orthodox Marxist, however! "Social classes and the nation, in that order, stand between the individual and humanity." Is that better?

---

[17] Padoa-Schioppa (2003).
[18] List (1909 [1841], p. 141).

But the greater part of capital is transnational... Yes, but labour isn't, one more reason for the national working classes to defend the sovereign state, the only barrier against the internationalist super-power of capital.

Nonetheless there is resistance, even by the Italian ruling classes, to a definitive end to sovereignty in exchange for crumbs. Thus Europe is in a dramatic impasse. A seriously federal Europe is historically unsustainable; the Europe of the crumbs is understandably resisted by peripheral countries; German mercantilism is an obstacle to a solution based on Keynesian cooperation. There are two possible outcomes:

(a) a (bitter) peal of laughter will bury us, in the sense of a new dramatic financial crisis that sweeps away the euro; it would be well to prepare for this event;
(b) the agony will continue and will involve sequelae of ordoliberal policies and impositions. Historical experience suggests that the resilience of social bodies to survive misery is enormous (refugee camps where millions of people live; the sad chapter of European policies in Greece; some districts of Naples). The price is of course the end of any social standard that can be defined as civil.

The European episode is one piece of the radical change in the balance of power between capital and labour since the end of the communist challenge and since globalisation. The global labour market has been flooded with billions of disinherited people, threatening the well-being that working classes had gained in countries where industrialisation had a longer history. The euro completes globalisation: not only does capital escape conflict by delocalising, but the state too becomes blurry—all that remains of it is the mocking smile of the Cheshire Cat, up there in Brussels or Berlin.

The discreet charm of the ordo-mercantilist state. Ordoliberalism is the German version of classical Anglo-Saxon liberalism, seen by ordoliberals as defective. There is nothing Keynesian in this, indeed the ordoliberals are fiercely anti-Keynesian. They simply hold that without strong public guidance, free-market forces can be overcome by powers such as oligopolies and unions. With ordoliberalism, the preservation of laissez-faire becomes a constitutional principle, as shown, for instance, by the imposition of the Fiscal Compact and an independent ECB with its primary mandate of stabilizing prices inscribed in the "European Constitution" (or Lisbon Treaty). The version of ordoliberalism for gullible leftists is the "social market economy". In practice, ordoliberalism is coherent with the German tradition that sees incarnation of the founding principles of the nation in the state. As we have noted, in practice the role of the German state goes well beyond mere defence of market rules. It goes in the direction of mercantilism, organisation of the technical and political resources of the nation to serve the real economy and exports. According to Friedrich List (1789–1846), Smith criticised the mercantilists, although British economic hegemony had been achieved through mercantilist policies. At the time the danger for Britain was that other nations, too, might give public intervention a leading role in economic development, threatening that hegemony. And so Adam Smith began to preach the virtues of free trade and criticise protectionism. List of course supported the opposite recipe for Germany, a recipe that can be recognised in the German mercantilist state. List, rather than the free-trade theorists, was also studied in Japan and the Asian tiger countries. As did Britain yesterday, today Germany praises the virtues of ordoliberalism to its partners, but would not dream of exporting the discreet role of the German state in support of industrial development.

6.12   Franciscan Italy

The narrative of Italy we hear from countries on the other side of the Alps is that of a fiscally dissolute country. This image is unfortunately shared by part of the Italian élite, especially in the centre-left area, who identify public debt as enemy number one. In a recent reconstruction, an excellent Dutch economist, Servaas Storm, tells us a different story. The titles of his articles are eloquent: "How to ruin a country in three decades" and "Lost in deflation".[19] The thesis is that Italy has observed the European rules on public accounts more than any other country, and this is why it has obtained the double failure of not improving the ratio of public debt to GDP, despite killing internal demand, employment and growth. Moreover, the progressive flexibilization of the labour market had a negative effect on real wages. This, together with an over-appreciation of the real exchange rate due to the euro, further depressed the demand for national products. According to Storm, Italy "may rightly be called the star pupil in the Eurozone class, as it radically transformed its political economy—abandoning its mixed economy, scaling down its health-care and social security systems, liberalizing its financial and industrial systems, and limiting democratic and parliamentary control over its macroeconomic policies".[20] The figures of the Italian fiscal effort are impressive, exemplified by the size of its primary surpluses—the difference between state revenue and expenditure excluding interest payments. These surpluses indicate the sacrifice that Italians have suffered on the altar of "sound public finance", since they measure how much they paid in taxes in relation to

---

[19] Storm (2019a, b).

[20] Storm (2019b, p. 202).

how much they received in exchange in public services. In the period 1995–2008, Italian mean primary surpluses were 3% of GDP against 0.7% of Germany and primary deficits of 0.1% in France. The Italian surpluses depressed growth and rendered the fiscal effort—only partly facilitated by falling interest rates, that in any case remained higher than the Eurozone average—largely ineffective. Nonetheless, this effort led to a decrease in the public debt-to-GDP ratio from 117% in 1994 to below 100% in 2007. Despite the crisis, the mean primary surplus in the period 2008–2018 exceeded 1.3%. It was 2% under the Monti government: Monti candidly admitted that it was "effectively destroying internal demand". Together with the ECB's deplorable delay in acting to sustain sovereign debts—which happened verbally only after Draghi's famous speech in summer 2012, and concretely in March 2015 with the start of QE—these policies took Italian public debt above 130% of GDP. In the meantime, France enacted primary deficit policies and Germany at least initially did the same. For an idea of the scale, in the decade after 2008, France expanded demand by 461 billion euro (2010 prices), the Italian governments contracted it by 227 billion. All these policies since 1995 are responsible for the collapse of investment and productivity: these *policies*, not the "absence of reforms".

Storm's voice is not completely alone. In 2018, David Folkerts-Landau, head economist at Deutsche Bank, wrote that "contrary to widespread belief, Italy has been a frugal country".[21] While this cannot be denied, it is certainly true that it was not always so. But history is not so simple. As we have seen, in 1979 Italy joined the European Monetary System, a system with fixed exchange rates, with the idea of ending the inflation-devaluation model, which substantially accommodated the high level of trade union conflict. A paper I wrote with Gennaro Zezza confirms that the resulting loss of external competitiveness had a negative impact on public debt: directly through undermining demand for Italian products, and hence wages and fiscal revenues; indirectly through the high interest rates that we began to pay to attract the capital necessary to finance external deficits. To prevent debt from growing, the governments should have reduced expenditure, but that would have further depressed growth. As Stiglitz observed (see Sect. 6.5), the search for external discipline can lead to foreign deficits and, as a rebound effect, to fiscal deficits to defend employment. With the euro, Italy has been more consistent, sacrificing growth on the altar of external discipline. The lesson is that self-imposed "external constraints" lead to disaster and that Italy should learn to

---

[21] Folkerts-Landau (2018).

regulate itself without "foreign popes". But today, like yesterday, it does not know how to do this. What can concretely be done?

In 2011, hundreds of Italian and international economists proposed a pact between Italy and Europe aimed at drastically reducing interest rates on Italian public debt in exchange for stabilisation of the debt-to-GDP ratio.[22] With low interest rates, let us say at the French level, the expenditure saved would allow primary *deficit* policies and a little growth, while allowing a stabilization of that ratio at the present level (for which there is no magic number: 60%, 130% or 230% for Japan). We already touched on this in Chap. 4. The institutional forms of the pact would need to be defined, but we do not see any other first step to get Italy out of this interminable suffering. Folkerts-Landau took up a moderate version of this proposal. Unfortunately, the attitude of the European élites is dominated by vindictive northern moralism that sees a sinner to punish in every corner.

The future of the Italian economy was already bleak when the coronavirus pandemic hit. Will European economic governance change after the coronavirus crisis? In the light of the experience recounted in this chapter, it seems to me that there is not much to add to the bitter gloomy considerations of Sect. 6.11. Europe is instrumental in sustaining backward liberalism and the subordination of some states in relation to others. It is incapable of being a collective instrument of solidarity and growth. This is very sad, but a European nation simply does not exist. The pandemic could have been an opportunity to forge a common experience, but it does not seem this will be the case. I will be happy to be wrong.

Further Reading

On the Italian economic development after World War 2, Graziani (2000) remains unsurpassed. I have taken up many of the themes of this chapter in Cesaratto and Zezza (2019a, b). These papers discuss the break at the end of the 1970s between the accommodative monetary policies adopted in that decade and the new monetary regime embraced in the early 1980s that culminated with the participation of Italy in the single currency. It is also shown that price stability was a victim of the policies of the seventies; public debt fell victim to the policies that followed Italian participation in the EMS and the divorce between the Bank of Italy and the Treasury; growth in income and productivity were the victims of the euro. Nikiforos et al. (2015) showed that

---

[22] http://documentoeconomisti.blogspot.com/2011/11/to-parliament-of-italian-republic-to.html. Accessed 6 May 2020.

external imbalances caused the rise in the ratio of public debt to GDP in the case of Greece. In the words of Alberto Bagnai (2012, p. 193): "The attempt to discipline the workers with the bogeyman of the foreign constraint... was successful, but reaped a victim: the sustainability of [public] debt".

Hirschman, whom we also mentioned for his metaphor of inflation as a tug-of-war, is an example of what economists should be: cultured, thoughtful and inspiring. After graduating from the University of Trieste, he fought with the Republicans in Spain. Among his most famous books, see Hirschman (1977), where he critically reconstructs the argument in support of the pursuit of individual interest through the marketplace, as put forward by Smith and others. According to that argument, the market can direct otherwise destructive human drives into beneficial channels (see Sect. 2.6). Hirschman (1991) criticises the conservative argument of the futility of social reforms as risky and counterproductive because human selfishness cannot change. In a final part of the book, however, he also criticises the naivety of many utopian views. He (1970) compares the three choices individuals may make about a group, organization or nation that makes them feel uncomfortable: exit, voice and loyalty. *Voice* is aimed at trying to change the situation, while *exit* (e.g. emigration) is implemented once it has been established that no satisfactory change is possible. *Loyalty* implies acceptance of uneasiness. Feel free to apply this scheme to the European situation.

Premonitory analyses on the unsustainability of the EMU without preliminary political union can be found in the work of two outstanding heterodox Cambridge (UK) economists: Nicholas Kaldor (1971) and Wynne Godley (1992). While the literature on "optimal currency areas" had long predicted the deflationary trend of a monetary union in Europe, no one had expected a debt crisis, as in developing countries. One exception was Paul De Grauwe (1998), who in an article in the *Financial Times* predicted a construction bubble in Spain financed by foreign capital.

The Frenkel cycle has also become the consensus view among orthodox economists, see: Baldwin and Giavazzi (2015). However, it has been contested by heterodox colleagues such as Marc Lavoie, Eladio Febrero and others who have taken my work as a representative of the heterodox version of the consensus view (as Oscar Wilde said: "There is only one thing in the world worse than being talked about, and that is not being talked about"). In this regard, see: Cesaratto, S. (2018a), where you can find many references to the debate. Carlos Diaz-Alejandro's paper "Good-bye financial repression, hello financial crash" is the classic paper on financial crises due to external debt (Diaz-Alejandro 1985). When a country allows foreign capital inflows, domestic credit becomes abundant (farewell financial repression) and the outcome is financial instability (welcome financial crashes). Under the Bretton Woods regime, in which capital movements were controlled, no financial crisis ever occurred. A fine book on the Greek events and the role played by the IMF is by the American journalist Paul Blustein (2016).

In the orthodox economic version, the Frenkel cycle begins with saving from core countries flowing to peripheral countries. In the heterodox version, the cycle is generated by endogenous production of money by peripheral banks (see above Chap. 5). This is well described in Febrero and Uxó (2013).

On the German model and monetary mercantilism see also Holtfrerich (1999), Cesaratto and Stirati (2011), Höpner (2019), and in a comparative perspective Baccaro and Pontusson (2016). The ordoliberal viewpoint on the euro crisis is expressed for instance in Feld et al. (2015). A German economist critical of ordoliberalism is Peter Bofinger, who was a very sceptical member of the "German Committee of Economic Experts" to the German government. He denounced the opportunism of being supported by the full employment policies of other countries (Bofinger 2016). Eucken was the main exponent of ordoliberalism; he taught in Freiburg, hence the name "Freiburg School" by which this approach is also known. On the German economic tradition, see Riha (1985) and Beck and Kotz (2017).

As we have seen, Von Hayek (1939) convincingly argued that the only possible European federal state is one with a minimal role of the state, and that federalism is therefore the Holy Grail of the liberals and not of the socialists. The theme of the link between political and monetary union is discussed in Cesaratto (2017). On the nation-state as a natural terrain of distributive conflict, see Massimo Pivetti (2019). The abstract of the paper does not give the European project a chance:

> Some critical economists appear to believe that the European monetary union (EMU) has gone somewhat astray, and that the working of the euro area could be made significantly better if only the flawed nature of a few key theoretical underpinnings of the project was duly recognized. Quite to the contrary, … [the] EMU has indeed been fully successful from the point of view of its actual objective, which has never been that of increasing the overall welfare of the majority of the population concerned. In the light of actual experience, EMU can be interpreted as a deliberate project to undermine wage earners' bargaining power throughout the Continent. …It is the removal of the nation state, coupled with the absence of a supranational political power, that the building of the euro system has largely achieved.

Marx was a fierce critic of Friedrich List (1909 [1841]), identifying economic nationalism as an instrument of the national bourgeoisies to co-opt and corrupt the working classes in their plans for national development, distracting them from deep commonality of interests with the working classes of other countries. "The proletariat has no nation! Internationalism! Revolution!" as we used to chant under Guido Carli's windows. Many left-wingers are still confident that German workers will take to the streets in solidarity with the workers of less fortunate European countries. While awaiting this event, we have plenty of time to read Robert Gilpin (1930–2018), one of the founders of International political economy, an interesting intersection between the disciplines of International Economics and International Relations. Gilpin classified liberalism and Marxism as cosmopolitan ideologies, and the mercantilist tradition taken up by List as economic nationalism. Despite being a liberal, political realism led him to sympathize with the latter tradition; see for instance Gilpin (2001).

On the proposal for "expansive stabilization" advanced, among others, by Folkerts-Landau (2018), see Cesaratto (2018b). To appreciate the moralistic animosity towards the South that drives the German élite (e.g. Wolfgang Schäuble), see Hien and Joerges (2018). A good review of the evolution of the Italian political framework in relation to Europe from Berlusconi's defenestration in 2011 to the pandemic can be found in Palombarini (2020).

References

Amato, G., & Ranci, P. (Eds.). (1974). *La Congiuntura più lunga: materiali per una analisi della politica economica italiana, 1972-1974*. Bologna: Il mulino.

Baccaro, L., & Pontusson, J. (2016). Rethinking comparative political economy: The growth model perspective. *Politics & Society, 44*(2), 175–207.

Bagnai, A. (2012). *Il tramonto dell'euro*. Reggio Emilia: Imprimatur.

Baldwin, R., & Giavazzi, F. (2015). *The Eurozone crisis: A consensus view of the causes and a few possible solutions*. Voxeu.org.

Basaglia, F. (1968). *L'istituzione negata. Rapporto da un ospedale psichiatrico*. Torino: Einaudi.

Beck, T., & Kotz, H.-H. (Eds.) (2017). *Ordoliberalism: A German oddity?* Voxeu.org.

Blustein, P. (2016). *Not so low: Inside the crisis that overwhelmed Europe and the IMF*. Waterloo, ON: CIGI Press.

Bofinger, P. (2016). *German macroeconomics: The long shadow of Walter Eucken*. Voxeu.org.

Carli, G. (1996). *Cinquant'anni di vita italiana*. Bari: Laterza.

Cesaratto, S. (2006). Spazio e ruolo di un riformismo coraggioso. In S. Cesaratto & R. Realfonzo (Eds.), *Rive Gauche – Critica della politica economica* (pp. 44–51). Roma: Il manifesto libri.

Cesaratto, S. (2017). Alternative interpretations of a stateless currency crisis. *Cambridge Journal of Economics, 41*(4), 977–998.

Cesaratto, S. (2018a). The nature of the eurocrisis. A reply to Febrero, Uxò and Bermejo. *Review of Keynesian Economics, 6*(2), 240–251 (working paper version: Quaderni DEPS, No. 752).

Cesaratto, S. (2018b). Italy: A question of interest rates and trust. *Intereconomics, 53*(6), 294–295.

Cesaratto, S., & Stirati, A. (2011). Germany in the European and global crises. *International Journal of Political Economy, 39*(4), 56–86.

Cesaratto, S., & Zezza, G. (2019a). What went wrong with Italy, and what the country should now fight for in Europe. In H. Hansjorg, J. Priewe, & A. Watt (Eds.), *Still time to save the Euro* (pp. 47–61). Berlin: Social Europe Publishing.

Cesaratto, S., & Zezza, G. (2019b). Farsi male da soli. Disciplina esterna, domanda aggregata e il declino economico italiano. *L'industria, 40*(2), 279–318.

De Cecco, M. (1994). L'Italia e il Sistema Monetario Europeo. In F. R. Pizzuti (Ed.), *L'economia italiana dagli anni '70 agli anni '90* (pp. 19–41). Milano: McGraw-Hill.

De Grauwe, P. (1998, February 20). The euro and the financial crises. *Financial Times.*

De Vivo, G., & Pivetti, M. (1980). International integration and the balance of payments constraint: The case of Italy. *Cambridge Journal of Economics, 4*(1), 1–22.

Diaz-Alejandro, C. (1985). Good-bye financial repression, hello financial crash. *Journal of Development Economics, 19*(1–2), 1–24.

Febrero, E., & Uxó, J. (2013). *Understanding target2 imbalances from an endogenous money view.* Department of Economics, University of Castilla-La Mancha, WP No. 2.

Feld, L. P., Köhler, E. A., & Nientiedt, D. (2015). *Ordoliberalism, pragmatism and the eurozone crisis: How the German tradition shaped economic policy in Europe.* CESIFO, WP No. 5368.

Folkerts-Landau, D. (2018, November 12). Europe must cut a grand bargain with Italy. *Financial Times.*

Frenkel, R. (2014). What have the crises in emerging markets and the Euro Zone in common and what differentiates them? In J. E. Stiglitz & D. Heymann (Eds.), *Life after debt—The origins and resolutions of debt crisis* (pp. 122–141). New York: Palgrave Macmillan.

Gilpin, R. (2001). *Global political economy—Understanding the international economic order.* Princeton: Princeton University Press.

Godley, W. (1992). Maastricht and all that. *London Review of Books, 14*(19). Retrieved February 20, 2020, from https://www.lrb.co.uk/the-paper/v14/n19/wynne-godley/maastricht-and-all-that

Graziani, A. (2000). *Lo sviluppo dell'economia italiana. Dalla ricostruzione alla moneta unica.* Boringhieri: Torino.

Hien, J., & Joerges, C. (2018). Dead man walking? Current European interest in the ordoliberal tradition. *European Law Journal, 24*(2–3), 142–162.

Hirschman, A. (1970). *Exit, voice, and loyalty: Responses to decline in firms, organizations, and states.* Cambridge, MA: Harvard University Press.

Hirschman, A. (1977). *The passions and the interests: Political arguments for capitalism before its triumph.* Princeton, NJ: Princeton University Press.

Hirschman, A. (1991). *The rhetoric of reaction: Perversity, futility, jeopardy.* Cambridge, MA: The Belknap Press.

Hirschman, A. (1994). Social conflicts as pillars of democratic market society. *Political Theory, 22*(2), 203–218.

Holtfrerich, C.-L. (1999). Monetary policy under fixed exchange rates (1948–70). In E. Baltensperger (Ed.), *Fifty years of the Deutsche Mark. Central bank and the currency in Germany since 1948* (pp. 307–402). New York: Deutsche Bundesbank and Oxford University Press.

Holtfrerich, C.-L. (2008). Monetary policy in Germany since 1948—National tradition, international best practice or ideology. In J. P. Touffut (Ed.), *Central banks as economic institutions* (pp. 22–51). Cheltenham: Edward Elgar.

Höpner, M. (2019). *The German undervaluation regime under Bretton woods: How Germany became the nightmare of the world economy.* MPIfG Discussion Paper No. 19/1. Köln: Max-Planck-Institut für Gesellschaftsforschung

Kaldor, N. (1971, March 12). The dynamic effects of the common market. *New Stateman.* Reprinted in N. Kaldor (1978), *Collected economic essays* (pp. 187–220). Vol. 6, London: Duckworth.

La Malfa, U. (1962). *Nota aggiuntiva alla Relazione generale sulla situazione economica del Paese.* Rome: Camera dei deputati, May.

Leibniz-Institut für Wirtschaftsforschung Halle. (2015). *Germany's benefit from the Greek crisis.* IWH Online 7/2015. Halle (Saale).

List, F. (1909 [1841]). *The national system of political economy.* London: Longmans, Green and Company. Retrieved February 20, 2020, from https://oll.libertyfund.org/titles/315

Nikiforos, M., et al. (2015). Twin deficits' in Greece: In search of causality. *Journal of Post Keynesian Economics, 38*(2), 302–330.

Padoa-Schioppa, T. (2003, August 26). Berlino e Parigi ritorno alla realtà. *Corriere della sera.* Retrieved April 30, 2020, from http://www.tommasopadoaschioppa.eu/europa/berlino-e-parigi-ritorno-alla-realta.html

Paggi, L., & D'Angelillo, M. (1986). *I comunisti italiani e il riformismo. Un confronto con le socialdemocrazie europee.* Torino: Einaudi.

Palombarini, S. (2020, April 10). Italy is discovering that European solidarity doesn't exist. *Jacobin.* Retrieved April 11, 2020, from https://jacobinmag.com/2020/4/italy-coronavirus-crisis-european-union-euro

Pivetti, M. (2019). The Euro System and the overall european project: Failure or fully-fledged success? *Revista de Economia Critica, 27*(primer semester), 112–121.

Reinhart, C. (2011). Series of unfortunate events: Common sequencing patterns in financial crises. *Rivista di Politica Economica, 100*(4), 11–36.

Riha, T. (1985). *German political economy: The history of an alternative economics*. Bradford: MCB University Press.

Stiglitz, J. E. (2010). *Freefall: America, free markets, and the sinking of the world economy*. New York: W. W. Norton.

Storm, S. (2019a). *How to ruin a country in three decade*. Retrieved February 20, 2020, from https://www.ineteconomics.org/perspectives/blog/how-to-ruin-a-country-in-three-decades

Storm, S. (2019b). Lost in deflation: Why Italy's woes are a warning to the whole eurozone. *International Journal of Political Economy, 48*(3), 195–237.

Von Hayek, F. (1939). *Individualism and economic order*. Chicago: University of Chicago Press.

7

Count Draghila

Abstract This chapter examines the European crisis from the point of view of monetary policy. Based on the monetary issues discussed in the previous chapters, we explain how monetary policy works in ordinary circumstances. We then look at non-conventional measures initiated by the ECB in 2008. The ECB's action became more effective with Draghi, but could only partially make up for the absence of appropriate European fiscal policy. In fact, European fiscal policy, based on pursuit of a balanced budget and obsession with public debt, does not work in tandem with monetary policy. From a Keynesian viewpoint, the central bank should primarily serve fiscal policy in the pursuit of full employment as well as price stability. Finally, we explain a controversy that raged in 2011–2012, but has never really died down: Target2, the European payment system. Appendix 1 completes our analysis of ECB monetary policy from a central bank balance sheet perspective. This is an excellent vantage point for reviewing conventional and unconventional monetary policies. Appendix 2 provides further details of Target2, discussing whether Target2 imbalances constitute real debt between EMU countries.

© Springer Nature Switzerland AG 2020
S. Cesaratto, *Heterodox Challenges in Economics*,
https://doi.org/10.1007/978-3-030-54448-5_7

7.1   An Unconventional Central Bank

Since 2011, when he became president of the ECB, Mario Draghi often seemed to be the only person tackling the European crisis, while most of the German élite in Berlin and Frankfurt seemed to be rowing against him. Clearly, Draghi was also representing the establishment and fulfilling his mandate as custodian of the euro. The aim of this chapter is to explain what the ECB did during the crisis. To do so, we require some notions of monetary policy.

As a preliminary synthesis, let us say that monetary policy normally consists in determination of the short-term interest rate by the central bank. In practice, this is the rate that ordinary banks apply to each other when lending reserves for short periods: a bank with excess reserves lends them to a bank short of reserves. This rate influences longer-term interest rates, the rates banks apply to their customers. In this way, the central bank influences economic activity in an expansionary sense by reducing interest rates and in a restrictive sense by increasing them. Interest rates also influence the exchange rate: when domestic interest rates increase, this attracts foreign capital and leads to an appreciation of the domestic currency; vice versa, falling interest rates make capital seek investment in financial activities in other currencies, which revalue, while the domestic currency depreciates. In turn, the exchange rate influences foreign trade: a depreciation of the euro can, for instance, favour European exports.

In the years of the crisis, the Federal Reserve immediately, and the ECB much later (and with temporary misgivings), brought interest rates to zero, the so-called "zero lower bound" or ZLB, in an attempt to revive their economies.

Prof, but once they've brought interest rates down to zero, the central banks have played their last card! The interest rate is indeed considered to be the main conventional tool of central banks. However, once ZLB had been reached, the central banks resorted to a series of unconventional instruments, the most famous of which is certainly quantitative easing (QE). Here again the Fed began QE immediately in 2008, the ECB 7 years later. Another unconventional instrument that central banks have used has been negative interest rates.

So let us begin by seeing the conventional instruments, namely how the central bank makes the short-term interest rate of its choice prevail in the economy: this rate is called the target or policy interest rate. We consider the ECB, but other central banks function more or less in the same way. Then we explain and assess the unconventional measures progressively adopted by the ECB since 2008.

7.2   Corridor Rates

In Chap. 5, we mentioned the system of interbank payments: when we have our bank pay a third party who has his account at another bank, as we do every day with drafts, cheques and credit cards, our payment order implies that a corresponding amount of reserves moves from our bank's reserve account to that of the other bank.

Yes, Prof, we remember: ordinary banks have a current account at the central bank, known as their reserve account, from which they pay other banks in order to fulfil the payment orders of their customers. Excellent! So you also remember that it can happen that on a given day, the customers of *Trust-Me Bank* make more payments to customers of *Rainy-Day Bank* than vice versa. *Trust-Me Bank* could thus run short of reserves while *Rainy-Day Bank* could have a surplus. According to the ECB regulations, over a period of 6 weeks (the maintenance period), banks must on average meet reserve requirements, currently 1% of deposits. The interbank market helps banks comply with this requirement: normally the bank in surplus lends reserves to the bank in deficit through the interbank market.

You will remember that banks also replenish their liquidity (i.e. reserves) from the central bank by taking part in periodic refinancing operations. There are short-term (1 week) refinancing operations known as Main Refinancing Operations (MROs), and longer-term (3 months or more) refinancing operations, known as Longer-Term Refinancing Operations (LTRO). The ECB's target interest rate is equal to the one applied to Main Refinancing Operations, that can therefore be considered a key interest rate.

Between one refinancing operation and another, however, a bank may find itself short of liquidity and revert to the interbank market. If it has difficulty in raising funds, it may have recourse to a central bank emergency desk.

For instance, *Trust-Me Bank*, which in the example is short of liquidity, can also apply to a window of the ECB known as the marginal lending facility. This emergency facility of the ECB will replenish liquidity of the banks at any time at an interest rate that is, however, higher than that on MROs. The central bank also offers a deposit facility to banks with a surplus of reserves, where the surplus can be kept and earn interest, lower than that on MROs, but (in normal times) positive.

Prof, you said that the ECB's target interest rate is equal to the rate on the Main Refinancing Operations. But how does this rate influence the rates that operators actually charge each other in the market? Let us consider a "normal" pre-crisis situation. Table 7.1 indicates, for example, that in mid-2007, the interest rate on main refinancing operations was 4%. The marginal lending facility (5%)

Table 7.1 ECB interest rates, effective since 13 June 2007

Marginal lending facility	5%
Main refinancing operations	4%
Marginal deposit	3%

Source: ECB

and the deposit facility (3%) interest rates represent the ceiling and the floor, respectively, of the so-called interest rate "corridor".

Going back to our example, *Trust-Me Bank*, short of reserves, could obtain a very short-term (24-h) marginal loan from the ECB at an interest rate of 5%. *Rainy-Day Bank*, with excess reserves, could park its surplus liquidity in a deposit facility at 3%. Bear in mind that if it becomes generally known that a bank resorts to a marginal loan, this can harm its reputation, because it suggests that other banks do not want to lend to it and that it, therefore, has balance sheet problems. Assuming the banks trust each other, it is natural to think that *Trust-Me Bank* would be willing to offer *Rainy-Day Bank* a little more than the 3% this bank receives if it keeps the money in the deposit facility. At an interest rate of less than 5%, *Trust-Me Bank* would save money and avoid the stigma of a marginal loan. One does not have to be an economist to guess that the two banks will agree to an interest rate around 4% precisely equal to the MRO rate targeted by the ECB. This is the rate at which *Rainy-Day Bank* lends its surplus reserves to *Trust-Me Bank*. And that is precisely the short-term interest rate that the ECB wanted to prevail on the interbank market where the central bank exerts its influence. This rate becomes the keystone of all the interest rates in the economy. As Claudio Borio of the Bank for International Settlements writes: "It is in this relatively unglamorous and often obscure corner of the financial markets that the ultimate source of the central banks' power to influence economic activity resides".[1] Well my friends, you have learnt the secret of monetary policy! It was not so difficult after all, was it?

Bank reserves are always held in two accounts at the central bank: in the reserve account, where required reserves are generally kept, and in the deposit facility, where excess reserves can be kept. Only the required reserves held in the reserve account are remunerated at the interest rate of MRO; if a bank held its excess reserves in this account it would earn no interest. That is why it normally keeps excess reserves in the deposit facility, or lends them to other banks that it trusts.

---

[1] Borio (1997, p. 14).

Prof, the central bank therefore relies on the corridor to make its target interest rate prevail on the interbank market, and this interest rate becomes the architrave of the whole edifice of interest rates, including longer term ones. If we understand correctly, the target rate is important, but so are the other two that define the interest rate corridor. Yes, that is correct. When the board of the ECB meets every 6 weeks, it fixes the interest rate on main refinancing operations and also decides the two "marginal" interest rates so that the rate at which banks lend each other money for short terms gravitates around the interest rate of main refinancing operations, which therefore becomes the keystone of all the interest rates in the economy. Figure 7.1 shows the interest rate corridor from January 2002 to December 2019.

Figure 7.1a shows that until mid-2008, that is before the financial crisis, the interbank interest rate, or EONIA (Euro Overnight Index Average),

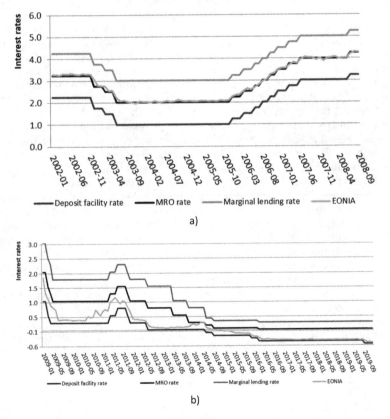

Fig. 7.1 BCE Official interest rate corridor, (a) 2002–2008, (b) 2009–2019. Source: Statistical Data Warehouse ECB, Eurosystem policy and exchange rates, Official interest rates, January 2020

oscillated around that of MROs. Figure 7.1b shows that after 2008, things changed somewhat and EONIA is down on the corridor floor. We shall see, in fact, that after 2008, banks stopped lending to each other because they no longer trusted the balance sheets of other banks (this should have raised EONIA); on the other hand, however, the ECB made a potentially infinite amount of liquidity available to the banks, and this abundance decreased EONIA. Though not officially, the ECB in fact used a version of the corridor known as the "floor system" in which the target rate coincides with that of the deposit facility. The Fed officially adopted the floor system in November 2008.

A decoupled central bank. *But Prof, macroeconomics textbooks say that monetary policy acts by varying the money supply through the so-called open market operations. When the central bank wants to lower the interest rate it buys bonds on the financial market, creating liquidity (i.e. reserves). More liquidity makes money cheaper, decreasing the interest rate. When the central bank wants to raise the interest rate, it sells bonds, decreasing the supply of money and increasing the price of liquidity, i.e. the interest rate.* This view is clearly wrong. As we saw, the demand for reserves, i.e. the liquidity the market needs, is governed by the amount of deposits that the banking system creates when prompted by the demand for credit that the market (households and firms) expresses at the interest rate chosen by the central bank. In "normal" times, the central bank aims to meet the need for reserves. In fact, an excess of reserves would make the interbank interest rate fall to the floor of the corridor, and a deficit of reserves would send it up to the ceiling. The central bank therefore cannot vary the amount of reserves as it pleases, as the textbooks say, otherwise the interbank interest rate would become unstable.

So how does the central bank vary the target interest rate? It announces the change by an *open mouth* operation (a mere announcement), not by an open market operation, as the macroeconomics textbooks say. As explained by Claudio Borio and Piti Disyatat,[2] there is "decoupling" between fixing of the interest rate and the quantity of money created by the central bank. The latter (verbally) fixes the target rate and passively adjusts the supply of reserves. The central bank is said to be a price maker and a quantity taker.

This is the so-called "interest-rate policy" normally applied by central banks. Since the recent financial crisis, central banks have adopted a second type of policy known as "balance-sheet policy" (a liquidity expansion policy). By acting as lender of last resort, since 2008 the ECB has for instance increased the liquidity

---

[2] Borio and Disyatat (2009, p. 3).

available to banks and this is reflected in the balance sheet of the central bank, as we shall see in Appendix 1—and has done so even more massively since 2015 with quantitative easing. In this case, decoupling is perfect. The central bank fixes the target interest rate, making it coincide with the floor of the corridor, i.e. with the interest rate on the deposit facility (floor system), and on the other hand, it creates as much liquidity as it sees fit. In this case, the central bank is both price and quantity maker.

Figure 7.2 shows that although the ECB suddenly reduced its interest rates between 2008 and 2009, the Fed did so more rapidly. In mid-2008, when the world was clearly falling into the worst recession since the 1930s (or perhaps the worst until the COVID-19 pandemic), the ECB was still raising interest rates because Germany was more worried about the increase in the price of oil. Figure 7.2 also shows the slow fall towards the zero lower bound, which was only reached in 2014.

Prof, there is another rise in interest rates in mid-2011. Could it be that Berlin …
Yes. Ig-Metal, the powerful German metalworkers union, asked for excessive wage increases, and in the middle of the spread crisis Berlin had the ECB raise

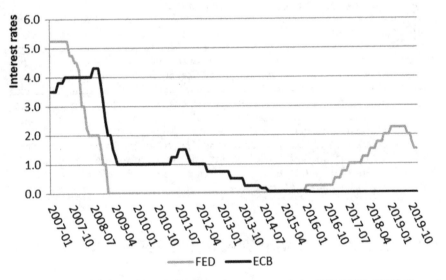

Fig. 7.2 Target interest rates of the Federal Reserve and the ECB (2007–2019). Source: Federal Reserve (effective federal funds rate), European Central Bank (main refinancing operations rate), January 2020

interest rates to threaten the unions. It was not until Draghi became president of the ECB on 1st November 2011, that the bank ceased to speak exclusively German. In fact, Super Mario never once increased interest rates during his mandate (2011–2019). In contrast, the Fed increased its rates over the same period, but the American economy, unlike that of Europe, had been back to normal for some time due to more aggressive monetary and fiscal policies.

Prof, why do German trade unions feel threatened by an increase in interest rates? At the time of the Deutschmark, the Bundesbank threatened the trade unions with an increase in interest rates if they made wage claims that were considered excessive. High interest rates discourage spending and make the national currency appreciate: domestic demand and exports decrease and unemployment increases. The Bundesbank was acting as guardian of German price stability and monetary mercantilism. In mid-2011, the German government imposed this policy on the ECB.

> **Short- and long-term interest rates**. Longer-term interest rates reflect the trend of the short-term interest rate, on which the central bank normally exerts its influence. They also reflect expectations regarding a possible change in the latter. For example, the 2-year interest rate is (approximately) the average of the interest rate of the current year (known) and that expected the following year (presumed). If I lend €100 for 2 years at an interest rate set now, and the current 1-year rate for loans is 5%, while that expected next year is 6%, it is reasonable to lend at an average interest rate of 5.5% (valid for 2 years). Operators generally expect that the central bank will increase the short-term interest rate if the economic outlook is positive. An upturn in the economy is in fact associated with a fall in unemployment and a consequent resumption of inflation following increased wage bargaining power of workers. Then one expects central banks to increase interest rates to moderate growth and undermine the increase in worker bargaining power.
>
> You can see that behind the idea of independent central banks (independent of political power) and with the prevalent objective of controlling inflation (particularly true of the ECB), there is the aim of controlling the distribution of income between wages and profits (see Sect. 3.9).

7.3 Unconventional Weapons: 2008–2009

It is hard to avoid the impression that the ECB adjusted interest rates "too little and too late", revealing a certain irresoluteness in dealing with the crisis. It is true, however, that interest rate adjustments may not be effective. During a recession, low interest rates may not suffice to induce households, already indebted, to increase their autonomous consumption (that financed by consumer credit). The investment decisions of firms, which as we know from Chap. 4 are insensitive to interest rates and very sensitive to expectations of future demand, were depressed by austerity policy.

One of the first effects of the financial crisis was the breakdown of trust between banks and consequently the interbank market, where banks lend each other liquidity for periods ranging from overnight to a few months.

The reason for this loss of trust may initially have been the famous American crisis of sub-prime mortgages that exploded in 2007. You will recall that in the financial orgy of the pre-crisis years, American banks or the shadow banking system began to provide mortgages to persons of uncertain income, but to whom the very growth triggered by the construction boom seemed to guarantee jobs. These mortgages were then packaged (securitised) with more reliable mortgages (the famous Mortgage Backed Securities), and sold on the market. The banks were in practice pocketing the mortgage fees and then selling them to other investors (a "buyer" of Mr. Smith's mortgage receives the interest payments). Many of these securities ended up in other American and European banks (especially German banks) according to the belief that a risk spread among many subjects is almost zero. But when the housing bubble burst, real-estate prices and economic growth collapsed and many loans became non-performing, not only sub-prime loans but also those of middle-class households who lost their jobs and were therefore unable to continue their mortgage payments. Since nobody knew exactly which banks were holding the "toxic" Mortgage Backed Securities, banks ceased to lend each other money. They also ceased to provide credit to the real economy, seeking rather to recover credit owed them in order to replenish the capital they needed to sustain any losses on non-performing loans. This is called a credit crunch. The Wall Street crisis, therefore, spread virulently to Main Street: from finance to industry.

A break-down of the interbank market can have severe consequences. Illiquid banks, perhaps due to a temporary lack of deposits or crisis-related late repayments, may be solvent but are forced to sell off assets to obtain the liquidity necessary to meet their obligations (such as paying back loans from other banks, or simply making payments for their customers) and at the same time have to tighten credit so as not to commit further liquidity. This shortage of liquidity makes interbank interest rates rise, together with the interest rates banks apply to their customers on new and existing indexed loans. This is what happened in Italy to mortgages indexed to Euribor, the interbank interest rate in the euro area for terms ranging from 1 month to 1 year. Whoever (like me!) had indexed mortgages in 2008–2009 remembers with horror the increase in interest costs that occurred for several months. Liquidation of assets by banks in search of liquidity caused the assets to lose value, impacting the wealth of consumers. The credit crunch, i.e. the reduction of bank credit to households and firms, transmitted the crisis to the real economy.

From the point of view of the central bank, the mechanism of transmission of monetary policy was broken: normally control of short-term interest rates is transferred to longer-term interest rates and turned into impulses to the real economy, expansionary or recessionary according to the monetary policy orientation. In practice, short-term interest rates ceased gravitating around the MRO interest rate and increased; this and the general difficulty of banks to refinance on the interbank market made longer-term interest rates rise.

Between summer 2008, when the American crisis exploded, and the end of 2009, when the Greek crisis began, the ECB's actions were mainly concerned with providing liquidity to the banking system at low rates of interest and for longer terms than usual, so as to reassure the public regarding bank solvency, decrease interest rates on the interbank market and restore bank credit to households and firms.

The ECB did this with a series of measures called Enhanced Credit Support and by decreasing the interest rate of main refinancing operations from 4.25% in October 2008 to 1% in May 2009 (see Fig. 7.2). These measures are defined as unconventional because they go beyond normal liquidity supply methods.

Summing up, by means of MROs (short term) and LTROs (the terms of which rose from 3 months to 1 year), the ECB supplied all the liquidity that banks needed at a predetermined interest rate. Since banks give assets (collateral) in exchange for liquidity, the ECB lowered the rating of the assets it considered acceptable, a necessary measure in view of the general decay of the financial instruments in circulation, due to the high toxicity of the financial market. By agreement with the Fed, the ECB even ensured liquidity in dollars to banks that had to pay back loans denominated in dollars and had trouble borrowing dollars from other banks: they were probably large German banks that had speculated on the American housing bubble. Finally, the ECB did a small QE, buying up covered bonds (i.e. bonds by which banks collect longer-term loans) in order to revive this important sector of interbank loans.

The initially small-sized QE of the ECB consisted in purchasing 60 billion euro of covered bonds in 2009 and more than 40 billion in 2011. In contrast, the Fed began QE, initially aimed at sustaining bank and semi-public bonds with purchases amounting to about 600 billion dollars in November 2008 and 750 billion in March 2009, incremented by the purchase of 300 billion dollars of government bonds. Two other QEs of similar size followed in 2010 and 2012. The success of the American strategy was certainly due to immediate monetary policy measures, as well as fiscal policy, which while not always sufficiently expansionary, was certainly very different from European budgetary rigour.

So Prof, if we understand correctly, the ECB did not want a citizen who had instructed his bank to make a draft, to have his request refused because the bank had no more liquidity in its reserve account. Precisely. A lack of bank liquidity would have triggered the classical run on banks, with people trying to cash the money lying in their accounts. Banks would have closed their counters. As we know, in his famous book *Lombard Street* (1873), Walter Begehot suggested that in such situations central banks should act as lenders of last resort.

Some other questions, Prof. Didn't the banks have an emergency window or marginal lending facility, that of the corridor ceiling, to replenish liquidity? Moreover, there was a run on banks in Greece in June-July 2015, wasn't there? Finally, why didn't the ECB implement QE immediately?

In reply to your first question, remember that "marginal loans" bring discredit and have relatively high interest rates. Instead, by reinforcing the instruments of main and longer-term refinancing operations, the ECB offered unlimited liquidity at a lower interest rate without discrediting the bank. In reply to your second question, yes, there was a run on the banks in Greece, because Greek banks saw deposits (and therefore reserves) fleeing the country for fear of redenomination of deposits in drachmas (or, equivalently, risk of outright default of corporations, banks and government). The ECB, however, limited liquidity supply to those banks as it was no longer sure of their solidity. So the banks had to limit how much cash Greek citizens could withdraw.

In reply to your third question, the ECB considered that in the euro area the transmission of monetary policy mainly relied on the banking channel, while QE was aimed at the financial market, which is relatively more important in the United States. In the United States, the stock market is more central for financing firms and household consumption. In the United States, firms and households hold many financial assets through investment funds: if the assets increase in value, they stimulate spending, the so-called "wealth effect". Importantly, however, in the United States, QE also backed US government bonds, thereby allowing expansionary fiscal policy leading to larger fiscal deficits to support the economy without burdening the government with an increasing cost of debt. This is almost anathema in the EMU.

If we were to judge ECB policy in this first phase, we could perhaps say that although it did not act aggressively or quickly enough to adjust interest rates, which after all are its main sign for orientation, it did fulfil its task of lender of last resort to the banks in a timely manner. The ECB's inadequacy manifested from 2010 until Draghi's famous speech in July 2012. In that period the ECB withdrew from acting as lender of last resort to European governments. American economic policy in 2008–2009, based on mutually supportive fiscal and monetary policies, quickly brought that country out of the crisis. The deplorable European choice of not letting fiscal and monetary policies work together made it impossible to limit the spread of the sovereign debt crisis that exploded in 2010. This failure has caused unnecessary suffering for some European countries.

7.4   Monetary Hypocrisy, Muddles and Tricks: 2010–2011

In 2010, the world economy began to come out of the crisis by virtue of Keynesian-style measures agreed at the G20 in London in April 2009 (unfortunately not confirmed in subsequent G20s). Between 2009 and 2010, in the euro area, the Greek question broke out. The huge foreign debt of certain peripheral countries, which we examined in the previous chapter, revealed the financial fragility of the EMU. In Greece, this foreign debt was mostly public debt, whereas in Spain and Ireland it was bank debt. But also in these countries, private debt was largely transformed into public debt once the states intervened to save the banks. The possible default of Greece, i.e. the impossibility of Greece to continue repayments due on foreign debt, was addressed in May 2010 by a lending package from European countries and the International Monetary Fund. Attention! "Bailing out" a country means saving creditor banks, in this case French and German banks that would have been in grave difficulty if the Greek government did not repay its debts on time. Countries like Italy, which had no credit towards Greece, were forced to participate in the bail-out of Franco-German banks. This was the first of the Greek bail-outs: others followed in spring 2012, accompanied by insufficient debt restructuring, and in July 2015, after the capitulation of Tsipras. It will long be debated whether Syriza could have done otherwise and whether the situation could have been tackled in 2010 by debt restructuring, cancelling a part of Greek debt and diluting repayment of the remaining debt at more affordable interest rates over time. It was decided not to do so, despite the perplexity of the IMF, because it could have caused losses for the French and German banking systems (already burdened with toxic American assets) and prompted similar requests for debt restructuring from Portugal, Ireland and possibly Spain. Be this as it may, the adjustment measures imposed by the Troika (as the EU, ECB and IMF envoys were defined) led Greece into a devastating crisis.

Faced with the prospect of market panic over the debt of other European countries as well, the ECB decided to do almost nothing. It set up a small asset purchasing programme called the Security Market Program (SMP) that ended up purchasing little more than 200 billion government bonds of peripheral countries (including Italy) until early 2012.

But Prof, the European treaties prevent the ECB from supporting the public debt of troubled countries! True, the ECB is not officially allowed to support government bonds. Its official justification was that interest rates of government bonds are a benchmark for bank credit to the private sector. Since the ECB's objective is to make credit conditions uniform in the different jurisdictions of the EMU, it has to sustain the government bonds of troubled countries so as to reduce their interest rates to the level of other countries. This story would not be worthy of further consideration, except for two other aspects. The first is that it confirms the hypocrisy, typical of moralists, of certain European élites. The ECB committed itself to draining the liquidity created with the SMP (technically, "sterilising the money supply"). In other words, when the ECB purchased a government bond from a bank, it did so by crediting the same amount of reserves to the bank's reserve account. Achtung! said Buba. The greater reserves (liquidity) held by the banks could generate new credit and inflation! Here one may ask if this is real or simulated stupidity. Since 2008, the banks have had infinite available liquidity (as we saw above), that did not give rise to more credit because there was no demand, as we already said. Nonetheless, the ECB was obliged to sterilise the liquidity created. It did this by offering the banks the possibility of parking it in an interest-earning account, to induce them to freeze it, as if they could do anything else with it. In June 2014, this hypocritical measure was abolished.

The second more technical aspect regards Draghi's famous "whatever it takes" announcement in July 2012, when faced with the imminent collapse of the euro due to the risk of exits by Italy and Spain. Draghi promised to buy government bonds under attack without any limit. As we shall see, the measure worked without any bonds actually being bought. By comparison, the ECB timid purchase of a handful of bonds through the SMP, without ever revealing the precise amount, was ineffective. Being a central bank means asserting authority over markets. The truth is that what some European capitals wanted was for the financial markets to assert their authority over certain national governments.

After the collapse of Portugal and Ireland, and after the Merkosy tête-à-tête at Deauville mentioned in Sect. 6.8, the sovereign debt confidence crisis was punctually transmitted to Italy and Spain. It manifested as the sale or as non-renewal at maturity of Italian and Spanish government bonds that foreign investors wanted to get off their hands. The sale of bonds depressed their value and raised the interest rate that the state had to offer on new issues in order to attract investors. In fact, if purchase of a bond is associated with a high risk that it could lose value, due to widespread lack of confidence in the solvency of the state that issues it, the purchaser will expect a much higher interest rate to cover that risk. This generates a vicious circle: high interest rates threaten the solvency of the issuing government, pushing up risk and interest rates even more. Increased risk discourages bondholders from rolling them over. When a batch of bonds matures, the state usually issues an identical batch, which is typically purchased by the holders of the mature bonds. If this does not happen, the state has to pay back euros, which it does not print. If it does not find new purchasers and is threatened with bankruptcy, a euro area country may decide to return to issuing its own currency. It dusts down the printing press, redenominates its bonds in the new currency and regains solvency. Clearly, redenomination of debt implies losses for foreign investors who purchased bonds in euro and find themselves with bonds in nuova-lira or nueva-peseta, currencies destined to depreciate to some extent against the euro.

In 2011, the famous spread crisis exploded. Ordinary Spaniards and Italians learned to assess the increase in interest rates of Italian and Spanish government bonds by means of the *spread*, i.e. the difference between the interest paid by Germany on the Bund, its 10-year government bond, and the yield of the corresponding Italian and Spanish 10-year government bonds, the BTP 10Y and the Bono 10Y, respectively. The words of Draghi in his famous speech also linked the risk measured by the spread with the risk of redenomination of debt: in other words, the risk that some big euro-area country, unable to meet its debt commitments, refuse to be put under politically and socially intolerable European tutelage. The risk of sovereign debt can also, however, be interpreted as a risk of default, while remaining in the common currency, as happened to the small peripheral countries Greece, Portugal and Ireland. For investors, there is little difference between a 20% cut in debt due to debt restructuring or a 20% loss on the value in euros once debt is redenominated in a new sovereign currency that depreciates with respect to the euro.

Glass half full? An early state rescue fund, the European Financial Stability Facility (EFSF) created by EU countries in May 2010, intervened with loans to Portugal, Ireland and Greece. The European Stability Mechanism (ESM) instituted in October 2012 replaced the EFSF for subsequent interventions: support for the Spanish banks (2012), Cyprus (2013) and Greece (2015). Both funds finance themselves on the market and are guaranteed by the countries of Europe (and ultimately by the ECB). In the case of the ESM, the countries contribute to equity capital.

In the light of the 2012 European agreements instituting the ESM, the Italian government, without any open parliamentary debate, accepted a clause that could make any contractual changes in the terms of the debt it issues more difficult. These contractual changes include debt restructuring through a cut in bondholders' claims and a lengthening of debt maturities, but also a mere redenomination of the debt in a new currency. Since 2013, all government bond issues contain a class action clause in the case of debt restructuring or redenomination in a new currency. The action must be moved by at least 25% of bondholders. The clause was added to *facilitate* debt restructuring, but it may equally be seen as an opportunity for a minority to oppose it.

7.5 Acronymia: 2012–2013

At the end of 2011, Mario Draghi introduced the Very longer-term refinancing operation (VLTRO) triggering an explosion of acronyms. We all learned the terms LTRO and VLTRO that we then had to distinguish from TLTRO I in 2014, TLTRO II in early 2016 and TLTRO III, announced in March 2019. The orgy of acronyms in these years included Target2, ASBPP, CBPP 1/2/3 and PSPP, not to mention the European funds EFSF and ESM, and the fiscal rules: European semester, Six-pack, Two-pack, Fiscal compact… a nightmare impossible for ordinary citizens to understand and for economics lecturers to teach. But let us see the substance.

With the VLTRO launched in late 2011, Draghi made about a thousand billion euro in liquidity available to European banks for 3 years. The measure was officially designed to stimulate banks to provide credit to households and firms; indeed, the complete mantra repeated on every occasion by Italian politicians was "households and firms, especially small firms". However, the banking sector did not suffer from lack of liquidity, it was rather the demand for credit that was missing, and also bank confidence in granting it. The horse led to water was not drinking. In fact, Draghi's VLTRO operation had another purpose. I know that in saying this, I will be doing Draghi's enemies a favour, but I will say it anyway: a secret bail-out of Italy and Spain.

Indeed, the main purpose of the VTRLO was to offset the flight of foreign investors from government bonds of peripheral countries. Peripheral commercial banks, especially Italian ones, massively used the 3-year liquidity made available by the ECB to replace foreign investors. They did so with a certain glee, since those bonds yielded well, helping to enhance their balance sheet—whereas VLTRO funds were cheap, offered at an interest rate equal to the ECB target rate, already down to 1%. Therefore, although home banks progressively replaced foreign investors, this did not decrease the spread. The only effect was to temporarily prevent the default of Italy (and Spain), otherwise unable to repay maturing loans to foreign investors or to find new lenders. The high interest rates were in any case likely to be unsustainable in the long term (it was a "loan shark" situation).

So Prof, correct me if I am wrong. The Italian Treasury could repay the debts on time by selling bonds of the same value to Italian banks that paid with VLTRO funds. The Italian banks were attracted to the operation because they were profiting from the spread between the low interest rates on ECB funds and the high rates paid by the Italian Treasury.

Exactly. Italian banks financed themselves at 1% and gained several times as much on government bonds (exploiting the spread). In the meantime, they swept the non-performing loans of austerity-hit households and firms under the carpet.

This led to what was called the "Balkanisation" of the public debt of European countries, namely national public debt, especially that of high-risk countries, ended up being held by the banks of the country itself. Gone were the days when European government bonds were considered equally safe. This led to what was called the doom loop between states and national banks: the states took on the debt of their banks (especially in Spain and Ireland); the banks then took on state debt (especially in Italy), like two who cannot swim trying to save each other. At the European summit on 29th June 2012, it was declared "imperative to break the vicious circle between banks and sovereign states". This implied European commitment to a true banking union (see Box below). Eight years down the track, a complete banking union still does not exist.

To save two who are drowning, you throw them a rope, possibly from a solid boat. The *austerian* solution was to let them both drown, but separately, each reflecting on his own sins. More recently, the senseless insistence by certain Nordic governments that banks should not be allowed to hold more than a certain amount of government bonds of their own country before completing the banking union, can be interpreted in this light. The Bank of Italy diplomatically judges this position to be "premature". (The large German banks, giants with clay feet, are still full of toxic American securities, but this is never mentioned.)

Returning to 2012, the VLTRO solution of outsourcing defence of public debt under attack to national commercial banks proved to be ineffective. In July 2012, with spreads very high, the euro had been given for dead. That was when Super Mario phoned Angela Merkel with a question something like: "Are you going to continue to listen to your ordoliberal advisors at the Bundesbank or can we be serious?"

7.6   The Arcane Target2

Just a minute, Prof. Before telling us what Super Mario did, could you explain something? You said that the most pressing problem for a country is foreign debt, not public debt, or in other words public debt is a problem if it is large and held by foreigners. So once the Italian banks had replaced a substantial amount of public debt that was in foreign hands, was the problem solved or not?

I was hoping you would not ask that question, but you are mischievous and want me to talk about Target2, the euro area's payment system. I will do so in Appendix 2, because it is rather complicated, but things should become clear to you if you bear with me for a moment.

In 2011, an astute and influential German economist, Hans-Werner Sinn, denounced a mechanism by which the Eurosystem allegedly enabled Mediterranean countries to continue accumulating debt with the core countries, especially with Germany, and to persist in living above their means. Sinn basically argued that despite the common currency, the peripheral countries continue to have their own printing presses, but instead of their feeble currencies they print solid euros that the Bundesbank is forced to accept for payment to German creditors. Sinn added another long series of nonsense designed to paint innocent Germany as the victim of the corrupt and lazy south, but with regard to the printing press, he is not completely wrong. As we saw, in fact, with the VLTRO, national banks could buy their country's public debt that foreigners no longer wanted, permitting indebted states to liquidate foreign creditors. With ECB refinancing, banks could in principle have also continued to supply credit to national citizens so that they could use it to buy German goods. Then if we add that refinancing was done by national central banks, i.e. the Bank of Italy refinances Italian banks, the Bank of Spain refinances Spanish banks and so forth, Sinn had enough ammunition to raise the indignation of the ordinary German citizen.

Excuse me, Prof, but what are the German citizens complaining about? First, they sold products to Spain and Italy and were paid in euros; then with that money, Andreas bought Spanish and Italian government bonds; finally, when he wanted to get rid of them, he got his money back. What more do they want? In fact, in a certain sense they should not complain. The point, not easy to grasp, requires us to go back to a key concept of these chapters: payments between subjects happen by shifting reserves from the payer's bank to that of the payee. Consider the case of an Italian bank that makes a payment to a German citizen, e.g. when the Italian state liquidates a German former investor, or an Italian pays for his new Audi. The Italian bank has its reserve account at the Bank of Italy. We have already recounted what happens several times: the commercial bank cancels the sum from the current account of the Italian subject who is making the payment and the Bank of Italy cancels the corresponding amount from the reserve account of the Italian bank. However, the Bank of Italy does not have the power to credit the reserves to the reserve account of the German commercial bank. It therefore asks the Bundesbank to please do so and this is done (it isn't a true favour, Buba is obliged to do it, and the German people are law abiding). When the German bank receives the credit entry (the new reserves that Buba has created), it transfers a corresponding amount to the account of the German payee. Does the Bank of Italy give anything to the Bundesbank? No. In exchange for crediting the reserves to the German bank, the Bundesbank obtains an accounting entry called "Target2 claim" (a credit) with the Eurosystem, while the Bank of Italy has a corresponding "Target2 liability" (a debt). The name Target2 is derived from the acronym of the electronic platform by which these intra-European payments are made, and on which these balances are recorded (it sounds like the name of a high-speed train network: "Trans-European Automated Real-Time Gross Settlement Express Transfer System").

Excuse me Prof, but how does the printing press come into the story? As a result of the payment, Italian banks have lost reserves, but can obtain new ones through Eurosystem refinancing operations at the Bank of Italy counter.

Prof, can we return to the example of the government bonds? The Italian state initially has a debt with Andreas who bought Italian government bonds. When the bonds mature and Andreas wants to cash them in, an Italian bank obtains a VLTRO, gets liquidity (reserves) from the Bank of Italy and (in place of Andreas) renews the loan to the Italian state, which can therefore give the money back to Andreas through Target 2 via Bank of Italy—Bundesbank—German commercial bank where Andreas has a current account. It was initially a debt of the Italian state towards a German citizen; after these Target2 passages by which Andreas takes his money home, that Italian debt has become official Target2 debt of the

Bank of Italy towards the Eurosystem, and symmetrically Andreas's private credit has become official credit of Buba towards the Eurosystem.

Exactly. Italian foreign debt still exists, but has gone from being towards a private person (Andreas) to being towards the Eurosystem, which has a corresponding debt towards the Bundesbank.

What irritated Sinn was not only that via the combination of Target2 and ECB refinancing operations, peripheral countries could accommodate capital flight from their bonds without incurring a financial crisis, but more in general that they could sustain foreign deficits by putting them on the Target2 account.

Let us take the example of Pedro, a Spanish citizen who buys a German car financed by a loan from a Spanish commercial bank (we already met Pedro towards the end of Chap. 5). The payment is made via Target2 and gives rise to a Target2 claim in favour of Germany and a Target2 liability for Spain. The Spanish bank that has lost reserves can replenish them at the Bank of Spain. Sinn asserts that Spain has not actually paid Germany anything, and what's more, it can repeat the game. Since, by definition, northerners are upright and southerners are crooks, Sinn cried scandal: the Club Med had found a way to cheat northern countries. They print euros and enjoy our products in exchange for a Target2 accounting entry. If the euro collapses and Target2 disappears, what remains of these claims?

Unfortunately for Sinn, however, this is not *exactly* how things stand.

Until the crisis, Spanish banks replenished the reserves lost due to net imports with loans from German banks. This is the concrete manifestation of the (ex post) flow of German saving to Spain that we met talking about Pedro at the end of Chap. 5. These loans, consisting of liquidity flows from Germany to Spain, cancelled the initial Spanish Target2 liabilities (due to the payment of net imports), so that until the crisis, Target2 balances were practically zero (see Fig. 7.6 in Appendix 2). With breakdown of the interbank market, these loans ceased. Although in principle Spain could have continued to borrow as described by Sinn (via Target2 liabilities and the printing press), it did not do so as a result of fiscal austerity measures (see next section). The negative Target2 balances for Spain arose from the repatriation of (mainly) German loans granted in previous years.

So Prof, what remains of Sinn's story is the fact that by using the "printing press" and exploiting Target2, Spain and Italy were able to avoid default on foreign debt in 2011–2012. Of course, and Sinn shouldn't complain about this since this default would have sunk the euro. Instead, he should complain about the monetary mercantilism and the consequent policy of vendor finance of his country, which is largely responsible for European financial imbalances.

7.7   The Meaning of Austerity

The European crisis of the first half of the last decade lay mainly in balance of payments problems and debt of certain peripheral countries towards core countries. These imbalances could even have continued, if we take Sinn at his word. Here, in my opinion, lies the key to austerity policies adopted then: fiscal austerity was not designed to reduce public debt in relation to GDP, but rather foreign debt. If Greek public debt was 300% of GDP and held by Greeks, it would be their problem. As this debt was largely held by non-nationals, the question became dangerous for foreign creditors. In Chap. 5, we learned that foreign debt arises from living above one's means (like it or not). To pay off that debt, it is necessary to live for a sufficient number of years below one's means. To do so, one way (certainly the worst) is austerity: cuts to the public sector and increased taxation lead to the collapse of aggregate demand and growth. The country begins to import less, and for a given level of exports, it begins to achieve a trade surplus, a sign that by now it is living below its means. The decrease in wages and prices should help external competitiveness: this is called "internal devaluation" in contrast to the classical external devaluation based on depreciating the exchange rate. These measures have to be sufficiently severe to obtain a large enough trade surplus to repay debt instalments and interest. Using what we saw in Chap. 5, it is not enough that the trade balance (the difference between exports and imports) be in surplus, but the current accounts must be in surplus as well (the current accounts include interest payments, among other things). With a large enough current account surplus, the country can begin to pay back its foreign debt (and not just the interest on it).

Are there less painful solutions? In a classic foreign debt crisis of the kind that has occurred repeatedly in developing countries with the debt denominated in foreign currency, if a country cannot manage to pay the instalments and interest, the IMF usually intervenes with the following measures:

- loans so that the country can pay its instalments to foreign creditor banks (we saw that in reality bail-outs concern creditor banks not debtor countries);
- debt restructuring, extensions for repayments and possibly lower interest rates; since what cannot be paid will not be paid, part of the debt can sometimes be condoned (usually after a rock concert with some famous star);

- fiscal austerity imposed on the country to reduce internal demand and generate a current accounts surplus so that the country can meet its repayments (now partly in favour of the IMF);
- a currency devaluation so that the resulting upturn in exports helps create a current account surplus, reducing the severity of austerity by sustaining demand and favouring the trade surplus.

The severity of the austerity that Europe imposed on southern Europe (and Ireland) can be measured by the fact that European adjustment was based on only the first and third of the four measures, while the fourth measure was replaced by internal devaluation (real wages cuts). Greek debt was restructured in 2012, but too little and too late. Besides, the public debt cut was all on the shoulders of the pension funds and the Greek banks, which the state had to recapitalise, incurring debt with the Troika. If the IMF has never been popular in the global south, it is because they never knew Schäuble!

Democratic devaluations. In autumn 2011 the Italian moderate left backed a government led by the mainstream Bocconi economist Mario Monti in order to oust Berlusconi. (This not exactly democratic manoeuvre was openly inspired by the European institutions.) The justification was that leftist austerity was better than right-wing austerity. "What is left and what is right?" sang Giorgio Gaber (an Italian chansonnier) long ago. Which type of devaluation is "less bad", external (of the exchange rate) or internal (of wages)? According to many economists, external devaluation, while involving a decrease in the real wage, affects everyone, whereas internal devaluation mainly affects workers' wages. As well, one can defend oneself from external devaluation by buying national instead of foreign goods. When your wage has been cut you buy less of both. Internal devaluation is also synonymous with deflation: a fall in prices and wages under the axe of austerity. This puts debtors in trouble, whether they are households or firms. Their wages and sales decline while the debt and relative interest payments remain the same. This is the origin of the non-performing loans that burdened Italian banks until recently (a new chapter is opened by the COVID-19 crisis). In short, internal devaluation seems "more bad".

Europe certainly could have done better than this, even without achieving the impossible political federation we spoke about in Chap. 6. But certain governments do not want to hear any talk of Keynesian concertation, Eurobonds and the like.

Now let us return to 2012, when the euro was on the brink of break-up.

7.8   Dragon of Last Resort

The VLTRO played for time but did not alleviate the confidence crisis towards Italian and Spanish sovereign debt. In July 2012, it seemed increasingly likely that the two countries would incur prohibitive interest rates and be forced to redenominate their public debt in a new sovereign currency. Thus we come to Draghi's famous euro-rescuing statement on 26th July 2012. On 2nd August, the ECB announced that it might resume purchasing government bonds, as it did in 2010 and again in 2011 with the SMP, but this time on an unlimited scale. The announcement was formalised on 6th September 2012. The purchase of bonds on the market was among the operations in the ECB arsenal, and we know from the previous chapter that it goes under the name of Outright Monetary Transactions, OMTs.

The official justification of OMT was still to ensure the transmission of monetary policy, but this time the aim of preventing a sovereign debt crisis was more evident, if not openly declared. Fears in certain European capitals that the OMT umbrella could induce troubled countries to suspend their fiscal adjustment efforts led to a number of conditions being attached to the rescue program. As I said in Sect. 6.9, the OMT would thus also involve support by the ESM, the state rescue fund, and a Memorandum of Understanding (MoU), consisting of severe fiscal adjustment measures, had to be signed with the European institutions.

In this way, ECB intervention is subordinate to coeval financial support from the ESM and to the country bailed out surrendering its fiscal sovereignty. Violation of the MoU is punished with interruption of the OMT programme. This calls its own bluff. How can the ECB interrupt support to a country in the OMT programme, when OMT was activated because failing to help that country could lead to break-up of the euro?

The complicated rules that accompany OMT make its effectiveness untimely in the face of a financial crisis, and unacceptable to the affected country. The OMT was also overshadowed by a case lodged with the German Constitutional Court alleging that the program violated the principle that the ECB was not to finance sovereign debt. The Karlsruhe court referred the final decision to the European Court of Justice which ruled in favour of the ECB. In June 2016, Karlsruhe finally endorsed OMT. With the prospect of Brexit materialising a few days later, it had little choice.

Even with these limits, the OMT was certainly effective in bringing long-term interest rates down to more sustainable levels for Spain and Italy. One result was renewed flows of capital between the core and the periphery and early repayment of VLTRO funds in 2013 and 2014. Target2 balances were effectively reduced (see Fig. 7.6 in Appendix 2). With OMT, the ECB went from reacting to acting, although the big bazooka, as OMT was called, did not fire a single shot. This demonstrates how unfounded some fears were: an unlimited guarantee by the ECB on Italian and Spanish bonds was enough to largely settle the spread crisis, without Frankfurt having to purchase a single one. Had it been done sooner, much unnecessary distress would have been spared.

Prof, I see that Target2 balances increase again from 2015. Yes, this has something to do with QE, so we shall deal with it later.

7.9   Hysterical Deflation: 2014

In contrast with the inflation hypochondria in certain quarters, in 2014 observers of the European economy began to fear deflation. It is not surprising that deflation should occur after years of hard austerity and increasing inequality. Again it was left to the ECB to fight it: deflation means falling prices, or a negative inflation rate. The main task of the ECB's mandate was to maintain the inflation rate "below but close to 2%", so the ECB was able to act and it did. However, since it could not remove the underlying causes of deflation, including the absence of a proactive European fiscal policy, ECB action proved difficult.

Deflation is the worst of all evils, above all because it troubles debtors, the most fragile link in the chain. In capitalism, economic expansions are associated with credit booms, and the heritage of booms is high firm and household debt. If with deflation prices and wages begin to fall, firm sales and household incomes collapse while the debt to pay remains unchanged. Many households and firms become unable to repay their debt, increasing the non-performing loans held by banks, and making banks more reluctant to grant credit to others. Many subjects react by cutting expenditure, or postpone it until prices fall, putting the economy into an endless deflationary spiral.

Draghi is an enigmatic, or perhaps simply astute personality. He often used the language of "structural reforms", famously in his unfortunate interview to the *Wall Street Journal* in 2012 when he declared: "The European social model has already gone".[3] However, since he knew how things stood, he could not lie, especially in front of his American mentors. This surfaced in an important speech he made at Jackson Hole in September 2014,[4] where he underlined

---

[3] https://www.ecb.europa.eu/press/inter/date/2012/html/sp120224.en.html. Accessed 10 May 2020.
[4] Draghi (2014).

that the risk of doing too little to sustain aggregate demand was much greater than the risk of doing too much; the risk being that cyclic (short term) unemployment in Europe become structural (long term).

Hysterical Europe. Hysteresis is what scientists call the persistent effects of events after removal of their cause. In economics, it may happen that protracted recessions destroy production capacity, since firms can stay afloat for a while, but eventually they have to close their activity and lay off their workers. Should there be a miraculous upturn in aggregate demand, it is often difficult to return to pre-crisis output levels simply because many plants and many professional skills have disappeared.

Draghi was referring to hysteresis when he said:

Demand side policies are not only justified by the significant cyclical component in unemployment. They are also relevant because, given prevailing uncertainty, they help insure against the risk that a weak economy is contributing to hysteresis effects. Indeed, while in normal conditions uncertainty would imply a higher degree of caution for fear of over-shooting, at present the situation is different. The risks of "doing too little"—i.e. that cyclical unemployment becomes structural—outweigh those of "doing too much"—that is, excessive upward wage and price pressures.

As noted by Marco Buti, a former Director General for Economic and Financial Affairs at the European Commission, the final words evoke those which Keynes addressed to the US president, Franklin D. Roosevelt in 1933: "I do not blame Mr Ickes [US secretary of the interior] for being cautious and careful. But the risks of less speed must be weighed against those of more haste. He must get across the crevasses before it is dark".[5]

Draghi's warning was accompanied by support to structural reforms, as expected. However, his observation on inadequate growth of wages, even in eurozone countries that were not under stress, was more important, as was his observation on the existence of room for expansionary budget policies backed by monetary policy, as happened in the United States and Japan:

Turning to fiscal policy, since 2010 the euro area has suffered from fiscal policy being less available and effective, especially compared with other large advanced economies. This is not so much a consequence of high initial debt ratios—pub-

---

[5] Buti (2020, pp. 7–8).

lic debt is in aggregate not higher in the euro area than in the US or Japan. It reflects the fact that the central bank in those countries could act and has acted as a backstop for government funding. This is an important reason why markets spared their fiscal authorities the loss of confidence that constrained many euro area governments' market access. This has in turn allowed fiscal consolidation in the US and Japan to be more backloaded.

This was widely read as a serious accusation to those European governments who rejected coordinated fiscal and monetary policies. The European economic constitution is fundamentally anti-Keynesian, with monetary policy concerned mainly with price stability and no pro-active fiscal policy at federal level (as exists in the United States). If someone breaks the rules and gets into trouble, the principle of responsibility enshrined by ordoliberalism holds: the person responsible pays. So no forgiveness in Europe for debtors.

But then Prof, who deals with employment? From the European perspective, the problem of full employment is fundamentally national: each country has to solve it by appropriate labour market reform, in the spirit of the most doctrinaire marginalism described in Chap. 3.

Prof, but Keynes... Yes, in Keynes the problem of full employment is international, *global* we would say today. We discussed it in Chaps. 4 and 5. Growth and employment should be pursued by internationally coordinated monetary and fiscal policies, as was done for a brief period in 2009, and that was essential to come out of the global crisis. But the dominant European power and its satellites have not yet learned the lesson. At the same time, the problems and conflicts in global trade that have emerged in recent years, and in 2020 after the COVID-19 pandemic, revealed that overdependence on foreign markets and "value chains" can be a major danger. But it is too early to say whether this will lead to a rethinking of monetary mercantilism.

But Prof, aren't international Keynesianism and Keynes's "national self-sufficiency"[6] contradictory?

No, International Keynesianism implies that countries in the first place develop their domestic demand and national production capacity, not entrusting their destiny completely to foreign trade. Europe has the ideal size to develop such a strategy, but it was constructed as a poor imitation of German monetary mercantilism.

In 2014, five long years after the Fed, the ECB brought interest rates almost to zero. This measure was accompanied by a commitment to keep them low

---

[6] See Chap. 5, Further Reading.

"for a long time". The idea was that long-term interest rates, those important for credit to "households and firms", depend on the current short-term interest rate and on expectations regarding its trend in future years. The ECB's promise to keep interest rates at zero in future was calculated to lower long-term interest rates. This was a policy used by the Fed since 2011, known as forward guidance. But again it is a case of bringing the horse to water, without being able to make it drink: unless austerity was brought to an end, there was no reason why the economy would show an upturn.

While the dreaded deflation was materialising, Draghi repeatedly alluded to the adoption of quantitative easing. In January 2015, 7 years after the Fed, Draghi announced that QE would begin in March. Known as the Public Securities Purchase Programme (PSPP), impressive in size, QE without expansionary fiscal policy is the proverbial mountain that gave rise to a mouse. QE is a way for the central bank to expand the liquidity of the system by purchasing long-term bonds, fundamentally public but also private, in order to decrease long-term interest rates. When the central bank purchases bonds on the market, it drives up their price and drives down their yield. It is said that with forward guidance, the ECB announced a long-term policy of low interest rates; with QE it put its money where its mouth is.

Let us take the case (Ricardian vice) of a bond worth €100 on 1st January and that will pay €5 on 31st December. If you buy at €100 at the start of the year, its yield at the end of the year will be 5%/year. However, suppose that QE drives up the price of the bond to €110 and that you buy it anyway. At the end of the year, the yield will have decreased to (5/110)% or about 4.5%.

With its refinancing operations in the period 2008–2014, the ECB only reacted passively, leaving it to the banking system to decide how much liquidity to absorb. When it finally began to operate pro-actively—virtually with OMT and then effectively with QE—it injected liquidity into the system by increasing its bond portfolio.

Carrots and sticks. When QE began in earnest at the start of 2015, it had been preceded by various mini-QEs aimed at sustaining the financial bond market (Covered Bonds Purchasing Programme 3, Asset Backed Securities Purchasing Programme). Already in June 2014, the ECB had decided to bring interest rates on excess reserves down to negative values (see below box Negative interest rates). Table 7.2 shows the interest rate corridor as of April 2020.

The ECB promised to maintain this policy until inflation returned to its target (forward guidance) and therefore did not exclude further decreases.

Table 7.2 ECB interest rates, effective since 18 September 2019

Marginal lending facility	0.25%
Main refinancing operations	0%
Marginal deposit	−0.50%

Source: ECB

7.10 Quantitative Fantasies

The objective of QE is to sustain aggregate demand—not to support employment (heaven forbid)—solely to bring inflation to its target level "below but close to 2%". The immediate effects of QE were to increase the value of the bonds purchased, decrease the long-term rate of interest and increase the liquidity available to the system, strengthening the promise to maintain short-term interest rates at zero, set out in the forward guidance.

The increase in value of the bonds can also occur via the "portfolio effect": subjects who sell bonds to the ECB find themselves with excess liquidity and inevitably buy others. Since the central bank mainly purchases government bonds, the portfolio effect essentially unfolds with transmission of the increase in government bond prices to the private segments of the financial market. From these first effects, others affecting aggregate demand were presumed to follow:

1. A first alleged effect was to stimulate credit creation by supplying extra reserves to banks: a clearly implausible effect, because since 2008, the banks had not been short of liquidity.
2. A second effect was an increase in the value of long-term bonds to support investment. This effect is based on the traditional idea of falling "marginal returns" on investment (or on capital), a flawed analytical concept that we met in Chap. 3. According to this theory, to be profitable, an investment must yield a marginal return almost equal (if not greater) than the long-term interest rate, which represents the cost of capital for entrepreneurs. A decrease in this rate, therefore, makes previously unprofitable investment projects profitable. In practice, QE should increase the market for financial assets that could therefore be issued offering lower interest rates. Non-financial (e.g. manufacturing and service) firms could therefore profitably finance additional investment. However, it can be excluded in theory and in practice that a decrease in long-term interest rates stimulates investment, especially under expectations of negative demand.
3. A third presumed effect is on consumption, elicited by wealth effects. This happens when an increase in real estate or financial assets prompts households to spend more. An increase in financial wealth probably has more

effect in the United States, where it is more widespread, than in Europe. The increase in value of financial wealth also favours the most affluent classes (who have a lower propensity to consume), and therefore has inappropriate redistributive effects and weak effects on demand.

4. According to the expectations view, QE transmits the message, to households and firms, that the central bank is absolutely determined to fight the recession. This creates expectations of future higher inflation. The idea is that if buyers expect an increase in prices, they purchase sooner (whereas if buyers expect deflation, they wait for prices to fall before purchasing). This game of expectations is also based on the popularity of the idea that more liquidity leads to more inflation, an idea corroborated academically by monetarism. This "autosuggestion game" is however fragile: inflation will only effectively increase if buyers believe it will increase, and if they hurry to spend enough to effectively increase it. People therefore have to have great confidence in the inflationary credibility of central banks that for years have sought to build an opposite credibility as guardians of monetary stability. This extremely imaginative game of expectations is a sign of the decadence of economic analysis and of the gradual predominance of subjective analyses that we have denounced since Chap. 2. There is also an underlying implication that the free market would lead spontaneously to full employment, were it not for people's wrong expectations. The objective truth is that in many parts of Europe, people do not spend because austerity policies and increasing social inequality have impaired the quality and quantity of jobs and have reduced wages, not merely because they have negative expectations.

On the basis of these first four presumed effects, QE seemed a desperate measure. Several years ago, Ulrich Bindseil, an excellent German economist in a position of responsibility at the ECB, commented on the first QE conducted by the Bank of Japan in distant 2001: "Although it may be unclear how exactly an excess reserves target is supposed to help a country escape from the deflationary trap, it at least seems unlikely to do any harm",[7] as if to say *why not, it can't hurt*. Referring to the Japanese experience of 2001, an eminent American-Taiwanese economist, Richard Koo, described QE as the twenty-first century's greatest monetary non-event.[8]

However, there are three other more plausible effects of QE:

---

[7] Bindseil (2004a, p. 41).
[8] Koo (2011).

5. The first is currency depreciation: excess liquidity in people's portfolios will also in fact be invested in foreign financial markets, so the greater demand for foreign currency to purchase foreign assets will cause depreciation of the national currency. Yet, in the case of the euro area, which already had a significant trade surplus towards the rest of the world (mainly from a single country), this strategy still sounds irresponsible: instead of reviving domestic demand and sustaining the global economy, Europe is dumping its problems on other world regions. The logic is one of competitive devaluations. The euro had indeed depreciated against the dollar even before QE began. The progressive decline in interest rates and the expectation of QE went in this direction.

6. The second was securing a part of sovereign debt and lowering the interest rates paid by Club Med governments with a consequent saving on expenditure (the interest rates of core countries went below zero bringing even greater advantages). Too bad this saving was not seized as an occasion for expansionary fiscal policy, but remained a bland attenuation of austerity. The Italian government, for instance, saved 30 billion in interest payments in 2013–2015 (Bank of Italy data), but deflation lowered tax revenues, consuming all or part of that saving. A further expansive effect of lower interest rates is to make household debt less onerous, so that households can consume more.

7. One final outcome of QE concerns banks. The increase in value of the sovereign bonds they hold benefits them because it increases the value of the assets on the balance sheet and because those bonds are collateral for borrowing on the interbank market. These effects predispose banks to grant more credit, though it should always be remembered that the amount depends on the demand for loans.

On the opposite side, critics of QE pointed out negative effects for savers: with low or negative interest rates, savers in core countries would earn lower yields on their pension funds, reacting with greater saving. In some countries, QE would therefore reduce demand instead of reviving it. As recalled in Chap. 6, this argument has been widely used by the German media to depict Draghi as a vampire of German savers. However, an ECB paper by Ulrich Bindseil et al.[9] counter-argued that the ECB's intervention was in the long-term interests of German savers because it supported the eurozone economy.

---

[9] Bindseil et al. (2015).

To accumulate savings by putting other countries into debt is in any case not a sign of wisdom or foresight. It could also be added that the German government's savings in interest payments could have abundantly covered income losses of low-middle income savers via tax relief or social transfers. Disproving the image of "Count Draghila"—a name borrowed from the German press[10] to indicate "expropriator of German savers"—the German member of the ECB's executive board, Isabel Schnabel, explains that for a loss of €500 a year for the German saver, the German debtor (well they exist!) saved €2000 and the German government €400 billion since 2017 (Schnabel writes in February 2020).[11] My German friends can be proud of such intellectual honesty!

Quantitative easing in practice. Draghi's QE began in March 2015 with the purchase 60 billion euro's worth of bonds per month until September 2016 and beyond, if the target inflation rate *below or close to 2%* was not achieved. The central banks of Eurosystem member countries were assigned a monthly target of their national government bonds to purchase—the targets were proportional to the countries' shares of ECB capital (the so-called capital key), roughly reflecting their demographic and economic weight. Since the inflation target was not in view, in December 2015 the ECB announced continuation until March 2017 and beyond, an increase in purchases to 80 billion per month, consisting of 64 billion in government bonds, and rollover of bonds at maturity. The types of asset purchased were also broadened so that in June 2016 it also included securities of large companies. The QE scheme envisaged that 80% of the bonds purchased by each national central bank would consist of domestic bonds. In this way, any associated losses would weigh mainly on national central banks. However, the idea that a drop in the value of a euro area country's government bonds falls exclusively on the central bank of that country contradicts the fact that in order to prevent a euro crisis, no major country is allowed to fail. In other words, if a large country is in difficulty, the ECB is forced to intervene to support it. The 80% clause thus appears to be another hypocritical measure designed to reassure public opinion in certain countries that they will not be involved in any rescue of unreliable partners.

Besides QE, in 2014 the ECB continued its passive policy of making cheap liquidity available to banks, renewing the LTRO of late 2011 that had lasted 3 years. It did so with TLTRO I, in which long-term refinancing granted to banks at low interest rates in 2015 and 2016 was made conditional on expansion of credit by the banks, with the usual idea of *pushing on a string* (the expression is attributed to Keynes); and TLTRO II in 2016 and 2017, even with negative refinancing interest rates (equal to the interest rate paid by the deposit facility). Hence a bank that borrowed from the ECB and left the liquidity in its account would break even.

---

[10] https://www.bild.de/bild-plus/geld/wirtschaft/politik-inland/ezb-leitzins-schlecht-fuer-sparer-frau-merkel-stoppen-sie-endlich-den-minus-zins-64669942,view=conversionToLogin.bild.html, accessed 4 May 2020.

[11] Schnabel (2020).

Prof, this is an upside-down world: one gains by borrowing and one pays to deposit! Indeed. With TLTRO II Draghi may have wanted to ensure liquidity at zero cost to all banks, especially those of the periphery, as a buffer against bank crises; and perhaps punish core banks who were the ones holding surplus liquidity. In March 2019, TLTRO III was launched, this time, however, not at negative interest rates. QE was gradually tapered (60, 30, then 15 billion in net monthly purchases) and temporarily terminated in December 2018. In September 2019, the Governing Council of the ECB decided to restart QE on 1st November at a monthly pace of €20 billion, just after the end of Draghi's presidency and Christine Lagarde's takeover. The ECB also confirmed that it will continue to hold the assets purchased under the programme "for an extended period of time", renewing purchases at maturity. The vampire's last bite?

Christine Lagarde's first challenge as president of the ECB in mid-March 2020 was handled in a clumsy manner. Instead of reassuring the financial markets regarding the impact of costly health and economic support measures on the countries with higher debt struck by the pandemic, she announced a reverse "whatever it takes". Perhaps inspired by Isabel Schnabel, she declared that the ECB was not there to narrow bond spreads.[12] Her declaration wreaked havoc on the Italian government bond market. Fortunately a few days later, inspired by the chief economist Philip Lane, the ECB increased the QE program by 750 billion (Pandemic Emergency Purchase Programme), giving up the "capital key" allocation of purchases and thus indicating a preference for purchases of the most troubled government bonds. This measure calmed but did not completely reassure the markets regarding the Italian government's ability to weather the crisis in the absence of a sharing (mutualisation) of at least the new debts by the rest of Europe. In other words, interest rates on Italian government bonds remain at unsustainable levels (see Sect. 4.7).

Manna from heaven. An extreme version of QE, backed by many well-known economists, is that of helicopter money, an expression attributed to Milton Friedman and made popular by Ben Bernanke in 2002. It consists in distributing a certain amount of money issued by the central bank to all citizens. In actual fact, it is a form of fiscal policy financed by the central bank, in which the state transfers a lump sum to its citizens. The objective is a positive shock to aggregate demand. However, it seems just another emergency measure, arising more from desperation than from a will to tackle the basic distributive and policy problems at the root of weak aggregate demand.

---

[12] Eurointelligence, 6 April 2020.

7.11   QE and Target2, or Buba Buys Italian Government Bonds

Prof, I see from Fig. 7.6 (Appendix 2) *that Target2 imbalances have been expanding again since 2015. Is this related to QE?* The ECB's official version is that it is a technical question linked to the QE procedure. An alternative explanation has to do with capital flight from peripheral countries. Whatever the correct explanation is, our old friend Werner Sinn has new reasons to be worried. Beginning with the ECB's version, we saw that QE was implemented with purchase of assets entrusted to individual central banks. Since many potential sellers were extra-European, for example American investment funds, purchases necessarily took place in Frankfurt where these bondholders operate. The Bundesbank therefore had to be in charge of the purchases, and it began to issue euros to buy the bonds, for example, Italian or Spanish bonds. The bonds were then transferred, for example, to the Bank of Italy in exchange for…

I can guess, Prof, in exchange for a positive Target2 entry (a claim) for Buba and a negative Target2 entry (a liability) for the Bank of Italy. Buba repurchased the Italian government bonds and returned them to the Bank of Italy in exchange for a Target2 liability. Exactly! As I wrote in 2017, the Bank of Italy, i.e. the Italian state, repurchased its bonds by issuing a Target2 liability, in practice obtaining a loan of unspecified term at zero interest from Germany. As Sinn wrote a year later,[13] the ECB had granted Italy an "asset swap" (which we could translate here as a shell or three-card game): i.e. the Italian Treasury swapped a debt towards private persons or companies, such as an American investment fund, with one between the Bank of Italy and the Bundesbank with no specified term and (currently) interest free.

OK Prof, but even if the euro broke down and Italy repudiated its Target2 balance, what does Germany lose? Plenty! The Bundesbank issued euros which are now in the hands of American investment funds, and these euros are a payment instrument with which German (or other eurozone countries') goods and financial activities can be purchased. To eliminate this threat, Sinn's proposal is for each country to settle its Target2 liabilities at the end of each year, if necessary with real or financial activities. This is unimaginable.

The second explanation of the rise in Target2 balances is complementary. It concerns capital flight by Italian (and Spanish) investors. Once an Italian investor, say, has sold her Italian government bonds to the Bank of Italy via QE, she might wish to park her money safely in Germany (fearing for

---

[13] Sinn (2018).

example an Italexit). As we know, when money is transferred from an Italian bank to a German bank, the Bundesbank is obliged to credit reserves to the German bank. In exchange, it obtains a Target2 claim on the Eurosystem.

In this case, Prof, Germany risks nothing. I'm not so sure. Buba created euros for Giovanna (an exporter of capital), and they are a payment instrument with which German goods (or goods of euro area countries) can be bought, while if Italy leaves the euro and reneges on its Target2 liabilities, Germany loses its potential claims on Italian products and assets.

And if Giovanna brings the euros into Italy? Giovanna gains because she converts the euros she has in Germany into nuova-liras with a good exchange rate as a result of nuova lira's depreciation from 1 nuova lira per euro to, say, 1.2 nuova lira per euro. Had she kept her euros in Italy, she would not have had this advantage: the euros would have been converted at the initial rate of 1:1. This is a classical exchange rate speculation. But Italy gains too, by finding itself with Giovanna's euros in its official reserves, and they are a medium of payment with which German (or other euro area) goods and assets can be bought. However, it is plausible that in the event of Italexit, Target 2 balances would be the subject of political negotiations.

Banking disunion. It is easier to explain economics when it intrudes into the lives of normal people. For many, *bail-in* and *deposit insurance* are now part of the general vocabulary. As mentioned above, in June 2012, intention to create a solid and supportive European banking union was announced. To make sense of this announcement, let us recall that bank crises occurring in single states of the United States are solved by federal financial intervention. This ensures that single states, which like European countries no longer have their own central bank, are not burdened with the task of saving banks; in this way, they avoid what has been defined as a "doom loop" (see Sect. 7.5). The European banking union that finally took form in 2014 is however very different from the American one. It is limited to making supervision of banks uniform, and not even completely, and this task is assigned to the ECB. The mechanism used to resolve bank crises is basically by bail-in, i.e. losses are paid by the bigger shareholders and creditors of the troubled banks (only customers with accounts below €100,000 are exempt, perhaps). After bail-in, any help to the banks comes from a European banking fund of "up to 55 billion euro". The details of further help from the ESM in case of systemic bank crises, and above all from the European Deposit Insurance System (EDIS) to safeguard deposits under €100,000, are still uncertain. Before EDIS can be launched, Berlin asks European banks (read Italian banks) to reduce the amount of domestic treasury bonds they are holding, so as to protect themselves against any domestic fiscal crisis. According to the Italian government, such a measure would destabilise its treasury bonds. The situation has therefore reached an impasse.

Negative interest rates (wonkish). It is not easy to explain the policy of the ECB and other central banks of lowering interest rates below zero. Official explanations are often unsatisfactory. Mainstream explanations are often plagued with the problems of marginalist theory. To focus on the problem, let us consider a lecture by a former Vice-President of the ECB, Vítor Constâncio. He came from the Club Med, was close to Draghi, and as we shall see, he endorsed some economic heterodoxy. In an unusual excursus on the history of economic thought (which takes us back over what we said in the initial chapters), Constâncio goes in search of the ghost of the natural interest rate, and refers to the results of the Cambridge capital controversy that we mentioned in Chap. 3. He does so correctly: mainstream economists associate the natural interest rate with the rate of return on the factor "capital", measured by its marginal productivity. However, Constâncio explains, how can "capital goods be aggregated in a variable called capital using prices that require an interest rate in order to be calculated, when at the same time it is supposed that the interest rate depends on the marginal productivity of capital?" This is precisely the vicious circle we talked about in Chap. 3. It is unfortunate that Constâncio did not force his staff at the ECB to sit for an examination in capital theory. In Chap. 3, we concluded that the natural interest rate, elusive in theory, is unknowable in practice. How can economics have credibility as a science if it recognises that its theoretical quantities are unknowable in practice? Were it the Higgs boson! So Constâncio refers to a goldfish guru (you will remember the forgetful goldfish in Chap. 1), Michael Woodford (Columbia University), the guru of mainstream monetary theory, who re-fishes the "Wicksell method" to pin down the boson, arguing that: "As the real equilibrium rate is unobservable, as in the case of Wicksell, evidence that the policy and market rates were deviating from the natural rate would be given by the change in inflation".[14] Here you will recognize the rule explained in Chap. 3: if prices increase, it means that aggregate demand is too strong, which means that the central bank is keeping the interest rate too low (below its natural level) and should raise it. If prices fall, it means that aggregate demand is too weak, which means that the central bank is keeping the interest rate too high (above the natural rate), and should lower it.

In this way, Constâncio exonerates the ECB of accusations that the bank was expropriating German savers with its policy of fighting deflation with low interest rates. No, he argued, the ECB does what theory demands, "because monetary policy is part of the solution and not part of the problem" (Isabel Schnabel uses the same argument). Naturally, we side with Constâncio in his common-sense battle against free criticism of the ECB, and it might be a good rhetorical strategy to contradict the adversary using its own (mainstream) theory. However, Lenin said that truth was revolutionary.

---

[14] As summed up by Constâncio (2016).

So we would have preferred Vítor to draw his conclusions from Sraffa, concluding that the natural interest rate (a sort of Plato's noumenon) does not exist and that the interest rate is therefore entirely a creature of central banks. In this sense, Vítor should have replied to the ECB critics: *Dear friends, you burden the euro area with exactly the opposite of the fiscal and wage policies necessary to pull it out of the crisis. We at the ECB do what we can to sustain aggregate demand by low interest rates. This is an act of responsibility that avoids a catastrophe of the euro and of your savings.* But clearly a central banker cannot say this (or can he? At Jackson Hole, Draghi went close). Be that as it may, according to Constâncio, persistent deflation indicates that the natural interest rate has become persistently lower. And why is it low? On one hand, he evokes the saving glut of Ben Bernanke, who found a scapegoat for the American financial crisis in the Chinese saving glut. (The standard argument is that due to the absence of a public pension system in China, ordinary Chinese have to save a great amount for their old age.) Turning the world upside-down, it was therefore not the accommodating monetary policy of the Fed, together with deregulation and tax incentives, that generated the American pre-crisis construction boom and upset the current accounts between the United States and China, but vice versa. It was the Chinese saving glut invested in American bonds that generated the fall in interest rates (Fig. 7.3). In other words, too much global saving is supposed to have reduced the marginal productivity of capital, and monetary policy was obliged to indulge it by reducing interest rates.

Constâncio then evokes another cause of the fall of the natural interest rate, namely "secular stagnation" and "chronic weakness of demand" (see Box in Sect. 4.10). In line with Paul Krugman, this may be described by an investment curve so depressed that it intersects the saving supply curve only at negative interest rates (at B instead of A of normal times; Fig. 7.4).

But Krugman himself confessed the dirty little secret that the interest rate does not affect investment. This confirms in practice what Sraffa explained in theory, namely that Figs. 7.3 and 7.4 are pure fiction. Leaving aside Bernanke's and Krugman's flawed arguments, we may therefore simply argue that interest rates, as creatures of central banks, are kept low to revive aggregate demand, keeping down interest rates on public debt, mortgages and consumer credit, sustaining financial markets and depreciating the exchange rate. But why negative interest rates?

Here Constâncio evokes Keynes's *liquidity trap*. If you recall Chap. 4, the trap concerns the central bank's attempt of keeping interest rates sufficiently low. As we said, the central bank controls short-term interest rates, but long-term interest rates are its real objective as they affect aggregate demand. Once short-term interest rates are at zero (the lower bound) they can only increase: this is how the market reasons, according to Constâncio. And since long-term interest rates depend on expected short-term interest rates (see previous box "Short- and long-term interest rates"), if the latter are expected to rise, attempts to lower long-term rates may fail. And here Constâncio quotes Sir John Hicks (1904–1989) perhaps the most ingenious marginalist after Knut Wicksell, initiator of the move to make Keynes a special case of mainstream theory: "In an extreme case, the shortest short-term rate may perhaps be nearly zero. But if so, the long-term rate must lie above it, for the long rate has to allow for the risk that the short rate may rise during the currency of the loan, and it should be observed that the short rate can only rise, it cannot fall".[15]

You will remember that the price of bonds has an inverse relationship to the interest rate (Sect. 7.9). I will not buy a bond if I expect higher interest rates, because my bond will lose value. But, Constâncio argues, Hicks is wrong to say that zero interest rates can only rise: the ECB and other central banks are demonstrating that they can continue to fall. Since 2014, the ECB has brought the interest rate on the deposit facility below zero and, Vitor reports, the ECB was ready to do so for the target interest rate, as it publicly declared in its forward guidance announcements. Naturally, Vitor does not fail to recite the mantra that negative rates on excess liquidity are designed to stimulate banks to expand credit and investment, and that the aim is certainly not competitive devaluation of the euro.

What is the moral of the tale? Taking interest rates below zero to obtain a true upturn is like tilting windmills, perhaps with the aim to force Berlin to endorse expansive fiscal policies, but not without utility for keeping interest rates low on sovereign debt and keeping the euro depreciated. However, it is irresponsible towards the global economy to keep the euro depreciated with European current accounts in surplus!

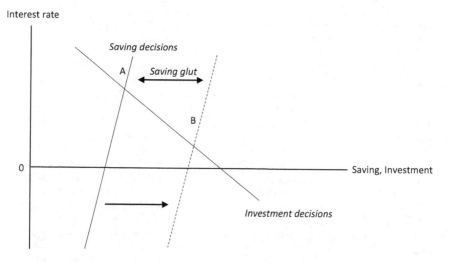

Fig. 7.3 In the world of Ben: negative equilibrium interest rates and saving glut

---

[15] Hicks (1937, p. 155).

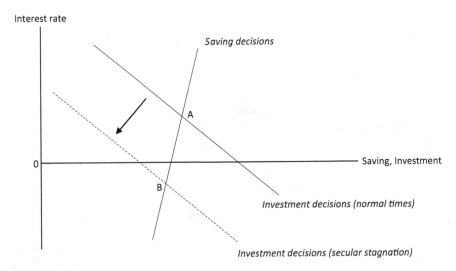

Fig. 7.4   In the world of Paul: negative equilibrium interest rates and investor pessimism

7.12 Ch€rnobyl

Before you leave us, Prof, what are the prospects? What should we do? In more recent years, it has been confirmed that Italy is the weak link in the euro. In 2016–2017, the governments guided by the Partito Democratico (a left-of-centre party) conducted a policy of stabilising the public debt-to-GDP ratio accompanied by modest positive growth. This policy was favoured by relatively (though still not sufficiently) low interest rates on public debt and by the European and world upturn, which allowed slightly less restrictive fiscal policy. A new neo-populist government (a coalition of Five-Star Movement and Lega) took over in late spring 2018, when the global economy was entering a slower phase. The German government had some responsibility for this deceleration, since its mercantilist policy continued through a restrictive fiscal stance (the government budget *schwarze Null* balance) that depressed the European economy and led to protectionist reactions by the United States. In Italy, anti-euro proclamations by the neo-populist government and announcements of very expensive fiscal measures (later scaled down), together with the imminent end of QE (December 2018), again pushed the spreads to high levels (above 250 points). Growth back down below 1%, reduced fiscal margins due to a fall in taxation revenue, an increase in expenditure for interest on public debt, and relatively ineffective fiscal measures made the results of the coalition government rather dismal. In any case, that coalition did not last, replaced in late summer 2019 by a Five-Star Movement—Democratic Party coalition. The resulting improvement in European and market confidence benefited the new government with lower interest rates on public debt (although still higher than French, German and Spanish ones). As we said, expansionary fiscal policies and growth are possible even with high public debt, but only if the mean interest rate on debt is less than the rate of growth. Italy was in the opposite situation, alone among European countries. At the beginning of 2020, against a bleak international economic background, with Italy oscillating between incoherent populism and servility to Brussels and Europe, the COVID-19 pandemic broke out.

The European "populist" right is now distinct from the classical liberal right. The cosmopolitan left is split into liberal-compassionate and radical-compassionate wings. The populist right is an ambiguous paladin of a welfare state where national citizens have precedence. It offers a partial response to the losers of cosmopolitan globalisation, promising privileged access to jobs and public services. According to the prevalent interpretation, the victory of Brexit was for instance based on this message. Classic fascism came to power on similar messages aimed at the masses of unemployed veterans and at people disinherited by absurd war debt and liberal policies. A disconsolate Austrian economist confided to me that big capital was counting on the liberal-compassionate left to implement its designs of globalisation of financial markets and labour, because the right had an excessively nationalist tradition.

The challenge for the non-liberal left is enormous. Its soul is divided between its inescapable ideals of international solidarity on one hand, and fear of globalization (including uncontrolled immigration) expressed by its traditional popular basis on the other. A new internationalism has to involve returning decisional space to nation-states and a strong drive for international cooperation, particularly in Europe.

As we said, the prospect of a Hayekian Europe with a minimal federal state that controls both monetary and fiscal policy, is unacceptable. Unfortunately, Europe can only move in this direction in line with Hayek's lesson on the impossibility of a federal, progressive Europe recalled in Chap. 6.

Prof, why then don't countries like Italy leave the eurozone? Ordinary people fear the consequences of a break-down of the euro. They are not completely wrong, because it would certainly be a dramatic event. Even calling a referendum or holding a parliamentary debate in which exit had a chance of victory would lead financial markets to panic for fear that Italian debt might be redenominated in a new currency. Spreads on Italian treasury bonds would hit the stars. At that point, Italy either leaves or backtracks, swearing allegiance to the single currency again, with its reputation for financial reliability in shreds (once a traitor, always a traitor). Italy would become a protectorate of the Troika.

Exit from the euro would bring at least three very serious questions with it:

(a) How much of the foreign and public debt can be legally redenominated in new lira in view of the class action clause mentioned above (Sect. 7.4)? If debt remains in euros (and this currency survives the earthquake), its cost in new lira will increase dramatically in proportion to depreciation of the new currency (plausibly 20–30%). However, redenomination of public debt may open serious legal issues.

(b) A country that leaves would be disconnected from the Target2 system of payments (remember that interbank payments rely on an IT platform called Target2). Does this mean that the national banking system would be blocked for a significant period of time, bringing economic activity to a standstill?

(c) The other countries could retaliate through trade: remember that German and French industrialists wanted Italy in the euro to prevent it from exploiting a competitive exchange rate outside the monetary union.

I have always thought that a country's exit from the euro can only be the result of a collapse of events. The COVID-19 pandemic could prepare the perfect storm. The storm could consist in an abrupt increase in the ratio of Italian public debt to GDP and a corresponding increase in interest rates; rejection of a radical mutualisation of sovereign debt (eurobonds) by Europe; Italian refusal to resort to the ESM and to sign a Memorandum of Understanding; the consequent refusal of the ECB to intervene with unlimited support for Italian government bonds.

Prof, does this mean that we have to remain inert in the face of events? Certainly not. Our task is to ensure that an intellectual black-out does not obscure what happens. This means continuing to explain that in some countries the élite's consensus regarding the single currency arose from a design to dismantle social conflict and welfare claims, and in others as a way to protect their mercantilist model. The EMU deprives nation-states of their autonomous levers of economic policy, which are handed over to supranational bodies, out of reach of national social conflict. We have to admit that international working class solidarity is little more than an ideal and that utopians often do a lot of damage (as taught by political realism).[16] Without utopias, we have to decline national autonomy in the sense of solidarity towards other peoples, for a new international economic and political order. In this framework, we also have to

---

[16] Cf., e.g. Zolo (2002).

explain that in theory we know how to make a monetary union work, and that even without achieving a redistributive Europe, other reasonable measures are possible. We discussed this towards the end of Chap. 6. Obstacles are political, starting with the German mercantilist model, but also prejudice between European populations. These obstacles are hard to overcome. Although cruel to accept, the truth about Europe is more useful to the pro-European cause than pointless appeals to European solidarity.

Finally, as an Italian, I do not forget that the "bel paese" is above all victim of itself and its historical vices, which are more accentuated in part of the country, where the purpose and virtue of the private sector is to swindle thy neighbour, and that of public employees is to swindle the state (i.e. the community). With this mentality one cannot go far. Since World War 2, part of the country has been able to drag Italy into the league of more advanced countries. The economic miracle failed in the sixties when an extremely mediocre Italian bourgeoisie was unable to regulate social conflict progressively, and to guide manufacturing in the necessary technological leap (probably possible at the time). All this can begin to change from querulous self-denigration to a virtuous circle, only if a different macroeconomic context helps the Italian economy to return to decent growth. These problems have obviously become more dramatic since the pandemic.

In the words of the poet:

Don't ask us for the phrase that can open worlds,
just a few gnarled syllables, dry like a branch.
This, today, is all that we can tell you:
what we are *not*, what we do *not* want.[17]

Appendix 1

Draghi's Concertina[18]

An intriguing way to follow the evolution of recent ECB monetary policy is through its balance sheet—a weekly financial statement that reports the ECB's assets and liabilities. Before launching QE, Draghi declared, for example, that his aim was to bring the ECB balance back to three trillion euro. What did he mean?

---

[17] Eugenio Montale, "'Non chiederci la parola che squadri da ogni lato'" ("'Don't ask us for the word to frame'"), translated by Jonathan Galassi, quoted by McKendrick (1999).
[18] This section was inspired by Mercier (2014).

Table 7.3 Consolidated balance sheet of the Eurosystem (€ billion) (29 June 2007)

Assets			Liabilities
Autonomous liquidity factors (assets)	449	730	**Autonomous liquidity factors (liabilities)**
Net foreign assets	318	633	*Banknotes*
(Gold and other foreign assets)		70	*Government deposits*
Domestic assets	131	27	*Other autonomous factors (net)*
Monetary policy instruments	464	183	**Monetary policy instruments**
Main refinancing operations (MRO)	313	182	*Current accounts (reserves)*
Longer-term refinancing operations (LTRO)	150		
Marginal lending facility	1	1	*Deposit facility*
Total	913	913	

Source: Mercier (2014); ECB Weekly financial statement

Table 7.3 shows the balance of the Eurosystem in June 2007 (before the crisis). The Eurosystem balance sheet consolidates those of the ECB and of the national central banks of eurozone countries. It is often simply called the ECB balance sheet.

Before you panic, consider the table as follows: on the left we have how liquidity is created (where it comes from) and on the right, its uses (where it is). We can also think of the left part as the supply of liquidity and the right side as demand. More specifically, the liquidity issued on the left-hand side corresponds to the assets held by the central bank *who* creates liquidity precisely in exchange for assets

The liquidity issued by the central bank takes the form of banknotes or reserves deposited in the accounts that the banks and the government hold with the central bank (banknotes and reserves are often called base money or monetary base). The banknotes issued and the deposits of the banks and the government are recorded on the right-hand side, where the liquidity takes the form of a liability, because from the central bank's point of view it is "money it owes". Be that as it may, let us note that the liquidity created up to that date was 913 billion euro, just under a trillion euro.

1. Money Comes and Goes

We already said that the liquidity created by the central bank includes reserves held by commercial banks, a "kind of money" that circulate exclusively among their current accounts at the central bank (only banks and the government can have current accounts at the central bank), and banknotes requested by the public, namely us.

How does the central bank create liquidity? In Chap. 5 and again in this chapter we saw that the central bank creates reserves on request for banks. You will remember the mantra of endogenous money: credit creates deposits and deposits create reserves. Normally, in fact, the central bank meets the demand for liquidity expressed by the economy in a relatively passive way. Its target is not the quantity of money but the *rate of interest*. Given the target interest rate, the central bank meets all demand for liquidity. If it did not, banks would go looking for reserves on the interbank market, soon causing the interest rate to rise above the target level set by the central bank.

However, liquidity can also be created through channels over which the central bank has little power and that are therefore called "autonomous factors". The principal autonomous factor is the foreign channel. Simplifying, when a eurozone company exports goods to the United States, for example, it acquires dollars that it normally changes into euro at its bank. The bank in turn changes the dollars back into euros at the national central bank (that belongs to the Eurosystem). As you can see, in this way the Eurosystem created euros in exchange for dollars in a completely passive way. By contrast, when we make a payment in dollars to the United States, we buy dollars from our bank, which in turn obtains them in exchange for euros from the central bank. This payment, made for example to import an American product, therefore involves the destruction of euros. The Eurosystem has again acted passively. This is why the "foreign channel" is defined an "autonomous factor" (for a more elaborate explanation, see next box).

Accommodating items. Things are actually more complicated. What we said applies to a certain extent to fixed exchange rate systems (such as Bretton Woods or the EMS). To simplify, let us examine only the two extreme cases of fixed and flexible exchange rates, ignoring intermediate monetary regimes, such as fixed but adjustable exchange rates.

In practice, transactions (e.g. international trade) take place through deposit transfers between international banks using "nostro/vostro" accounts (these financial instruments, including double-entry bookkeeping, were Italian inventions). For instance, Bank A has an account with a foreign Bank B in Bank B's domestic currency. From the point of view of Bank A this is a "nostro", indicating "our account on your books", while to Bank B, it is a "vostro", standing for "your account on our books".

Fixed Exchange Rates

For convenience, let us go back to the time of the lira and assume fixed lira/dollar exchange rates, as in the Bretton Woods monetary system.

An Italian bank has an account "nostro" at an American bank in New York. Through this account, the bank makes payments in dollars (when an Italian imports an American good) and receives dollars (when she exports a good).

Now let us suppose that imports exceed exports, so that the Italian bank's account does not have sufficient funds in dollars. What can it do? The bank can seek dollars on the international foreign exchange market, offering lira in exchange for dollars, but this weakens the lira, making the Bank of Italy intervene on the foreign exchange market, offering dollars (as long as it has them in the official reserves). In practice, it is as if the Bank of Italy sold dollars through the market to the Italian bank, in exchange for lira.

In summary:

> If the government operated a fixed exchange rate system, it would seem more reasonable to regard the change in reserve assets as an accommodating item as it would result from the government [through the central bank] (passively) satisfying the private sector's need for foreign exchange. [19]

Flexible Exchange Rates
Under flexible exchange rates, the Bank of Italy does not intervene in the foreign exchange market. In the above example, the lira/dollar exchange rate is allowed to fluctuate (the lira depreciates) and ideally, this leads to a commercial rebalancing. (The exchange rate may not change if the Italian bank obtains a loan in dollars; if Italy's total debts accumulate creating distrust among foreign creditors, however, an exchange rate crisis might only be postponed.)

Note now that the amount of money created via the foreign channel may or may not be able to meet the demand for central bank liquidity (banknotes and reserves) coming from the economy. If the liquidity is not sufficient, the central bank creates it by other channels. We shall soon see what these channels are. How much liquidity depends on the size of the supply already available through the foreign channel and the size of the demand:

Liquidity created by the central bank = Liquidity demand of banks (reserves) and the public (banknotes) − Liquidity created autonomously through the foreign channel

To sum up, the central bank sets its target interest rate; this rate, together with many other economic variables (fiscal policy, economic cycle, etc.), influences the demand for credit (deposits) and, together with the demand for banknotes, the demand for liquidity of the system. Part of this liquidity is met by the foreign channel; the central bank must meet the remaining net demand. If this were not the case, the lack of liquidity would raise the actual short-term interest rate above the target rate. We already know that this net demand is normally met through refinancing operations.

---

[19] Chaundy (1999, p. 12).

Table 7.3 shows the elements of the ECB's balance sheet (assets and liabilities) most important for us to know. It shows the situation at mid-2007 just before the world financial crisis hit.

On the left side of Table 7.3, we see that the central bank created 449 billion euro by "autonomous liquidity-creation factors". The main "autonomous factor" is the so-called "foreign channel" of liquidity creation, shown in the table as "gold and foreign currencies".

In rough terms, the presence of foreign assets indicates that in the past the ECB collected more dollars, yen, pounds sterling, etc. than it gave. Net import of dollars, yen, sterling, etc., exchanged at the ECB, gives rise to net creation of liquidity. The dollars and so forth, but also gold reserves, are in the official reserves of the Eurosystem, so they are written up as assets: 318 billion in Table 7.3. Autonomous factors also include domestic assets held by the Eurosystem, but this interests us less.

The ECB actively creates liquidity through monetary policy operations. It does so by supplying liquidity on a temporary basis—a week, 3 months and now even longer periods—in exchange for bonds deposited with the ECB, often termed "collateral". In the assets column we, therefore, have the value of bonds deposited by commercial banks as collateral in their short-term Main Refinancing Operations (MRO), Longer-term Refinancing Operations (LTRO) and emergency refinancing operations (marginal loans). The latter are relatively unimportant. By 29th June 2007, 464 billion euro of reserves had been created by these "monetary policy operations".

Prof, I understood that these operations are normally done to meet the demand for liquidity (reserves and banknotes) not already met by liquidity creation via the autonomous channel. That's right, although on closer inspection, the central bank is also somewhat passive in this respect too: it sets a short-term interest rate, which in turn influences all the interest rates in the economy, starting from the interbank interest rate (remember the "interest rate corridor" for short-term money market rates that we mentioned in Sect. 7.2?); at that rate, a certain demand for reserves is generated (remember: credit generates deposits and these generate demand for reserves); the central bank has to meet this demand for reserves, otherwise, interbank interest rates shoot up for lack of liquidity.

Now looking at the right side of Table 7.3, the demand for banknotes constitutes most of the demand for liquidity (it was 633 billion) and it is classified as an autonomous factor because the central bank cannot do much to influence it: it depends on seasonal factors, national customs regarding the use of cash, and alas on the pervasiveness of illegal activities and tax evasion. The demand for liquidity for reserves purposes was 182 billion euro due to the compulsory reserve requirement which was 2% at the time. The amount of required reserves to be held by banks is considered a monetary policy operation because the central bank can influence it by reducing the reserve coefficient, as it did (halving it) in December 2011. There are also excess reserves that the banks park in the *marginal deposit*. They do not amount to much (one billion), but see what happens next!

Prof, am I right in thinking that the central bank creates liquidity in exchange for foreign currency (autonomous channel) or in exchange for bonds (refinancing)? Liquidity is then held in banknotes (especially by the public), or it is held in the banks' reserve accounts, of which there are two: the required reserve account and the "marginal deposit"? Yes, that's right. In the next section we shall see that during the crisis, the banks that refinanced themselves at the ECB were not necessarily the ones that ended up with liquidity.

For the moment we can conclude this: in June 2007, the demand for liquidity at the target interest rate, which we know from Table 7.1 stood at 4%, was 913 billion euro. It normally coincides with commercial banks' liquidity requirements to meet the compulsory reserve and the public's demand for banknotes. These requirements were partly met via the autonomous channel (449 billion) and the gap was filled by monetary policy operations (464 billion), otherwise the banks would have sought reserves on the interbank market, pushing up the target interest rate.

Repetita juvant. *Demand for liquidity of banks and the public—Demand for liquidity created through the autonomous channel = liquidity created by monetary policy operations*

$$913 - 449 = 464$$

This last figure, 464, is called the *net liquidity deficit* of the system, or the liquidity that the system itself cannot meet by autonomous factors alone. The net liquidity deficit has to be covered by money offered by the central bank through its refinancing operations. In this way, commercial banks do not have to seek the liquidity they need on the market, stressing the interest rate. Indeed, if you sum the liquidity created by the central bank via monetary policy operations (left side of Table 7.3 MRO + LTRO + MLF) you will get exactly 313 + 150 + 1 = 464.

Now we know what the Eurosystem balance sheet is and in the meantime, we have learned many things that will be useful later. The Eurosystem balance sheet was below one trillion euro in 2007. It rose to 2.5 trillion in 2012 and went back down to 2 trillion in 2014. On launching QE, Draghi declared his intention to increase it to 3 trillion. Why does the balance of Frankfurt am Main stretch and shrink like a concertina?

2. The Main in Flood

The Main is a beautiful river. Walking or cycling along its banks or having a beer by the waterside is a popular pastime. The river seems to have a very regular flow, to the envy of Italians who are used to the whims of their temperamental rivers. This may be why with Mario Draghi, but actually since 2008, the liquidity created by the ECB has fluctuated widely.

Indeed, at the beginning of this chapter, we saw that in the period 2008–2011, the ECB made much liquidity available so as not to leave the banks short of reserves when the interbank market broke down. What happened to this liquidity? Everything flows, the philosopher said. Actually, except for the banknotes, the liquidity created by the central bank never leaves its premises. At most it flows from one reserve account of a bank to the reserve account of another bank. Let us see this in more detail. Exogenous money theory, (still) taught in many textbooks, says that liquidity created by the central bank is the precondition for the creation of bank credit (the terms base money or monetary base evoke this presumed role). The reasoning goes as follows: whenever a commercial bank grants credit, it creates a new deposit for a client (e.g. an overdraft). However, because of that new deposit, the bank needs liquidity to meet its reserve obligations. So the more liquidity the bank has to meet its reserve obligations, the larger the volume of deposits/credit it can create. Reserves create deposits; deposits create credit. This is the exogenous money mantra. I leave it to you to find a central banker who believes it. We have seen that according to endogenous money theory, reserves are created by the central bank on demand and therefore do not determine the quantity of deposits/credit that commercial banks can create. Actually, the amount of liquidity made available by the ECB after 2008 was much greater than the demand for compulsory reserves of credit institutions: this demand remained relatively constant around 200 billion euro from 2008 to 2011. At the end of 2011, it halved when the ECB reduced the compulsory reserve coefficient from 2 to 1%. Yet, the abundance of central bank liquidity, well over the required reserves, has not led to greater credit creation.

The stability of the demand for compulsory reserves shows that despite declarations to the contrary, the aim of the ECB's unconventional measures was not to expand credit, but something else. Not that the expansion of credit was not hoped for in order to pull the economy out of the bog, but the ECB itself admits in its *Annual Report* 2012 that "the amount of central bank reserves held by a bank is not the determining factor in its ability to generate new loans".[20] Credit is what creates reserves and not vice versa. This confirms that central banks do not believe in the multiplier of bank deposits, i.e. in the idea that an increase in reserves increases the amount of deposits and credit in the economy. Alas, economics textbooks still offer this explanation.

(To be fair, the next passage in the ECB Annual Report is less promising: "Factors influencing a bank's loan supply are, among other things, its capital position, its monitoring technology and its cost structure". All supply side factors. Conversely, Keynesian common sense suggests that the supply of credit depends on the demand for finance expressed by firms and households, and this in turn depends on aggregate demand).

The initial reason the ECB made so much liquidity available was the collapse of the interbank market. Later, with the sovereign debt crisis, it was peripheral countries' need to liquidate foreign financial funds that no longer wanted to remain invested in those countries' bonds. Collapse of the interbank market largely coincided with the interruption of capital flows from core to peripheral banks, flows that financed current account deficits of the latter countries (see the box in Sect. 5.10). In addition, in 2010 core countries' financial investors began to withdraw their investments in government bonds of peripheral countries, selling or not rolling them over at maturity. This affected small peripheral countries in 2010, and Italy and Spain in 2011 and 2012. As we explained in Sect. 7.6, the banks of peripheral countries relied on ECB refinancing to support their Treasuries in liquidating foreign capital, allowing it to go home. For example, Italian banks used Eurosystem finance, especially VLTRO funds, to buy back government bonds that German investors no longer wanted, and this enabled the Italian Treasury to liquidate foreign investors. It also enabled the banks to profit from the spread between the low interest rates on refinancing operations and the high yield of State bonds. (Perhaps this was why in those years, Italian banks were described as solid, despite increasing distress.) The liquidity initially created for Italian banks, therefore, ended up in German or Dutch banks, going from the reserve accounts of Italian banks to those of banks north of the Alps. This is where a good part of the liquidity created ended up: as excess liquidity in the reserve accounts of transalpine banks. Readers will already have recognised the link with the Target2 saga, which is explained in more detail in Appendix 2.

Table 7.4 Shows the Eurosystem balance sheet at the beginning of March 2012.

---

[20] European Central Bank (2012, p. 36).

Table 7.4 Consolidated balance sheet of the Eurosystem (€ billion) (2 March 2012)

Assets			Liabilities
US$ Repos	53	53	Claim US Federal Reserve
Autonomous liquidity factors (assets)	**1013**	**1283**	**Autonomous liquidity factors (liabilities)**
Net foreign assets (Gold and other foreign assets)	621	871	Banknotes
		135	Government deposits
Domestic assets	379	277	Other autonomous factors (net)
Monetary policy instruments	**1414**	**1132**	**Monetary policy instruments**
Main refinancing operations (MRO)	29	91	Current accounts (reserves)
Longer-term refinancing operations (LTRO)	1100		
Securities held for monetary policy purposes (mainly SMP)	284	220	Absorbing operations related to Security Market Programme
Marginal lending facility	1	821	Deposit facility
Total	**2468**	**2468**	

Source: Mercier (2014); ECB Weekly financial statement

The assets side—where we have items such as foreign currency and public and private bonds, in exchange for which the ECB created liquidity by refinancing operations—shows the shift, with respect to Table 7.3, in the importance of the short-term Main Refinancing Operations (MRO 29 billion) in favour of the Very longer-term Refinancing Operations (LTRO 1100 billion). The securities acquired by the ECB by purchasing peripheral state bonds (Securities Markets Programme) and bank obligations (Covered Bonds Purchase Program), operations explained in Sect. 7.3, also appear on the assets side of the balance sheet (for a total of 284 billion).

The liabilities side shows where the liquidity created is. As in 2007 (Table 7.3), the liquidity created by the central bank (2468 billion) is largely in the form of banknotes (871 billion), most in the hands of the public. It is also in the reserve account (91 billion) which is halved with respect to 2007 due to halving of the required reserve coefficient. It will not escape you that this means that the total credit to the economy has remained substantially unchanged since 2007! The liquidity is also in specially remunerated accounts instituted by the ECB to soak up the liquidity created by the Securities Markets Programme (220 billion), to reassure certain governments, who in the midst of a flood of liquidity were worried about a dripping tap. Much of the liquidity was also in the "marginal deposit" (821 billion), where most of the liquidity flood ended up. And from what we have said, it is mainly the transalpine banks that parked liquidity in the marginal deposit. This liquidity roughly amounts to the financial investments that German and French

Table 7.5 ECB interest rates, effective since 14 December 2011

Marginal lending facility	1.75%
Main refinancing operations	1%
Marginal deposit	0.25%

Source: ECB

Table 7.6 Consolidated balance sheet of the Eurosystem (€ billion) (13 October 2013)

Assets				Liabilities
Autonomous liquidity factors (assets)	932	1426		**Autonomous liquidity factors (liabilities)**
Net foreign assets (Gold and other foreign assets)	551	919		Banknotes
		71		Government deposits
Domestic assets	381	436		Other autonomous factors (net)
Monetary policy instruments	996	503		**Monetary policy instruments**
Main refinancing operations (MRO)	91	269		Current accounts (reserves)
Longer-term refinancing operations (LTRO)	658			
Securities held for monetary policy purposes (mainly SMP)	247	188		Absorbing operations related to Security Market Programme
Marginal lending facility	0	46		Deposit facility
Total	**1929**	**1929**		

Source: Mercier (2014); ECB Weekly financial statement

investors (the latter, however, acting as intermediates for German foreign saving) withdrew from European peripheral countries. This liquidity, vastly in excess of compulsory reserve requirements, was held in the "deposit facility" where it still enjoyed a positive interest rate, whereas holding excess liquidity in the reserve account paid zero interest. Indeed the latter account only remunerates compulsory reserves at the ECB policy rate, not excess reserves. Table 7.5 shows the interest corridor in March 2012:

In July 2012, the interest rate on marginal deposits was finally brought to zero, so that it made no difference to banks whether they held reserves in their reserve account or in their *marginal deposit*. But above all, in July 2012 Dragonball launched the *whatever-it-takes* operation also known as Outright Monetary Transactions. The effects of Draghi's reassurance regarding the solidity of the euro led to a resumption of loans from core to peripheral countries. In other words, the transalpine banks began to lend to southern banks and investors again began to purchase public "Club Med" bonds. Peripheral banks therefore began to repay their LTRO loans. Table 7.6 shows these developments. In October 2013, the overall liquidity created falls to 1929 billion.

Table 7.7 Consolidated balance sheet of the Eurosystem (€ billion) (27 February 2015)

Assets			Liabilities
Autonomous liquidity factors (assets)	994	1445	**Autonomous liquidity factors (liabilities)**
Net foreign assets	590	1006	Banknotes
(Gold and other foreign assets)		52	Government deposits
Domestic assets	404	385	Other autonomous factors (net)
Monetary policy instruments	723	272	**Monetary policy instruments**
Main refinancing operations (MRO)	165	234	Current accounts (reserves)
Longer-term refinancing operations (LTRO)	323		
Securities held for monetary policy purposes (mainly SMP)	234	0	Absorbing operations related to Security Market Programme
Marginal lending facility	0	37	Deposit facility
Total	**1717**	**1717**	

Note: Net foreign assets: (A1/2/3) − (L7/8/9); Domestic assets: A7.2 + A8; MRO + LTRO: A5.1/2; Securities held for monetary policy purposes A7.1; Banknotes L1; Government deposits L5.1; Other autonomous factors (net): (A4/6/9) − (L3/4/5.2/6/10/11/12); Reserves L2.1; deposit facility L2.2. See ECB, *Monthly Bulletin*, May 2002
Source: ECB Weekly financial statement

Compared to 2012 (Table 7.4), LTROs are almost halved, while the corresponding *deposit facility* swells, partly also due to transfer of excess reserves into the reserve account, since remuneration became zero in both reserve accounts.

Table 7.7 shows the Eurosystem balance sheet on 27th February 2015, just before QE began. Despite the new TLTRO I initiative, the item LTRO is well below what it was in October 2013, indicating that all VLTRO funds had been paid back. The TLTRO I initiative was used less than expected. Note the interruption of Securities Markets Programme sterilization operations on the liabilities side, decided in June 2014.

3. Towards Infinity and Beyond

Table 7.8 shows the situation in May 2019, after QE ended in December 2018. As we can see, the Main Refinancing Operations (MRO) have become secondary, whereas the LTRO operations, relaunched in various forms (I and II), return to considerable levels. Between 2015 and 2018, QE (item "Bonds held for monetary policy") rocketed to more than two and a half trillion euro. The Draghi concertina expanded enormously and paved the way for the upturn in the European economy in 2015–2018 through a weak euro and partial support for the public accounts of countries like Italy.

Table 7.8 Consolidated balance sheet of the Eurosystem (€ billion) (3 May 2019)

Assets				Liabilities
Autonomous liquidity factors (assets)	947	2258		**Autonomous liquidity factors (liabilities)**
Net foreign assets (Gold and other foreign assets)	690	1229		Banknotes
		203		Government deposits
Domestic assets	257	826		Other autonomous factors (net)
Monetary policy instruments	3349	2038		**Monetary policy instruments**
Main refinancing operations (MRO)	6	1404		Current accounts (reserves)
Longer-term refinancing operations (LTRO)	719			
Securities held for monetary policy purposes (mainly QE)	2624	0		Absorbing operations related to Security Market Programme
Marginal lending facility	0	634		Deposit facility
Total	**4296**	**4296**		

Note: See Table 7.4
Source: ECB Weekly financial statement

By definition, the liquidity created by QE ends up in the reserve accounts of banks. In the period 2008–2012, the expansion of liquidity should be seen in the light of collapse of the interbank market, and later of the flight of foreign investors from Italian and Spanish bonds, enabled by the combination of Target2 and recourse of Italian and Spanish banks to VLTRO (see Appendix 2). The ECB acted somewhat passively while the initiative came from the banks. With QE, the expansion of liquidity is due to the initiative of the ECB (albeit flanked by new LTRO funds). European banks therefore again found themselves with a formidable excess of reserves in their accounts at the ECB at a negative interest rate (−0.4%). This had a negative effect (albeit relatively marginal) on bank profits.

But Prof, can't banks get rid of this costly excess of reserves? There is talk of a hot potato effect. The banks as a whole cannot get rid of these reserves. If bank A invests the excess liquidity in bonds bought from Mr. Rossi, the same reserves end up in the reserve account of bank B, where Mr. Rossi has his current account. Excess reserves can only be reduced if:

• The amount of credit created by banks increases so as to transform part of the liquidity into compulsory reserves, but we know that the theory of the multiplier of bank deposits is untrue, and this is by now generally recognised; moreover, to absorb excess liquidity in this way, the amount of credit needed would be stratospheric (hundreds of trillions, since 100 euro of credit/deposits would have to be created for every euro of reserves).

- The banks buy bonds outside the Eurozone, exchanging reserves with foreign currency at the Eurosystem and making them disappear; this was an undeclared aim of QE (weaken the euro).
- The banks use the superfluous reserves to pay back other ECB funds, like LTRO.
- Of course, reserves disappear if the ECB decides to reduce them by selling bonds: this tapering is the reverse of QE. In 2013, the president of the FED Ben Bernanke did this prematurely and it had negative effects on financial markets. The ECB will never be able to resell the government bonds of the high debt countries it has bought and will continue indefinitely to buy them back at maturity. Tapering is therefore taboo in the eurozone, if common sense prevails.

Obviously, some banks are better than others at passing hot potatoes to other banks. As well, the distribution of excess liquidity is not uniform but concentrated in core countries. This, too, is related to QE, and as we said before, it has to do with the growth of Target2 balances and with capital flight from the periphery. This is why periphery banks, especially those of Italy, continued to have recourse to LTRO funds. Among other things, excess liquidity was a reassuring buffer against non-performing loans.

Summing up, we can distinguish four phases of expansion of the ECB balance (Fig. 7.5): the first (2008–2010) in which the ECB, like other big central banks, was lender of last resort when interbank credit broke down. It did so effectively through so-called Enhanced Credit Support. In a second phase (2011–2013) the ECB buffered the crisis of the bank systems and sovereign debt of certain big countries, subject to massive flight of capital, through the combination of Target2 and refinancing operations (VLTRO). From the point of view of liquidity creation, in these first two phases the ECB acted passively, accommodating the demand for liquidity expressed by the banking system. Later it began to actively acquire bonds. With the Outright Monetary Transactions, the ECB actually limited itself to the mere threat of purchase, but it was sufficiently credible to enable an upturn from the worst stage of the crisis in the third phase (2012–2014), and the later resumption of core-periphery capital flows. Growth did not return for good reasons, since no fiscal expansion measures were undertaken to sustain aggregate demand; indeed, the fiscal policy of the eurozone has systematically resisted such measures, giving rise to deflation. In the fourth phase, inaugurated by QE in March 2015, the ECB set out to expand its balance sheet to bring inflation to its target level, *below but close to* 2%. It is, however, questionable whether QE and repeated LTRO operations have bolstered aggregate demand by making more liquidity available to banks. In fact, in the light of the theory of endogenous money, we know that the amount of credit generated by banks is unrelated to the amount of reserves available, as in the theory of the deposit multiplier, but instead it is credit that generates demand for reserves. Naturally, an abundance of liquidity can be good for banks, making them more amenable to conceding the credit needed by the market. But it is still the market, on the basis of current and expected aggregate demand, that decides how much it wants. Invested abroad, liquidity kept the euro weak, and this was good for demand for European products, although such a policy seems irresponsible from the point of view of the global economy. Finally, purchase of public bonds by the central bank—plausibly almost permanent—has partially reassured markets about the sustainability of public debt of highly indebted countries.

In conclusion, if QE did no harm, there was a surprising disproportion between its size and its relatively modest results. Its impact would have been different, had it been used to support expansive fiscal policy. Draghi found himself conducting an orchestra in which the musicians (core eurozone countries, the European Commission, etc.) refused to play the music of fiscal policy, and in which the producer in Berlin did not want to contribute a single euro. Draghi did his best with his concertina (Fig. 7.5, see a colour version on the web). I doff my hat to him.[21]

---

[21] Note: The figure shows the Eurosystem's monetary policy operations from a balance sheet point of view from 2007 to July 2018. In the upper part, there are the liquidity providing operations for the various types of MRO, LTRO and QE (outright purchases) (see glossary at the beginning of the volume). The dashed line represents the system's net liquidity requirements due to factors such as demand for banknotes and compliance with minimum reserves (see box "Repetita iuvant" in appendix 1). If we subtract this liquidity requirement from the liquidity created by monetary measures, we obtain excess liquidity. The lower part shows where this excess lies, typically in the deposit facility or as an excess in the reserve and settlement account (daily reserve surplus).

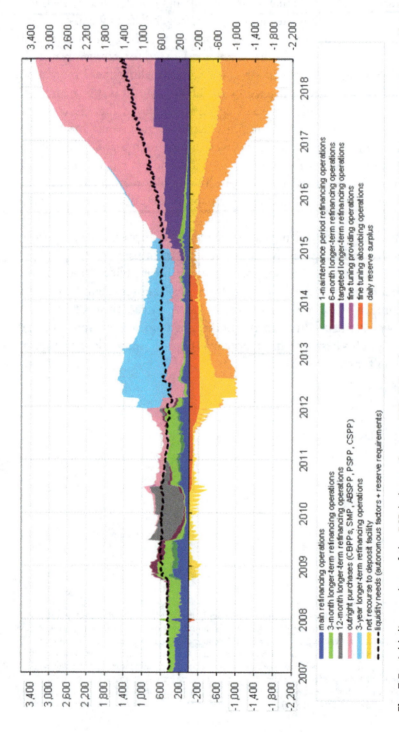

Fig. 7.5 A bird's eye view of the ECB balance. Source: ECB, WP series, n. 2219, December 2018, Fig. 16 (ecb.www.europa.eu > pdf > ecb.wp2219.en.pdf)

Appendix 2

The Strange Case of Target2

In 2011, Hans Werner Sinn, one of the most influential German economists, raised a media and academic storm by claiming that the ECB was engaged in a stealth bail-out of peripheral countries through an arcane mechanism known as Target2. Target2 was initially a brain teaser for economists, as most of us were unaware of its existence. Target2 is a platform that governs interbank payments: when we send money abroad, e.g. for a €100 bottle of champagne, our bank transmits this payment to the French supplier's bank via Target2. We have already outlined how it works; now let us see in more detail.

1. How It Works?

To understand the role of Target2 in the crisis, we recall one *leitmotiv* of these chapters: payment orders of clients from one bank to another, such as drafts, give rise to a transfer of funds from the reserve account at one bank to that of another. The eurozone is organised in such a way that each bank keeps its own reserve account at its national central bank (which acts as a local subsidiary of the Eurosystem). So it happens that when a bank makes a payment to another bank, in the example it transfers €100 from our current account at Unicredit to that at Paribas where the French wine producer has its account, our bank loses an equivalent amount of reserves from its account at the Bank of Italy, reserves that the French bank sees credited to its account at the Bank of France. On the basis of this, Paribas in turn credits €100 to the current account of the wine company. In the transaction, the Bank of Italy, that cancelled €100 from Unicredit's reserve, asks (so to speak) the Bank of France to credit €100 to Paribas's reserve account. In reality, all this happens automatically via the platform Target2. But what does the Bank of France obtain in exchange from the Bank of Italy? It obtains an accounting entry at the ECB saying that the Bank of France has a claim of €100 on Target2, while the Bank of Italy has a liability of €100 on Target2. Innocent accounting entries? Up to a certain point. At this stage, it is true that we lost €100 from our current account and Unicredit's reserves were reduced by the same amount. However, the Bank of Italy did not transfer anything to the Bank of France. Apparently no problem: the Bank of Italy and the Bank of France are branches of the same "company", the Eurosystem, so while tracing liquidity transfers between the two branches is sensible, not much importance should be ascribed to these accounting entries: we are part of the same family.

Or are we? The members of the European Monetary Union kept their national banks, which is hardly compatible with the irreversibility of the euro.

If national central banks were abolished, there would be no need for accounting entries. Rather, in the spirit of sibling rivalry, national central banks and Target2 entries exist to remind us, as in the transaction described above, that Italy owes France something.

> **Divided we stand**. If as residents of Rome, we bought a bottle of vintage Barbera (a famous wine from Piedmont) by making a bank draft to Banco di Torino, the Bank of Italy would transfer reserves from Banca di Trastevere to Banco di Torino without any strange accounting entries between Latium and Piedmont that showed that the branch of the Bank of Italy in Latium had a debt and the Piedmont branch had a credit with the Bank of Italy headquarters in Rome. This does not mean that within a country, problems of balance of payments (external constraint) between rich and poor regions do not exist, as many believe (see Sect. 5.7). The Banca del Mezzogiorno cannot freely give credit that translates into imports from Polentonia (the land of polenta, i.e. northern Italy). To rebuild reserves lost in South-North transactions—remember? payments imply that reserves are transferred between banks—the Banca del Mezzogiorno will need loans from the Banca del Lombardo-Veneto. If this debt grows it will come up against obvious limits. As happens in all monetary unions that are also political unions, imbalances are made sustainable by fiscal transfers between regions. These top up southern bank reserves and enable southern people to spend more than they produce and to pay back their loans. Regions that live beyond their means either borrow or are supported by official transfers.

Prof, if I understand, when there is a bank transaction between countries of the eurozone on the Target2 platform, for example Italy and Germany, a corresponding amount of reserves are cancelled at the Italian bank and credited to the German bank. At the same time, the Bank of Italy acquires a Target2 liability and the Bundesbank a Target2 claim on the Eurosystem. On target! As well, in Chap. 5 we said that if a bank loses reserves (Banca di Trastevere in the preceding example), normally it may have to make them up with an interbank loan. Symmetrically, there is a receiving bank that acquires reserves (Paribas in our initial example), that willingly lends its excess reserves.

> Paribas received a new deposit of €100 (the credit entry to the wine company) and the same amount in reserves. But for that new deposit, it only needs an extra euro of mandatory reserves and can therefore lend €99 on the interbank market. This is exactly what Unicredit needs: symmetrically it has lost a deposit of €100 (our draft) and the same amount of reserves. Unicredit has to make up €99 of reserves (not €100, because it no longer needs one euro of reserves since it has €100 less in deposits).

In the example, Paribas will send €99 to Unicredit via Target2; the Bank of Italy will return the favour to the Bank of France by crediting €99 to the reserve account of Unicredit. This favour means that the Target2 claim of the Bank of France is reduced to one euro. As we can see, Paribas's loan to Unicredit largely cancels the strange accounting entries "Target2 claims/liabilities" that reminded us that Italy owed something to France in exchange for the bottle of champagne. Instead of those accounting entries that resembled an *official loan* of the Bank of France to the Bank of Italy, there is now a loan of Paribas to Unicredit. In other words, now the Italian commercial liability has the more tangible form of a *private loan* by Paribas to Unicredit.

In the years leading up to the euro crisis, as in the example, increasing imports by some European peripheral countries that gave rise to Target2 liabilities were compensated by bank loans from European core countries. Target2 balances were therefore about zero (Fig. 7.6). What was not zero, but was growing progressively, were loans from core banks to peripheral banks, reflecting the worsening of the foreign accounts of peripheral countries (technically a worsening of current accounts and of their net international investment position, as we know from Chap. 6, see Figs. 6.1 and 6.2).

2. Was It True Debt?

A document of the European Commission defined Target2 balances as "the equivalent of foreign currency reserves", specifying that "unlike reserves, and although Target2 flows are recorded as central bank transactions with the rest of the Eurosystem, they do not involve concrete transactions between the national central bank and a foreign central bank since the liquidity is provided at the national level".[22] In other words, I, peripheral central bank (say, the Bank of Greece), create liquidity for my commercial banks (say, for Alpha-Bank) that provide credit to and make foreign payments on behalf of my citizens (e.g. for Athanasios), when for example they buy fine German cars. You, Bundesbank, credit the amount to your car producers. In the meantime you "take note" of our debt (as the Roman shopkeeper would once have said to the penniless old lady), and one day we shall see. Or in other words, peripheral central banks issue a reserve currency, let me call it T2/€, a virtual currency that eurozone central banks must accept and record as an asset (of course this currency is an invention of mine). As Bagnai observed regarding Target2, "In economic madness, there is always method".[23]

---

[22] European Commission (2015, p. 9).
[23] Bagnai (2012, p. 392).

Very well Prof, but basically the German car producers were paid and with those euros they can buy olive oil from peripheral countries. This is true, and they would do well to hurry to buy it instead of accumulating Target2 claims, because real problems arise only if the euro disappears and the peripheral countries repudiate their Target2 balances.

But Prof, even if that should happen, the German creditors would still have euros in their accounts (or neu-DM if the euro disappears). Ah no! Suppose that Fritz buys olive oil with the neu-DM and that Athanasios uses this revenue (neu-DM) to buy a fine German motorbike. At the end of the story, Athanasios has a car and a motorbike and Fritz only has olive oil. The periphery would pay one and get two. Greece did not pay for the car.

But Athanasios paid for it, Prof. That's true, but in principle when the peripheral central bank repudiates its Target2 liabilities (cancels a liability), it could at the same time credit the corresponding amount of reserves back to Athanasios's bank and the Alpha Bank could cancel our friend's debt. Disowning Target2 liabilities means not paying for the car.

But then the statement that Target2 balances are "mere accounting entries" as some say—another way of saying they are of a fake nature—is not true. Debts and credits always give rise to accounting entries, which demonstrates that we are talking about something serious. What Sinn said was not stupid, except that he forgot that if Fritz had immediately used what he earned from selling the car to buy olive oil or a Mediterranean holiday instead of accumulating Target2 claims, the storm would never have been raised.

3. Target2 in Flight

As we have said, in 2008 the interbank market collapsed: no new loans were made and existing loans were no longer rolled over. The crisis of confidence not only concerned interbank loans but later also sovereign bonds of peripheral countries, and this made the famous spreads skyrocket (see Sects. 7.5 and 7.6).

At that point, while capital flight from peripheral countries gave rise to negative Target2 balances, refinancing of peripheral banks that were losing deposits (and therefore reserves) was implemented by the Eurosystem.

> Remember that the refinancing operations are decentralised to the national central banks of the Eurosystem. This is just a technical organisational aspect. The reserves created by the central banks for commercial banks are a liability, which like the corresponding assets, namely bonds obtained from banks as collateral, are entries on the Eurosystem balance sheet.

Capital flight first mainly involved the three small peripheral countries (Greece, Portugal and Ireland), but in 2011, Italy and Spain also began to be affected. Ordinary refinancing, without which peripheral countries could not accommodate the transfer of funds from their accounts to those of core country banks, was later strengthened by the ECB 3-year Very longer-term refinancing operations (VLTRO). Banks that were losing liquidity due to capital flight were therefore thus restocked by the central bank.

As Minenna, Dosi and Roventini observed:

> Between 2011 and 2012, at the peak of the Italian debt crisis, core country banks sold a significant amount of Italian debt on the secondary market due to increased perception of a credit risk. The sale of a financial activity from abroad amounts to capital leaving Italy, recorded with a minus sign on the Target2 balance. Italian state bonds were then repurchased at low prices by Italian banks, thanks to the massive flow of liquidity that the banks borrowed via LTRO from the ECB. This operation was successful in ensuring refinancing of the Italian government, but at the cost of internalising the sovereign credit risk in the Italian financial system.

At the same time, German banks were reducing their long-term loans to Mediterranean countries. The authors conclude: "The combined effect of selling off state bonds to Italian banks [...] and contraction of interbank credit [...] fully explains the explosion of Target2 balances".[24]

These authors appropriately highlight that this "buffer operation" towards the Italian and Spanish sovereign debt crisis made Target2 balances rise—replacing foreign debt towards the private sector with debt towards the Eurosystem—and created the "mortal embrace" between banks and peripheral country governments that we already mentioned (Sect. 7.5).

Figure 7.6 shows the fluctuations of Target2 claims and liabilities. The contrast between Germany's surplus (upper part of the figure) and the deficit of the peripheral countries (lower part) is evident.

The figure also shows the two peaks in the divergence between the core/periphery balances. Both phases of the Target2 affair raised hot disputes. In the course of 2010 and 2011, and then more markedly in the first half of 2012, the balances diverged dramatically only to shrink again in the second half of 2012. Draghi's famous announcements on 28th July 2012 marked the watershed. The graph shows that in 2015 the Target2 balances began to diverge again in concomitance with QE. Let us look at the first phase of the

---

[24] Minenna et al. (2018, p. 152).

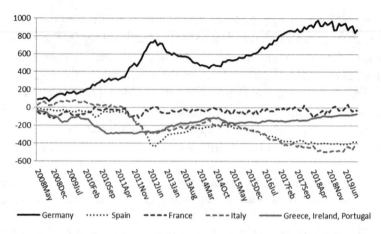

Fig. 7.6 Target2 balances of some eurozone countries (2008–2018), in millions of euro. Source: ECB Eurosystem policy and exchange rates, Target balances of participating national central banks, June 2019

controversy, which is probably the more interesting of the two (we dealt with the second in Sect. 7.11).

4. The Controversy

Let us first reflect on the difference with respect to what would have happened in a peripheral country that had its own currency and was faced with a foreign debt crisis. Let us consider an emerging country with net foreign debt (technically with a negative net international investment position) denominated in a foreign currency, usually dollars, due to past current account deficits. If foreign investors refuse to continue to finance new deficits or roll over pre-existing loans and if the country cannot pay back these debts due to insufficient official reserves, the country will default, namely declare that it cannot repay the principal and interest. As we saw in Sect. 7.7, this is normally followed by IMF intervention: the country is lent money to pay its debt to foreign creditor banks. The IMF also imposes external debt restructuring on the country and its creditors, extending the deadlines at reasonable interest rates, and imposes conditions. This "conditionality" requires the country to implement restrictive fiscal policies aimed at creating a current account surplus so as to obtain a net inflow of dollars with which to service the restructured debt. Devaluation of the national currency can soften the austerity of these policies.

With respect to the classical balance of payments crises experienced by dozens of emerging countries, the combination of Target2 (that enables an ordered repatriation of international loans) and refinancing operations (that do not cut off liquidity to peripheral banks), radically changes the picture. It does so in a way that greatly resembles Keynes's proposed *Currency Clearing Union*, in which the latter has the task of recycling surplus liquidity of countries with current account surpluses to countries with current account deficits. However, there is a difference. In Keynes's proposal, countries with current account deficits had to try to restore equilibrium—although the recycling of liquidity would give them time and avoid drastic restriction of internal demand with consequent increases in unemployment—but they would be helped in doing so by expansive policies implemented by countries with current account surpluses and by a possible realignment of exchange rates. In Europe, it seems that only the first measure, restriction, is undertaken, whereas exchange rate adjustments are impossible by definition and German expansion is hindered by its mercantilist model.

On these questions, two positions have emerged. The first, proposed by Sinn,[25] is that the combination of Target2 and refinancing operations are a silent bail-out of peripheral countries, enabling them to avoid adjusting their external balances (but this adjustment has taken place in any case through severe social hardship, see Sect. 7.7). The second position is that all this takes place in accordance with pre-existing rules aimed at ensuring the smooth functioning of a monetary union through the possibility of freely transferring deposits between one country and another, with replenishment by the central bank of reserves of banks that are short of them.

An excellent ECB economist, Philippine Cour-Thimann,[26] in a sense gives credit to both positions. Basically, she holds that when the European interbank credit bank collapsed, it was as if the Eurosystem intermediated interbank loans: capital withdrawn from the periphery via Target2 was deposited with national central banks of core countries, i.e. with branches of the Eurosystem; and when peripheral central banks of the Eurosystem regenerated reserves lost by peripheral banks, it was as if the Eurosystem reloaned the excess liquidity of core commercial banks to peripheral commercial banks (and indirectly to struggling states), roughly in line with the Keynes Clearing Union concept. If the reserves lost by the periphery to capital flight were not regenerated, peripheral commercial banks (and troubled states) would default, and this would force peripheral countries to re-emit their national currencies to refinance them. So in order to maintain financial stability and protect the euro, Cour-Thimann somehow admits that the Eurosystem ended up helping

---

[25] Sinn (2018).
[26] Cour-Thimann (2013).

peripheral countries to roll over their foreign debt. There is nothing wrong with this, the economist concludes. It gave Europe time to remove the causes of imbalance. Too bad that it has acted only in the unilateral direction of imposing restrictive measures on peripheral countries, contrary to the symmetrical adjustment that Keynes had in mind: a symmetrical adjustment all the more necessary in the absence of an exchange rate correction.

5. Crisis, What Crisis?

Prof, but if Target2 prevented the European crisis from degenerating into a classical balance of payments crisis, the European crisis could have been avoided if the ECB had intervened earlier and decisively in support of sovereign debt? Yes, a more timely intervention by the ECB would certainly have mitigated the adjustment, but a rebalancing of the balance of payments would still have been necessary, although this is less dramatic if carried out symmetrically by countries in surplus and countries in deficit. However, I don't feel like following authors, such as Paul De Grauwe, Marc Lavoie and Randall Wray, who go as far as to say that one cannot speak of a balance of payments crisis in a monetary union equipped with systems like Target2 and refinancing instruments at the central bank. In their view, well-managed monetary unions cannot suffer from balance of payments crises and the euro crisis has been due to constraints imposed on the ECB, preventing it from intervening strongly to restore confidence in sovereign debt. Lacking ECB support, they conclude, peripheral countries were forced to tackle the confidence crisis with austerity measures, which only made things worse.

To test the truth of this stance, let us do a mental exercise. Let us imagine a monetary union, as conceived by these scholars, without large inter-regional transfers that permit poorer members to "live beyond their means", but with a central bank that acts as lender of last resort for regional governments, which by assumption are not subject to budget constraints. To sustain their economies, the poorer members increase their public deficits. Peripheral banks, especially if backed by a central bank policy of low interest rates, will begin to offer cheap credit, confident that their regional governments will bail them out if things turn sour. Governments in turn are confident that the central bank will bail them out. This policy will lead to large foreign debt, but this is no great problem. Even if private loans from richer states are not forthcoming, payments can continue via Target2, while the central bank recharges the bank reserves of indebted countries by refinancing mechanisms. In this land of plenty, not only are commercial banks sure of government support, but governments are certain that the banks will buy their bonds. A mortal embrace?

No, there is central bank support. Of course, public opinion of the core states is sooner or later likely to cry "¡Ya basta!" and impose austerity measures on the prodigal states: austerity measures meant to enable the spendthrift states to repay their foreign debt by virtue of current account surpluses. Contrary to the ideas of the above authors, austerity is not a method (ineffective) for adjusting public accounts, but a method (effective, albeit controversial) for correcting foreign imbalances.

The fact is that a monetary union of economically heterogeneous countries can only survive if it is based on political union, namely the willingness of richer members to aid poorer members through a large redistributive federal budget and a central bank that underpins federal fiscal policy, while local states keep their budgets balanced: in other words, the fiscal constraints of Maastricht would make sense if completed by a large federal redistributive budget. Of course the poorer members, sustained by federal transfers, are a market for richer members. But this market will always need hand-outs from the people of wealthy states. The latter will therefore think twice about joining a *political* union that would have such consequences, and indeed, in Europe it will never happen (see Sects. 6.11 and 7.12). They prefer to *lend, not give*, to poorer states, although history teaches that the outcome of loans is often a debt crisis.

So, Prof? So in the absence of any leanings towards political union, it would have been better if all the states of Europe kept their own currencies and made agreements to stabilise exchange rates, which could be adjusted when the "fundamentals" no longer warranted them. It would be necessary to ensure that fixed exchange rates do not stimulate international lending culminating in debt crises, and to correct the asymmetries of European monetary system governance. The tragedy is that German mercantilism would still pose a problem in this context. Trying to govern it with a single currency, however, was the classical leap from the frying pan into the fire.

Further Reading

On the effective functioning of monetary policy, I recommend the following three authoritative articles that diverge from the explanations found in textbooks: Bindseil (2004b), Disyatat (2008) and Fullwiler (2017).

On ECB monetary policy see: Eser et al. (2012) (for the period 2008–2011), Alvarez et al. (2017) (for the period 2012–2017) and Hartmann and Smets (2018) (for the period 1999–2018), all available on the ECB website, where there is also much introductory material on monetary policy. A critical overview of European monetary and fiscal policy can be found in Ashoka Mody (2018) (rather cliché on Italian problems) and Yanis Varoufakis (2017). On the role of the Bundesbank as guardian of price stability with particular regard to trade union wage claims, see Franzese and Hall (2000). Adalbert Winkler (2015), an eminent and impartial German economist, denounces the fact that German protests against the Security Market Programme limited ECB action as lender of last resort to states.

On the basic philosophy of European fiscal policy, consisting of prohibitions rather than policies aimed at sustaining aggregate demand, see Otmar Issing (2002), a former chief economist at the ECB (1998–2006). In his opinion, it is not necessary to coordinate fiscal and monetary policy to achieve full employment; it is enough that member countries obey the rules and liberalise the labour market. On the ordoliberal (and protestant) foundations of these ideas, see Hien and Joerges (2018). Their definition of the European Union as a "stateless market" is accurate. Mainstream economist Daniel Gros (2015) acknowledges that the principal aim of austerity policies is to realign external imbalances. I am embarrassed to say that I am unable to suggest a good guide in English to the jungle of European fiscal governance with its infernal invasive congeries of rules for national balances, made even more intrusive by the presumed fiscal nature of the crisis. A good text in Italian is Fantacci and Papetti (2013). But you can always consult the European Commission's website, https://ec.europa.eu/info/business-economy-euro/economic-and-fiscal-policy-coordination/eu-economic-governance-monitoring-prevention-correction/european-semester/framework/eus-economic-governance-explained_en. Good luck!

There is abundant literature on the Target2 saga. The data is continuously updated at: http://www.eurocrisismonitor.com/. On "sudden stops" of capital flows into Italy and Spain in 2011, see Merler and Pisani-Ferry (2012). I recommend Febrero and Uxó (2013) for their clarity on Target2 mechanisms. The *summa summarum* of the debate is Philippine Cour-Thimann (2013). As already mentioned, Target2 and the nature of the European crisis have been the subject of controversy among heterodox economists, see the references in Cesaratto (2018). On the similarities between the Target2 payment system and the *clearing union* proposed by Keynes at the Bretton Woods conference in 1944, see Lavoie (2015). Regarding Target2 and QE, see Eisenschmidt et al. (2017), Sinn (2018), and for a post-Keynesian perspective, Febrero et al. (2019). On the effects of QE, see Demertzis and Wolff (2016). Dolan (2013) and Gros (2013) are two simple texts on what a banking crisis is and why a viable monetary union entails a solid banking union.

On exit from the euro, see Nordvig and Firoozye (2012). The authors were finalists for the *Wolfson Economics Prize 2012*, a prize instituted by a wealthy English businessman for the best study on how the eurozone could be safely dismantled. This study is in my opinion better than that of the winner, Roger Bootle.

References

Alvarez, I., Casavecchia, F., De Luca, M., Duering, A., Eser, F., Helmus, C. et al. (2017). *The use of the Eurosystem's monetary policy instruments and operational framework since 2012*. ECB Occasional Paper, No. 188/2017.

Bagnai, A. (2012). *Il tramonto dell'euro*. Reggio Emilia: Imprimatur.

Bindseil, U. (2004a). *Monetary policy implementation. Theory, past and present.* Oxford: Oxford University Press.

Bindseil, U. (2004b). *The operational target of monetary policy and the rise and fall of reserve position doctrine*. ECB Working Paper Series, No. 372.

Bindseil, U., Domnick, C., & Zeuner, J. (2015). *Critique of accommodating central bank policies and the 'expropriation of the saver'—A review*. ECB Occasional Paper Series, No. 161.

Borio, C. (1997). *The implementation of monetary policy in industrial countries: A survey*. BIS Economic Papers, No. 47.

Borio, C., & Disyatat, P. (2009). *Unconventional monetary policies: An appraisal*. BIS Working Papers, No. 292.

Buti, M. (2020). *Economic policy in the rough: A European journey*. CEPR Policy Insight No. 98.

Cesaratto, S. (2018). The nature of the eurocrisis. A reply to Febrero, Uxò and Bermejo. *Review of Keynesian Economics, 6*(2), 240–251 (working paper version: Quaderni DEPS, No. 752).

Chaundy, D. (1999). *What is the accommodating item in the balance of payments?* Working Paper No. 122, ESRC Centre for Business Research, University of Cambridge.

Constâncio, V. (2016, June). *The challenge of low real interest rates for monetary policy. Utrecht School of Economics.* Retrieved February 20, 2020, from https://www.ecb.europa.eu/press/key/date/2016/html/sp160615.en.html

Cour-Thimann, P. (2013). *Target balances and the crisis in the euro area*. CESifo Forum—Special Issue April, Ifo Institute for Economic Research at the University of Munich.

Demertzis, M., & Wolff, G. (2016). *The effectiveness of the European Central Bank's Asset Purchase Programme*. Bruegel Policy Contribution, No. 10.

Disyatat, P. (2008). *Monetary policy implementation: Misconceptions and their consequences*. BIS Working Papers No. 269.

Dolan, E. (2013). *Bailouts, bail-ins, haircuts and all that: Program notes for the Cyprus banking drama*. Retrieved February 20, 2020, from http://archive.economonitor. com/dolanecon/2013/03/22/bailouts-bail-ins-haircuts-and-all-that-program-notes-for-the-cyprus-banking-drama/

Draghi, M. (2014). *Unemployment in the euro are. Annual Symposium of Central Bankers in Jackson Hole*. Retrieved February 20, 2020, from https://www.ecb. europa.eu/press/key/date/2014/html/sp140822.en.html

Eisenschmidt, J., Kedan, D., Schmitz, M., Adalid, R., & Papsdorf, P. (2017). *The eurosystem's asset purchase programme and target balances*. ECB Occasional Paper No. 196.

Eser, F., Amaro, M.C., Iacobelli, S., & Rubens, M. (2012). *The use of the Eurosystem's monetary policy instruments and operational framework since 2009*. ECB Occasional Paper Series, No. 135.

European Central Bank. (2012). *Annual report*. Frankfurt.

European Commission. (2015). Recent developments in cross-border capital flows in the euro area (Section prepared by Alexis Loublier). *Quarterly Report on the Euro Area, 14*(1), 7–18.

Fantacci, L., & Papetti, A. (2013). *Il debito dell'Europa con sé stessa. Analisi e riforma della governance europea di fronte alla crisi*. Costituzionalismo.it, n. 2/2013.

Febrero, E., & Uxó, J. (2013). *Understanding Target2 imbalances from an endogenous money view*. Department of Economics, University of Castilla-La Mancha, WP No. 2.

Febrero, E., Uxó, J., & Álvarez, I. (2019). Target2 imbalances and the ECB's Asset Purchase Programme. An alternative account. *Panoeconomicus*. Advance online publication, 1–21. Retrieved March 9, 2020, from https://panoeconomicus.org/index.php/jorunal/article/view/798

Franzese, R. J., & Hall, P. A. (2000). Institutional dimensions of coordinating wage bargaining and monetary policy. In T. Iversen, J. Pontusson, & D. Soskice (Eds.), *Unions, employers, and central banks: Macroeconomic coordination and institutional change in social market economies* (pp. 173–204). Cambridge: Cambridge University Press.

Fullwiler, S. T. (2017). Modern central bank operations—The general principles. In L. P. Rochon & S. Rossi (Eds.), *Advances in endogenous money analysis* (pp. 50–87). Cheltenham, Edward Elgar.

Gros, D. (2013). *Banking union: Ireland vs Nevada, an illustration of the importance of an integrated banking system*. Voxeu.org.

Gros, D. (2015). *The Eurozone crisis as a sudden stop: It is the foreign debt which matters*. Voxeu.org.

Hartmann, P., & Smets, F. (2018). *The first twenty years of the European Central Bank: Monetary policy*. ECB Working Paper Series, No. 2219.

Hicks, J. R. (1937). Mr. Keynes and the 'Classics'; a suggested interpretation. *Econometrica, 5*(2), 147–159.

Hien, J., & Joerges, C. (2018). Dead man walking? Current European interest in the ordoliberal tradition. *European Law Journal, 24*(2–3), 142–162.

Issing, O. (2002). On macroeconomic policy co-ordination in EMU. *Journal of Common Market Studies, 40*(2), 345–358.

Koo, R. C. (2011). *The holy grail of macroeconomics: Lessons from Japan's great recession.* Singapore: Wiley (Asia).

Lavoie, M. (2015). The eurozone: Similarities to and differences from Keynes's plan. *International Journal of Political Economy, 44*(1), 3–17.

McKendrick, J. (1999). Two Jackals on a Leash. *London Review of Books, 21*(13).

Mercier, P. (2014). *The Eurosystem, the banking sector and the money market.* Cahier d'études, no. 92, Banque Centrale du Luxembourg.

Merler, S., & Pisani-Ferry, J. (2012). Sudden stops in the Euro Area. *Review of Economics and Institutions, 3*(3), 1–23.

Minenna, M., Dosi, G., & Roventini, A. (2018). ECB monetary expansions and euro area Target2 imbalances: A balance-of-payment-based decomposition. *European Journal of Economics and Economic Policies: Intervention, 15*(2), 147–159.

Mody, A. (2018). *Euro Tragedy: A drama in nine acts.* New York: Oxford University Press.

Nordvig, J., & Firoozye, N. (2012). *Rethinking the European monetary union.* Wolfson Economics Prize 2012—Final submission. Retrieved February 20, 2020, from https://jensnordvig.com/

Schnabel, I. (2020, February 11). *Narratives about the ECB's monetary policy—Reality or fiction?* Speech at the Juristische Studiengesellschaft, Karlsruhe. Retrieved February 20, 2020, from https://www.ecb.europa.eu/press/key/date/2020/html/ecb.sp200211_1~b439a2f4a0.en.html

Sinn, W. (2018). *The ECB's fiscal policy.* NBER Working Paper No. 24613.

Varoufakis, Y. (2017). *Adults in the room: My battle with Europe's deep establishment.* London: The Bodley Head.

Winkler, A. (2015). The ECB as lender of last resort: Banks versus governments. *Jahrbücher für Nationalökonomie und Statistik, 235*(3), 329–341.

Zolo, D. (2002). *Invoking humanity: War, law, and global order.* London: Continuum.

Epilogue

Prof, in this book you talk a lot about economic growth and social justice, but you never talk about the environment, and yet a better society is impossible without safeguarding the environment.

You are absolutely right. The two things, a better society and environmental protection, go together, and in some ways they face a similar challenge: how to get the necessary social values to prevail, social values based on respect for other people, animals and the environment. Unfortunately, the battle against the theoretical and practical implications of laissez-faire ideology has diverted the energies of heterodox economists away from these fundamental themes.

A radical approach to the environmental collapse of the planet requires a major change in the current lifestyles which are based on massive consumption of goods and services. However, this must be accompanied by social justice, giving priority to the things that really matter, healthy food and a healthy environment, access to healthcare, education and culture. Producing less to produce better would reduce working time, leaving room for community work and individual creativity. The quantitative growth mindset must be replaced by an ethic of qualitative growth.

We cannot rely on technological development to bail us out: environmental degradation is happening much faster and "green innovations" are never at zero environmental cost. Science and technology must, however, remain a priority.

© Springer Nature Switzerland AG 2020
S. Cesaratto, *Heterodox Challenges in Economics*,
https://doi.org/10.1007/978-3-030-54448-5

The problem is how to achieve a new social project. Could it be achieved by returning to the presumed primitive innocence of the hunter-gatherers? It is not clear how environmentally friendly those communities were, if it is true that they were able to exterminate the poor mammoths. And it hardly seems applicable to complex societies. We already touched on these issues in Chap. 2 (Further reading).

Real socialism does not seem to have been a happy experience from an environmental perspective, and was not helped by the hostility it met with. Real socialism failed to offer an alternative to capitalism, but competed with it to expand mass consumption, and lost. The failure of real socialism is also measured by the rigid social stratification it produced. But how do you avoid hierarchies in complex societies? Moreover, the full employment achieved by the socialist countries created disaffection for work and laxity. The Chinese model appears to replicate Western consumerism and has authoritarian elements alien to our democracies. Cuban healthcare, however, is an example that the world should perhaps study. At the moment, the best model to begin with seems to be the social democratic compromise, based on a combination of state and market, with an enhanced role of government in social and environmental protection.

The scale of the problem is global and it is not easy to find solutions that satisfy everyone, particularly given the fact that there are huge differences in levels of consumption and pollution between countries. Achieving significant agreement between hundreds of countries is a complex task.

Prof, is it hopeless then? The questions are complex and the answers we have gathered so far are probably not up to the task. Certainly economists who move in the marginalist sphere are not structurally able to think about economic models and mechanisms other than laissez-faire. Environmentalists sometimes dodge the complexity of the economic and political problem, and often slip into hasty green utopianism. Mass awareness of the environmental problem remains limited, even in the wealthiest countries, where people have no real willingness to question their lifestyles, while if we are to remain democratic, we have to find solutions accepted by most of the population.

Prof, do the coronavirus pandemic and lockdown teach us anything? In the long emergency some may have revalued the importance of small things: we did not miss the tropical island holiday but the walk in the park. Some may have learnt that many things can be given up for the common good. This means that more people might accept to do without many seriously polluting goods, such as environmentally and culturally poor tourism, cruises, excessive meat consumption and car ownership, if faced with an imminent environmental emergency. But how can we do this democratically without waiting until these measures have to be imposed by law, and probably too late, as in the case of the epidemic? And don't most people just want to go back to their prior style of consumption and with renewed gusto?

If we abolish devastating products and processes, many industries and those related to them will disappear or will be downsized, e.g. tourism and the car industry. Greening the economy and infrastructure, including transport and cities, and of course redistributing working time between those who have lost and those who have maintained employment, is no small task. Who, and with what know-how and what consensus, could guide this process? The downsizing of polluting industries could adversely affect international trade, and some countries will suffer more than others. How can this conversion be managed on a global scale?

Could the surplus approach you explained help find solutions? The surplus approach could help reshape environmental economics towards policy proposals no longer based on marginalism and its faith in market mechanisms, but on a deeper understanding of the real workings of human societies, rival social interests, the centrality of public intervention and the limits of laissez-faire.

Input–output tables are an example of a tool typical of the classical approach to analysis of the real economy, but are hardly taught in universities any more. These statistical tables illustrate the dense network of technical and trade connections between different industries. Many sectors do not work for the final consumer, but for other industries, producing industrial machinery, components and so on. These tables are estimated at national and even global level. Through them we can evaluate the ultimate effects on production and employment of downsizing certain polluting industries or expanding other cleaner ones. Input–output tables were conceived by Wassily Leontief (1906–1999), a Russian-American economist and (deserving) winner of the Sveriges Riksbank Nobel Prize in Economics. Leontief studied classical economists and Marx, in particular the famous *Tableau économique* of the French physiocratic economist François Quesnay (1694–1774). The analytical schemes of Sraffa and Leontief show significant similarities; they actually have the same classical roots.[1]

We ultimately need to stop being dominated by laissez-faire economics and, through it, by our less noble instincts, such as the ostentation of wealth, profit and power. Unfortunately, we still have neither the concrete planning capacity nor the full mass awareness necessary to take our destiny into our own hands. To conclude, in my opinion, it is not enough to complain about

---

[1] See Kurz and Salvadori (2000).

environmental problems, the technical solutions for which we often already know (from more sustainable technologies to outright downsizing of certain types of production). We lack the political solutions: how to build a fairer and more environmentally friendly society and the most appropriate social coalition to fight for it.

The COVID-19 pandemic is unlikely to trigger any profound changes in European economic governance either. The events of the crisis of the last decade as described in Chaps. 6 and 7 have left Europe divided economically and politically. The pandemic will perhaps leave an even deeper divide. We can only hope that the younger European generations will do better. I hope this book will help. And in this respect let me briefly return to what I consider to be its deepest contribution, the construction of a solid challenge to mainstream economics.

In the 1980s, two Cambridge (UK) economists, scholars of the classical surplus approach, staged a coup. They recruited a tolerant mainstream economist and succeeded in having a re-edition of a famous dictionary of economics, the *New Palgrave*, assigned to them. It came out in three large volumes.[2] Shortly after, a very conservative leading American economist and Nobel Laureate, George Stigler, wrote in a review of the work[3] that if a future economist were to judge the state of economics at the end of the 20th century on the basis of the dictionary, he would deduce that Italy ranked global third in economic research and that Marx and Sraffa were at the centre of economic debate, when in fact, heterodoxy only touched a tiny minority of modern economists and had no impact in major English-speaking universities. A few years later the editor charged more reliable economists with the *New Palgrave 4.0*.[4]

A somewhat similar criticism will be levelled at me. Certain stories told here, it will be said, reflect the ideas of a minority (Sraffians) of a minority (heterodox economists). It is true. However, I have no doubt that what I have reported here, inspired principally by the lessons of Sraffa and Garegnani, constitutes the solid core of economic heterodoxy, the only line of thought that at least for a few years—in conjunction with a wave of social uprisings— put orthodox views on the ropes (disproving Stigler's judgement of insignificance). Nevertheless, this book bears the influence of other heterodox currents of thought, for example the lesson of Luxemburg–Kalecki and the theory of endogenous money. Yet, I have to admit that my opinion on some parts of

---

[2] Eatwell et al. (1987).
[3] Stigler (1988).
[4] Durlauf and Blume (2008).

economic heterodoxy is somewhat severe, especially with regard to certain post-Keynesian traditions with their insistence on subjective elements such as expectations, uncertainty and animal spirits. Mainstream theory has long incorporated these concepts, which play an essential role in supporting the Walrasian theory. After criticism of the theory of capital, neoclassical theory has in fact had to give up the determination of long-period equilibria, i.e. of the natural prices underlying the invisible hand of Smith. It has therefore taken refuge in so-called short-period Walrasian equilibria, thus avoiding a measurement of the value of capital (see Sect. 3.10.2). In this way, neoclassical theory fails in predicting the outcome of the invisible hand: the economy will go where its heart takes it, under the influence of subjective and therefore unknowable elements. Can you imagine a physicist sustaining theories of this kind?

Dixi et salvavi animam meam as old Marx said.[5]

References

Durlauf, S. N., & Blume, L. E. (Eds.). (2008). *The New Palgrave dictionary of economics* (2nd ed.). New York: Palgrave Macmillan.

Eatwell, J., Murray, M., & Newman, P. (Eds.). (1987). *The New Palgrave: A dictionary of economics* (1st ed.). New York: Palgrave Macmillan.

Kurz, H. D., & Salvadori, N. (2000). 'Classical' roots of input-output analysis: A short account of its long prehistory. *Economic Systems Research, 12*(2), 153–180.

Marx, K. (1875). Critique of the Gotha Programme. In K. Marx (Ed.), *The First International and after. Political writings* (Vol. 3, pp. 339–359). Middlesex: Penguin Books.

Stigler, G. J. (1988). Palgrave's dictionary of economics. *Journal of Economic Literature, 26*(4), 1729–1736.

---

[5] "I spoke and saved my soul", Marx (1875, p. 359).

Index

© Springer Nature Switzerland AG 2020
S. Cesaratto, *Heterodox Challenges in Economics*,
https://doi.org/10.1007/978-3-030-54448-5

CPSIA information can be obtained
at www.ICGtesting.com
Printed in the USA
LVHW080925130421
684346LV00001B/4